New Curriculum MATHEMATICS for Schools

KEY STAGE 2

Consultant Editor: **Sir Wilfred Cockcroft**

Coordinator: **John Marshall**
Authors: **John Armstrong, Anne Bartel,
David Bootherstone, Ian Lusk, John Page,
Linda Parton, Gwyn Price**

Teacher's Guide 2
Pupil's Book 2

Acknowledgements

The authors and publishers would like to thank the many headteachers, teachers and pupils who have helped so much in the development of this material over a number of years. Particular thanks are due to Jim Lennon, Margaret Barclay and the staff of Muirtown Primary School, Inverness, to the numerous contact schools throughout the country, to those schools in the authors' neighbourhoods, especially Staffordshire, and to those international friends whose advice has been so constructive. Special thanks are also due to Susan Langhorne for typing the manuscript so effectively.

Designed and illustrated by Cauldron Design Studio, Berwickshire.

Oliver & Boyd
Longman House
Burnt Mill
Harlow, Essex,
CM20 2JE, England
and Associated Companies throughout the world
An imprint of Longman Group UK Ltd

© Sir Wilfred Cockcroft, John Marshall, John Armstrong, Anne Bartel, David Bootherstone, Ian Lusk, John Page, Linda Parton and Gwyn Price 1992. All rights reserved. No part of this publication (with the exception of the Pupil Record Sheet on pages 148–9) may be reproduced, stored in a retrieval system, or transmitted in any form or by any means, electronic, mechanical, photocopying, recording or otherwise, without either the prior written permission of the Publishers or a licence permitting restricted copying in the UK by the Copyright Licensing Agency Ltd, 33-34 Alfred Place, London WC1E 7DP.

ISBN 0 05 004423 0
First published 1992

Typeset on Apple Macintosh SE/30 in Palatino 10/12pt
by Word Power, Berwickshire.
Printed in Great Britain
by The Bath Press, Avon

Preface

The Department of Education and Science and the Welsh Office's document *Mathematics in the National Curriculum* (HMSO 1991) lays down levels, attainment targets and programmes of study to be observed in all state-supported primary and secondary schools. At primary level, Key Stage 1 came into operation in September 1989, and Key Stage 2 in September 1990.

The Report *Mathematics Counts* (HMSO) foreshadowed many of the recommendations now being made for the teaching of mathematics and our own series *Mathematics for Schools* was already moving in the right direction but what teachers need, and children deserve, is a mathematics package written *for* the National Curriculum. A package which takes *Mathematics in the National Curriculum* as its starting point and covers every attainment target at every level and yet does not focus on these targets only but on the complete mathematical well-being of every child. A package which recognises first and foremost that mathematics is best appreciated and knowledge gained by activity, and that any series of books, however good, can only be a small resource to the one essential element – good teaching.

New Curriculum Mathematics for Schools, written under the guidance of Sir Wilfred Cockcroft, is such a complete package. It will set a high standard for the implementation of the National Curriculum in Mathematics.

New Curriculum Mathematics for Schools covers Key Stage 2 with five sequential Pupils' Books, each one supported by a Teacher's Guide, Activity Cards and Copymasters. In each Teacher's Guide, we have given some indication of the attainment targets (ATs) covered and, where possible, the level and subsection. We have also reproduced an outline of these (from *Mathematics in the National Curriculum* 1991) on page 11 of this Guide.

The ATs are only markers, however, and the Guide should be used as a rich source for the achievement of much more than the bare essentials. We leave this suggestion with you, the teacher, the real source of your children's mathematical progress!

New Curriculum Mathematics for Schools Key Stage 2

Contents

Introduction			5
National Curriculum Attainment Targets			11
Section 1	(pages 2-7)	Data Handling	13
Section 2	(pages 8-10)	Tens and Units	20
Section 3	(pages 11-14)	Position Value (H.T.U.)	26
Section 4	(pages 15-19)	Time	33
Section 5	(pages 20-27)	Addition (H.T.U.)	40
Section 6	(pages 28-31)	Shape, Space and Position	47
Section 7	(pages 32-34)	Negative Numbers	53
Section 8	(pages 35-37)	Shape, Space and Position	58
Section 9	(pages 38-46)	Multiplication	64
Section 10	(pages 47-51)	Sharing	80
Section 11	(pages 52-53)	Measurement: Area	87
Section 12	(pages 54-55)	Pattern	90
Section 13	(pages 56-63)	Difference (H.T.U.)	96
Section 14	(pages 64-65)	Measurement: Capacity	104
Section 15	(pages 66-69)	Data Handling	108
Section 16	(pages 70-74)	Take Away (H.T.U.)	112
Section 17	(pages 75-78)	Money	117
Section 18	(pages 79-80)	Data Handling	124
Answers			128
List of Activity Cards and Copymasters			145
Glossary			147
Pupil Record Sheet			148

Introduction

Towards the end of the introduction to the Teacher's Guide to Key Stage 2, Book 1, I quoted paragraph 329 from *Mathematics Counts* on the subject of what our aims in teaching mathematics should be:

> 'The overall aim must be to develop in children an attitude to mathematics and an awareness of its power to communicate and explain which will result in mathematics being used wherever it can illuminate or make more precise an argument or enable the results of an investigation to be presented in a way which will assist clarity and understanding.'

In Key Stage 2, Pupils' Book 2, and in the associated material, we continue to keep this aim in mind as we develop in our pupils the skills and techniques which will enable them to solve ever more varied problems and to explain the world around them in increasingly sophisticated mathematical terms.

Such skills can only be developed on the basis of the work dealt with in Key Stage 1. In this sense we recognise the essential need for the children to begin to acquire the so-called basic skills from the start of their work. We follow *Mathematics Counts* in defining such 'basic skills' as those skills which are 'needed as a basis for the mathematics required in employment or in adult life or for further study'.

These skills cannot be restricted to the operations of arithmetic in isolation from applications. Again quoting *Mathematics Counts* (paragraph 278), 'the ability to carry out a particular numerical operation and the ability to know when to use it are not the same: both are needed'.

If the children are to gain both an understanding of the necessary basic computational skills, and confidence in using them in applications, we must engage them in discussions about the methods which they can use in their calculations, arguing about alternative ways of proceeding in solving problems arising in applications of their work. We must persuade them to take for granted how one can explicitly discuss ways of working. By such means we develop further their appreciation of how to communicate in mathematical terms.

It is this explicit discussion of 'ideas' which we aim particularly to begin to develop at this stage of our work, alongside the natural extension of the range and scope of the problems we raise with the children in the light of their broadening interests.

But, as we cannot say too often, the interests and enthusiasms of the individual child, and his or her particular problems in deploying the necessary mathematical skills at the right time and in the right place, are known only to the class teacher. What we have to offer is overall support not just in book form, but also (and never to be forgotten), in the form of supporting classroom material for individual and general class use, for you the teacher to use in association with the Pupils' Books.

As we continue to produce our material, debate also continues about the most efficient and appropriate ways to assess progress of pupils through the detail of the National Curriculum in mathematics. For our part we cannot believe that the difficult problems of assessment of all pupils, particularly at the earlier ages, will be easily solved; further debate and change in the light of experience will, we believe, continue to be inevitable.

This does not deter us. We see our role as supporting the teachers in their efforts to educate their pupils to work in mathematics with enthusiasm and confidence, following a course of study developed in the light of the National Curriculum in the subject. The abilities and attitudes we wish to aim to instill in the pupils are such that they should be able to face assessment at any appropriate level, and in whatever form, confident about what they know, understand, and can do.

Sir Wilfred Cockcroft

About the Series

New Curriculum Mathematics for Schools offers children an integrated approach to mathematics. It has six main strands: pattern, number, data handling, shape and space, measurement, and algebraic relations. All are intended to be taught in the first place through activities and all are interrelated. Understanding is fundamental to our course. We believe that to understand something it should be seen in a variety of situations which have as many inter-connections as possible. Each piece of work begins with children being encouraged to model their mathematics with apparatus. Only after work with appropriate apparatus should the children turn to the books.

'The transition from the use of concrete

materials to abstract thinking takes place slowly and gradually; and even those children to whom abstract thinking appears to come easily often need to undertake practical exploration at the beginning of a new topic.' (*Mathematics Counts:* paragraph 296)

The Materials

Key Stage 2 materials consist of five Pupils' Books, each supported by a Teacher's Guide, a pack of Activity Cards and a pack of Copymasters. Figure 1 shows how the materials cover Levels 3 to 6 of the National Curriculum. A Curriculum Leader's Manual covering the whole of Key Stage 2 will also be available.

	Level 3		Level 4		Level 5/6
Key Stage 1 overlap	Pupils' Book 1	Pupils' Book 2	Pupils' Book 3	Pupils' Book 4	Pupils' Book 5
	Teacher's Guide 1	Teacher's Guide 2	Teacher's Guide 3	Teacher's Guide 4	Teacher's Guide 5
	Activity Cards 1	Activity Cards 2	Activity Cards 3	Activity Cards 4	Activity Cards 5
	Copy-masters 1	Copy-masters 2	Copy-masters 3	Copy-masters 4	Copy-masters 5

Figure 1

The Teacher's Guides

The Teacher's Guides are fundamental to the series. They are designed to offer detailed help to teachers as they plan the programmes of study for the children. Each Guide is divided into sections covering the topics in the Pupils' Book. These sections contain advice on the purpose of the work, the materials required, the necessary pre-page activities, key page points for each page of the Pupils' Book, further activities and check-ups (figure 2).

It is *not* intended that pupils attempt all the activities suggested. Teaching is about making selections, and teachers will need to find those activities which suit their children best.

The following is an introduction to the work which will be encountered in this Guide.

NUMBER

In Section 2, links are made with earlier tens and units work related to money. The essence of this section is to encourage children to explore ways of performing the calculations. Estimating and mental skills are required to play Sue at her own game on page 10.

Position value moves into hundreds, tens and units in Section 3, with the use of

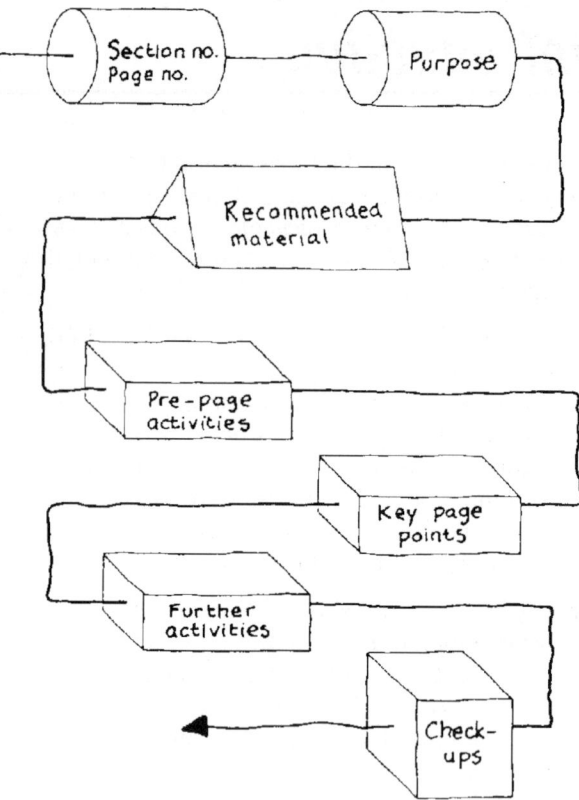

Figure 2

materials to model the hundred, ten and one relationship.

Section 5 introduces the addition of hundreds, tens and units, where situations are modelled, in the first instance, with size-related materials. Throughout the series there are a number of single concept pages in the Pupils' Books which highlight the process of the mathematics instead of the result of the process. It is intended that on these pages pupils will recount the experiences of the children shown in the illustrations. It is vital, therefore, that pupils have had similar experiences themselves before attempting the pages, and suggestions for suitable activities can be found in the pre-page activities. As these single concept pages can only illustrate one method, children should be encouraged to explore others.

Negative numbers are introduced in Section 7 through the topic of the weather and the use of calculators. Looking at the weather across the USA offers a range of temperatures for the children to study. Comparisons can be made and in question 3 on page 32 these comparisons need to be illustrated on temperature/thermometer charts. It will be up to individual teachers to decide if these comparisons should be developed to include number sentences such as $24 - ^{-}24 = 48$ (for Minneapolis). Types of numbers are introduced on page 34 when children are asked to find as many ways of

About the Series

writing ⁻5 as they can. Logic activities are also recommended.

Multiplication is developed in Section 8 to extend the product range considered in Book 1 (the 5 x 5 matrix and the 2, 5 and 10 tables) to include the full range of products with the use of the 'x' sign predominant. In this series pupils are encouraged to read, interpret and model number sentences. Thus 4 x 8 = 32 should be read as 'four multiplied by eight equals thirty-two' and can be modelled by taking a set of four objects eight times to produce thirty-two altogether. Children are encouraged to recognise situations where such sentences appear. The laws of mathematics are built into the activities throughout the series. The commutative property of addition has been considered (1 + 2 = 2 + 1), and recurs for multiplication, where we stress that 4 x 8 and 8 x 4 produce the same result in mathematics but illustrate a different image in reality. The use of the distributive property of multiplication over addition {6 x 9 = (6 x 5) + (6 x 4)} is vital in understanding the multiplication algorithm, and is considered in the activities leading into and out of page 45 in the Pupils' Book. The committing to memory of number facts is important and the following paragraph from *Mathematics Counts* (paragraph 298) seems most appropriate: 'The learning of number facts to which we have referred needs to be based on understanding, but understanding does not necessarily result in remembering. A time comes, therefore, when most children need to make a conscious effort to commit these number facts to memory'. Teachers need to plan to include appropriate work in the programmes of study for their pupils. It should also be stressed that number facts are not the only elements of mathematics which need to be remembered.

'Difference', 'take away' and 'adding on' are aspects of subtraction covered in Sections 13, 16 and 17. The single concept pages 56–9 typify the approach suggested in the activities. As we have already said, pupils are expected to have had similar experiences to those outlined on these single concept pages before attempting to complete them. Sharing in Section 10 develops experiences based on 'lower' products/quotients to feature those 'higher' products encountered in the multiplication section. Section 10 again uses models which are designed to emphasise the repeated subtraction aspect of the sharing process. Picture stories and number stories are also used. Again the children are asked to record sentences such as '36 ÷ 9 = 4 because 9 x 4 = 36', for in doing so they should gain a better understanding of the type of sharing situation the sentence represents. When using a calculator in 'real' sharing situations, whole number results may not always occur. This section deals with this aspect of 'between-ness', which is also developed in Section 15.

PATTERN (leading to Algebra)

'At all ages children should be encouraged to look for "pattern" in the results they obtain and to explain this in words even though they may not be able to express in algebraic terms what they have observed' (*Mathematics Counts*, paragraph 227). This series takes this advice to heart and in both the Pupils' Book and the suggested activities, teachers will find ample opportunity to discuss mathematical patterns with the children. The frequently recommended 'ways of writing' activity provides opportunities for children to investigate a sequence which may well take them into those parts of mathematics which they 'haven't done yet'. In other circumstances

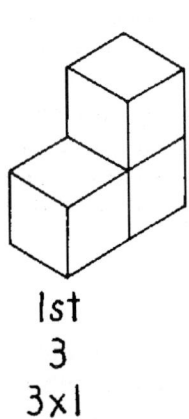
1st
3
3 x 1

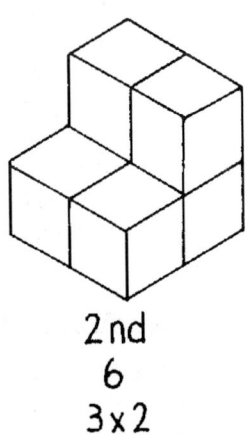
2nd
6
3 x 2

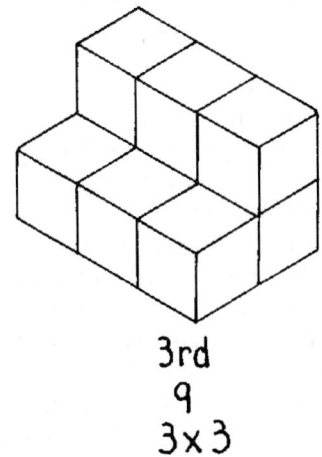
3rd
9
3 x 3

Figure 3

what appears to be a routine practice exercise may have something which the children can generalise about. Laws of mathematics, such as the distributive property in multiplication, can be articulated if the children can see the pattern in their results. Section 12 is a specific pattern section where pupils are asked to create sequences (as in figure 3), discover relationships and make predictions such as 'I think the tenth in the sequence will be …'.

MEASUREMENT

Work on the 24-hour clock is provided in Section 4 using bus and flight timetables. The ordering of events is consolidated on pages 18 and 19 where children are introduced to time zones around the world. The juxtaposition of this time sequence with an addition algorithm is deliberate, to link with the ordering of the addition algorithm mentioned earlier. Work on timetables provides the opportunity to see how many buses/planes are needed to operate a route. The conservation of the square metre leads into using this larger unit to find areas in Section 11. Modelling the number of square metres which cover the area of the classroom floor provides an opportunity to link arrays with area, leading into multiplication. As well as counting squares, children may see the chance to use the distributive laws to discover a way to calculate the result.

Small units of capacity are used in Section 14 with millilitres being featured. Children are encouraged to find relationships between 'small' containers such as cups, container caps and spoons. The relationship between the amount a container holds and its cost is also considered when looking at, for example, the cost of a large and a small drink. We encourage children to 'think metric', yet be aware of the units of measure in common everyday use. The approximate nature of measurement is a feature of all work in this section.

SHAPE AND SPACE

Devices to measure 'horizontal' and 'vertical' are suggested in Section 6 with positions pinpointed by coordinates. Rotational symmetry in Section 8 encourages children to explore similarities and differences as shapes fit, or don't fit, onto themselves, first by looking at container lids and then the plane shape derivatives. Solid shapes are investigated in terms of sides, faces, vertices, angle features and other geometrical properties. Logic activities in the notes are intended to develop 'critical' thinking, challenging the children to consider whether, for example, a square belongs in the set of rectangles!

DATA HANDLING

Collecting and analysing data is the opening section in Book 2. Pages 2 and 3 of the Pupils' Book provide a game board for the children to use, analyse and then improve on, using multiplication facts learned earlier. The analysis in this section includes the use of pictograms, where the uncertainty of interpreting some of these is highlighted. An investigation into the frequency of letters is used to see how this information is useful in the design of 'Letraset' type products and 'Scrabble' board games.

Section 15 provides a simple introduction to finding the mean average, while Section 18 looks at situations involving collecting sets of 'free' gifts within supermarket products, and encourages the children to set up their own enquiries.

'The mere drawing of graphs should not be over-emphasised. It is essential to discuss and interpret the information which is displayed in graphs which the children have themselves drawn and also in graphs which they have not.' (*Mathematics Counts*, paragraph 293).

A number of the activities which are suggested require the children to survey 100 events. In the analysis of the data the children should be encouraged to say things like '20 in 100 scored …'. Our intention is, of course, to lay a foundation for the introduction of percentages later in Book 3. Throughout this series we often recommend that a class graph is made and displayed. This will involve contributions from the whole class and may well evolve over a period of time, providing ample opportunities for discussion. When making a class block graph, the children may like to colour-code the squares they fill in so that individual contributions can be easily identified.

It is recommended that teachers keep a selection of graphs made by different groups from year to year so that they can be compared by other children performing similar tasks. In this way the children will develop a better understanding of the general nature of these surveys and not be influenced totally by a single activity.

The Pupils' Books

These are not books to 'get on with', but have rather been designed to stimulate joint activity between pupil and pupil, and pupil and teacher. The single concept page is a feature which builds on experiences children have had in class. Comments on each page of the Pupils' Book can be found in the *Key page points* for each section.

The Activity Cards

The Activity Card Pack for Pupils' Book 2 contains 64 cards, most of which should be cut up along the broken lines and used in conjunction with the notes. Some of the cards can be used together to form a board for a game.

The Copymasters

The 94 copymasters for Pupils' Book 2 provide both support for some of the Pupils' Book pages and extra material. The page support masters should help the children with their recording of the work on certain pages of the Pupils' Book. A symbol is included on those pages so that the pupil will know that a master is available. Suggestions for when to use the copymasters are included in the activity notes. Teachers will need to make selections of the material both in the Guide and from elsewhere.

The Course as a Whole

In creating this integrated course the authors have been concerned throughout their work to support classroom activity in all possible ways.

ACTIVITY

First and foremost it is expected that children's participation will be active. In whatever form the work takes – either through extended practical work, for the child who takes a long time to understand the processes he or she is involved in, or in work with symbols, on paper, which comes more easily for some children than for others – there must be active participation by all, each at an appropriate level. Better delay a while to firm up ideas than hurry on in the name of traditional expectations.

INVOLVEMENT

Activity of the kind we envisage can only come about if everyone is involved. The natural curiosity of the children must be exploited to the full. Even at the earliest stages the questions 'why?', or 'but what if?', need to be encouraged. 'Whatever their level of attainment, pupils should not be allowed to experience repeated failure' is how *Mathematics Counts* describes the situation which can so easily come about if pupils are not involved, i.e. working within their competence and being appropriately stretched by well-guided activity.

CONCRETE AND ABSTRACT

It goes without saying that this series constantly advocates concrete introductions to abstract ideas. Problem solving in practical situations, followed by discussion between pupils and with the teacher, are an essential beginning at each level. Do not be afraid of a sideways move to different topics, rather than pursuing ideas for too long a period. Ideas take time to mature before they can be seen to have been taken in at an abstract level.

DISCUSSION

It is in discussion with the teacher that the level of understanding of the individual child can be examined. The dialogue which is needed must not only enable the teacher to diagnose difficulties, but also stimulate confidence in what the child understands. Improvement of memory can be helped, by questioning the child in ways which show how connections between remembered facts can 'jog one's memory' and help the recognition of forgotten, or indeed new, information.

AT-HOMENESS

Through involvement in activities, and discussion of both concrete and abstract ideas, there can develop that at-homeness with 'numbers and the ability to make use of mathematical skills' which *Mathematics Counts* sees as essential in developing numeracy. Playing games involving counting on in a board game, or adding numbers on a pair of dice are both examples of situations in which children can be seen to be taking for granted, at the earliest stages, their number skills. There is more to numeracy than skills with numbers, and the understanding of information presented in diagrammatic or graphical form is part of our intention.

APPLICATIONS

The world around us is full of applications of mathematics. The shapes we pick up and use every day of our lives illustrate pattern in three dimensions. Our earliest explorations of the world around us form the background to our mathematical developments; we cannot divorce ourselves from the use of the subject outside and inside the classroom.

DISPLAY

The activities in the Teacher's Guides provide many opportunities for devising mathematical displays. Teachers should take every opportunity to develop material both for display in the classroom and around the school. This can take various forms:
- exhibits which are a record of the work

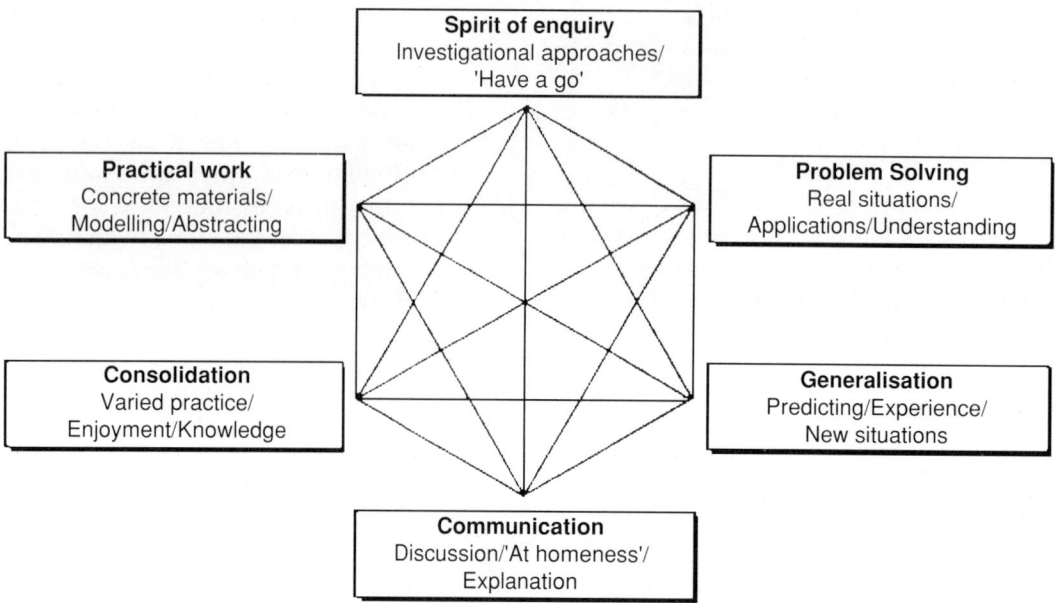

Figure 4

children have done;
- material which poses questions or suggests participation is some activity;
- publicity which is a point of reference for the children and may well remain on exhibition for quite some time.

Of course the three categories are not mutually exclusive. However, do make sure the display is in a prominent position to suit its needs. As one walks round the school, even when the children have gone home, the quality of the wall display will indicate not only the excellence of the mathematics going on in the school but also the importance the subject has in the life of the pupils.

'During every mathematical lesson a child is not only learning, or failing to learn, mathematics as a result of the work he/she is doing but is also developing his/her attitude towards mathematics. In every mathematics lesson his/her teacher is conveying, even if unconsciously, a message about mathematics which will influence this attitude .... The challenge for the teacher is to present mathematics in ways which continue to be interesting and enjoyable, and so allow understanding to develop.'
(*Mathematics Counts:* paragraphs 345-7)

CONSOLIDATION

When work is put together for display, we are in one way consolidating our work. Practical work, abstract work, problem solving, discussion, recognition of use, have to be put together and considered as a whole, as we move on. Time to reflect on 'where we are' and 'what we are now able to do', is as essential as first developments of what we might like to be able to do. Only through practice and recognition of routines do we come to be at home with our skills.

CONFIDENCE

The aim throughout the course must be to instil confidence. If we are to improve standards pupils need to be given a belief in their ability. For most children this means recognising that they do have mathematical skills in practical situations, that they can solve problems in the world around them. Not that they can reproduce in rote fashion ideas which they cannot use.

So, once again, the *Pupils' Books* are only a part of the work of this course. They cannot stand alone and are useful only in the context of practical work with concrete materials. As paragraph 243 of *Mathematics Counts* says:

'Mathematics teaching at all levels should include opportunities for:
- exposition by the teacher;
- discussion between teacher and pupils and between pupils themselves;
- appropriate practical work;
- consolidation and practice of fundamental skills and routines;
- problem solving, including the application of mathematics to everyday situations;
- investigational work.'

We cannot think of a better summary of the kind of teaching we hope the series will lead to and support.

National Curriculum Attainment Targets in Mathematics for Key Stages 1–4 (1991)

Attainment Target 1: Using and Applying Mathematics

Pupils should choose and make use of knowledge, skills and understanding outlined in the programmes of study in practical tasks, in real-life problems and to investigate within mathematics itself. Pupils would be expected to use with confidence the appropriate mathematical content specified in the programmes of study relating to the other attainment targets.

Attainment Target 2: Number

Pupils should understand and use number including estimation and approximation, interpreting results and checking for reasonableness.

Attainment Target 3: Algebra

Pupils should recognise and use symbolic and graphical representation to express relationships.

Attainment Target 4: Shape and Space

Pupils should recognise and use the properties of two- (2-D) and three-dimensional (3-D) shapes and use measurement, location and transformation in the study of space.

Attainment Target 5: Handling Data

Pupils should collect, process and interpret data and should understand, estimate and use probabilities.

Key Stage 2 Pupils' Book 2   Reference and Matching of National Curriculum Attainment Targets, Statements of Attainment and Levels

Note: **AT 5 3b** refers to Attainment Target 5, Level 3b.

Game Boards	p2–3	**AT 5 3b. AT 1 3b, 3c.**
A Watch Survey	p4	**AT 5 3a, 3b. AT 1 3c.**
Can It be Right?	p5	**AT 4 4d. AT 1 3a, 4c. AT 5 3a, 3d.**
Making Letters	p6	**AT 5 3a, 3b. AT 1 3b, 3d.**
The Hidden Message	p7	**AT 3 3a. AT 1 3a.**
At the Grocer's / At the Fruit Shop	p8–9	**AT 2 3e. AT 1 3a, 3b, 3c.**
Sue's Game	p10	**AT 2 3a. AT 1 3a, 3c.**
Choc Ices	p11	**AT 2 3c. AT 1 3c.**
Scoreboard	p12–13	**AT 2 3a. AT 1 3c.**
Targets	p14	**AT 2 3a. AT 1 3c.**
The Watchmaker's Shop Window	p15	**AT 5 3a. AT 2 3e. AT 1 3a, 3c.**
The Bus Station / The Classroom Travel Agent	p16–17	**AT 5 3a. AT 1 3a, 3b, 3c, 3d.**
Around the World	p18–19	**AT 5 3a. AT 1 3a, 3b, 3c.**
The Best Kept Village	p20–21	**AT 2 3a, 3d, 4a. AT 1 3b, 3c.**
The Best Kept Village	p22–23	**AT 2 3a, 3d, 4a. AT 3 2b. AT 1 3b, 3c.**

Find the Sum / Waste Paper	p24–25	**AT 2 3a, 4a.** AT 3 2b. AT 1 3b, 3c.
Travel Service / Tell Me a Story	p26–27	**AT 5 3a.** AT 2 3a, 3e, 4a. AT 1 3c.
Matchstick Maths	p28–29	**AT 4 2b, 4b.** AT 3 4a. AT 1 3c.
Moving a Shape / How Do They Look?	p30–31	**AT 4 4a, 4b.** AT 3 4a. AT 1 3c, 3d.
World Weather: The USA	p32–33	**AT 5 3a.** AT 2 3e. AT 1 3a, 3c.
Everybody Counts	p34	**AT 2 3e.** AT 3 2b. AT 1 3a, 3c, 3d.
The Solid Shape Quiz	p35	**AT 4 2a, 3a.** AT 1 3b, 3c, 3d.
Boxes / Quick Fit	p36–37	**AT 4 2a, 3a.** AT 1 3b, 3c, 3d.
Party Time	p38–39	**AT 1 3a, 3b, 3c.** AT 2 3c.
Situations / Have a Go	p40–41	**AT 2 3b, 3c.** AT 3 2b, 3a. AT 1 3a, 3b, 3c, 3d.
At the Baker's / At the Toy Shop	p42–43	**AT 2 3b, 3c.** AT 3 3a. AT 1 3a, 3b, 3c, 3d.
Tiles / Grow It Yourself	p44–45	**AT 2 3b, 3c.** AT 3 2b, 3a. AT 1 3a, 3c, 3d.
Bingo	p46	**AT 2 3b, 3c, 4a.** AT 3 2b. AT 1 3b, 3c.
The Apple Orchard	p47	**AT 2 3b, 3c, 4a.** AT 3 2b, 3a. AT 1 3a, 3b, 3c, 3d.
The Bakery / Make the Shares Equal	p48–49	**AT 2 3b, 3c, 4a.** AT 3 2b, 3a. AT 1 3c, 3d.
Do It and Undo It / A Two-stage Function Machine	p50–51	**AT 2 3b, 3c.** AT 3 2b, 3a, 3b, 4a. AT 1 3c, 3d.
The Classroom Floor	p52–53	**AT 4 4d, 5d.** AT 2 3c, 3e, 4e. AT 3 2b. AT 1 3a, 3b, 3c, 3d.
Puzzle Patterns	p54–55	**AT 3 2b, 3a, 4a.** AT 1 3a, 3c, 3d.
A Petrol Survey	p56–57	**AT 2 3a, 3d, 4a, 4b.** AT 3 2b. AT 1 3a, 3b, 3c, 3d.
A Petrol Survey	p58–59	**AT 2 3a, 3d, 4a, 4b.** AT 3 2b. AT 1 3a, 3b, 3c, 3d.
What's the Difference? / Card Games	p60–61	**AT 2 3a, 3d, 4a, 4b.** AT 3 2b, 3a, 4a. AT 1 3a, 3b, 3c, 3d.
Weighing in the Kitchen / Fly Away	p62–63	**AT 2 3a, 3d, 4a, 4b.** AT 3 2b. AT 5 3b. AT 1 3a, 3b, 3c, 3d.
Full Measure / The Lemonade Stall	p64–65	**AT 4 4d.** AT 2 3e, 4c. AT 3 2b. AT 5 3b. AT 1 3a, 3b, 3c.
Holiday Pocket Money / The Charity Stall	p66–67	**AT 5 3a, 3b, 4c.** AT 3 4b. AT 2 3c, 3d, 4a. AT 1 3b, 3c, 4a.
Clearing the Playground	p68–69	**AT 5 3a, 3b, 3c, 3d, 4c.** AT 2 3c, 4a. AT 1 3b, 3c.
The School Newspaper / Ways of Writing	p70–71	**AT 2 3a, 3d, 4a, 4b.** AT 3 2b. AT 1 3a, 3b, 3c.
Sentences to Read / Other Ways of Doing	p72–73	**AT 2 3a, 4a, 4b, 4d.** AT 3 4a. AT 1 3b, 3c.
The Maths Class	p74	**AT 2 3a, 4b, 4d.** AT 1 3a, 3b, 3c, 3d.
Shopping for a Present	p75	**AT 2 3e, 4a, 4c.** AT 1 3a, 3b, 3c.
At the Supermarket / Mother's Day	p76–77	**AT 2 3d, 3e, 4c, 4d.** AT 1 3a, 3b, 3c.
At the Station	p78	**AT 2 3b, 3c, 3d, 3e, 4a, 4c, 4d.** AT 1 3a, 3b, 3c.
Collecting Badges	p79–80	**AT 5 3b, 3d, 4d.** AT 1 3c, 3d, 3e.

Section 1

AT 1 3a, 3b, 3c, 3d, 4c. AT 3 3a. AT 4 4d. AT 5 3a, 3b, 3d.

Pages 2–7 Data Handling

Pages 2 and 3 Game Boards

Page 4 Watch Survey

Page 5 Can It Be Right?

Page 6 Making Letters

Page 7 The Hidden Message

Purpose

To provide the children with practice in reading and drawing bar graphs, and using the information in their mathematics.
To encourage the children to predict the outcomes of random events.
To introduce the pictogram as a means of data presentation.
To encourage the children to practise the multiplication facts within the 2, 3, 4 and 5 tables.
To give the children practice in finding multiples.

Recommended material

1. The Multiplication Race Track is included on pages 2 and 3 of the Pupils' Book. To play the game you will require a good supply of blank dice and counters.

2. Spinners and overlays as shown in figures 1.2 and 1.6.

3. Examples of pictograms from newspapers and magazines.

4. **Copymasters 1.1–1.12.**

5. 1 cm squared paper and tracing paper.

6. Scrabble game.

Pre-page activities

Note In *New Curriculum Mathematics for Schools* we often suggest a class graph is made. This can take the form of a block graph where all the children make a contribution by completing a 'square' with their own colour code or mark. The graphs illustrated on pages 2 and 3 of Pupils' Book 2 are examples of class graphs. A bar chart can also be created from a class frequency/tally chart where all the children have contributed to the frequency/tally chart before the bar chart is made.

1. Have the children turn to pages 2 and 3 in the Pupils' Book and play the Multiplication Race Track Game (figure 1.1). The game requires two dice, both marked with the numbers 2, 3, 4 and

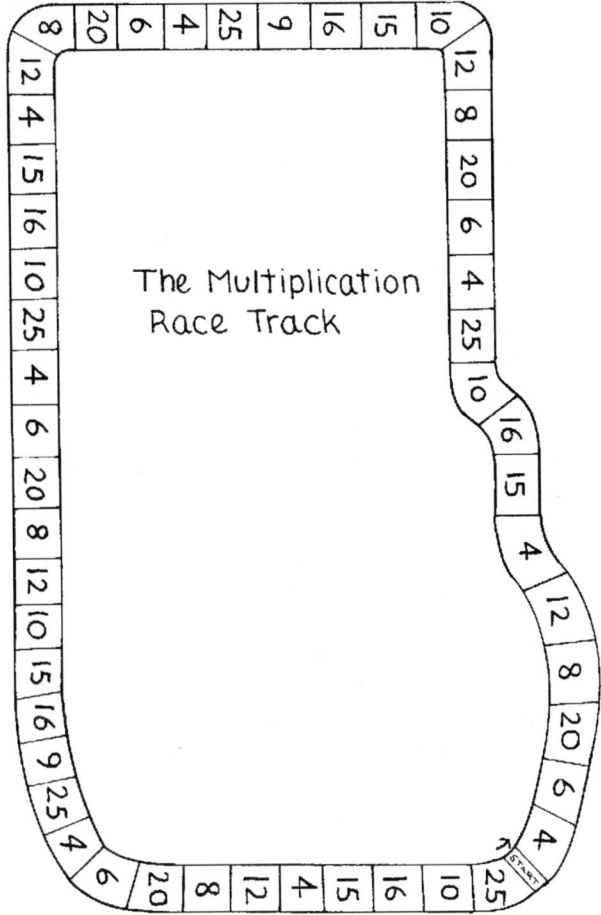

Figure 1.1

5, and with the remaining two faces blank. The players have to decide which numbers to repeat on the blank faces, e.g. a player may decide to include an extra 2 and 3, in which case both the cubes will be marked 2, 2, 3, 3, 4 and 5. To play the game the first player rolls the two dice and finds the product of the numbers shown. He/she then moves a counter along the track to where that product number appears ahead of them on the track. Players take it in turns to throw the selected dice. The first player to pass the chequered flag wins.
You may like to discuss the page with the class and decide on a number of dice to use. Make sure the children play with a variety of dice, marked according to the rules, and have them record on a class graph how many throws they took to finish the game with their particular dice. Check that the class graph displayed indentifies the pair of dice used in that particular game. Get the children to analyse the class graph 'as it grows'.

2. Ask the children to investigate the frequency of obtaining 5 and 10 using a spinner with an overlay as shown in figure 1.2. Note that on this

New Curriculum Mathematics for Schools Key Stage 2

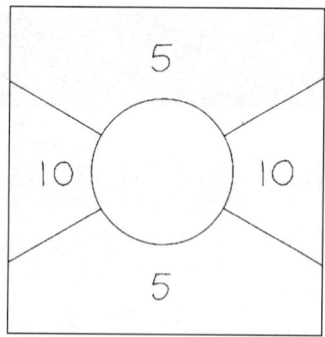

Figure 1.2

overlay the '5' sectors cover twice as much area as the '10' sectors.

Let the children design their own data collection chart, and make a graph of their results. If they conduct 100 trials, they will probably encounter the difficulty of drawing a bar with a length of, say, 68 units on the paper available. If small units are chosen, they might find it tedious and time-consuming to label every unit. Discuss with the children how such difficulties might be overcome. They may well decide that a 1 cm length can be used to represent five tally marks, in which case discuss with them how to label the axes, and where bars showing lengths of, say, 68 and 32 will be drawn. Their graph might well look like the one shown in figure 1.3.

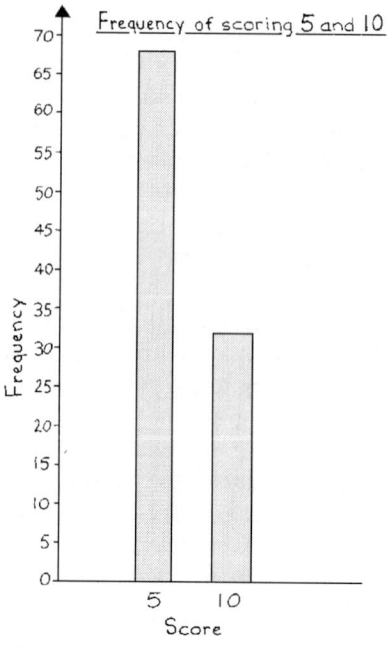

Figure 1.3

Encourage the children to write about their results, e.g. '68 times out of 100 a 5 was scored. 32 times out of 100 a 10 was scored. I think I am twice as likely to get a 5 as a 10'. Ask the children to make predictions based on their observations, e.g. 'If I spin the spinner 30 times, I think that I will get 5 about 20 times, and 10 about 10 times'.

3. Have the children make a collection of pictograms from newspapers and magazines. Discuss with them what each picture represents, e.g. a complete 'picture' may well represent ten items, in which case a part of the 'picture' may represent five. Discuss the possible multiples used in these representations.

4. Get the children to conduct a survey to find out how many apples, oranges, pears and bananas would be needed if each child in the school is to be given his or her favourite of these fruits on a special occasion such as Christmas or Sports Day. (If there is a real situation analogous to this, so much the better.) Discuss with the children how the information can be collected. Does everyone need to be asked? Have the children record the results of the survey on a pictogram. The fruit pictures on Copymaster 1.1 can be used to help the children produce their pictogram. Each picture should represent the preference of more than one child. The scale used will obviously vary according to the number of children being surveyed, but considering a range of multiples (2, 3, 4, 5, 10) will encourage the children to make use of their 'tables'. Discuss with the children how they can represent less than the number of units represented by one picture (figure 1.4). Make sure the children write about their findings. (Note: there are two types of pictogram. In the type being used here the frequency is denoted by the number of pictures. The pictures should all be the same size. A less desirable type of

Figure 1.4

pictogram is one where the size of picture indicates the frequency. This can be misleading, as a doubling in one dimension of the picture results in a quadrupling of the area of the picture. See page 5 of the Pupils' Book.')

5. Have the children complete Copymaster 1.2. Here they are given a copy of a child's survey report, and they are asked to draw the graph and interpret it. Get the children to conduct their own yogurt survey by taking a sample of children in the school. Encourage them to discuss their findings with the school cook. Does he/she serve yogurt? If so, how often and what flavours? Is there ever any left over?

6. Have the children conduct their own survey into the frequency of letters used in a passage of English. Copymaster 1.3 can be used, or a passage from a book or newspaper. The children should make a graph of their results, and comment on what they found. Get them to arrange the letters in rank order, the most used letter being placed first. Did every survey produce the same order?

7. Repeat activity 6 with other languages. Copymasters 1.4 and 1.5 can be used for French and German respectively. Have the children compare their results.

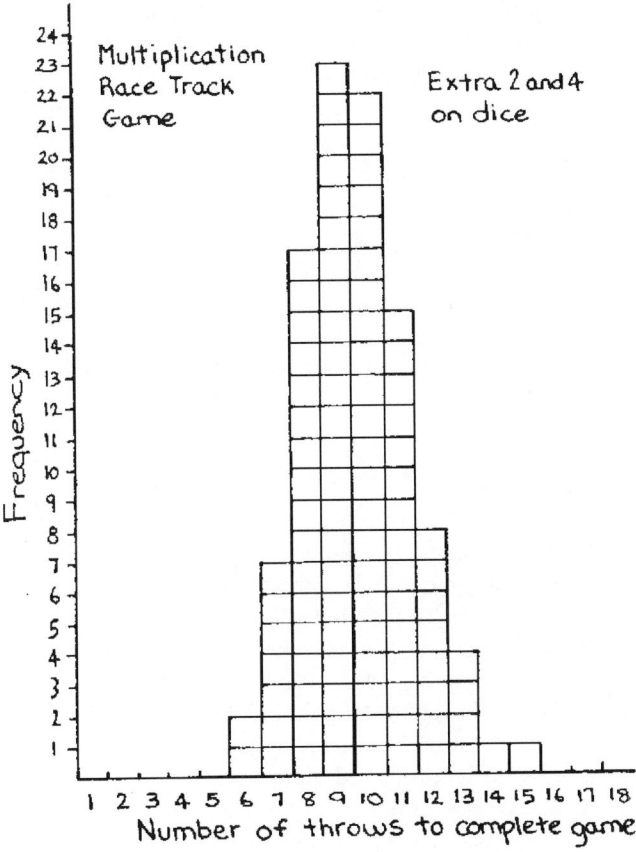

Key page points

Pages 2 and 3 Make sure the children are familiar with the game and its rules (see Pre-page activity 1). As the children consider the questions on the pages make sure they realise that Ming and Hannah have used their own special cubes to play the game a number of times and that they have recorded their results on their class graphs. Have the children complete an outcome chart for the dice Ming and Hannah used. (Copymaster 1.6 can be used.) Encourage the children to enlarge on the reports Ming and Hannah have started, using the information they found in question 1 on likely outcomes for given dice and the two class graphs shown (figure 1.5). Neither Ming nor Hannah has made reference to likely outcomes ... yet. Ask the children to use some cubes marked like Ming and Hannah's to see if they get similar results. Hannah is quoted as saying that she feels her cubes will produce a quicker result than Ming's. (Hannah has found that about 90 out of 100 of her games are over in less than ten throws whereas Ming finds 50 out of 100 take less than ten throws!) Have the children test Hannah's statement by allowing them to play the game again with the two sets of cubes and make their own class graph. See if they can say how the graphs may indicate that one set of cubes will have a faster result than the other.

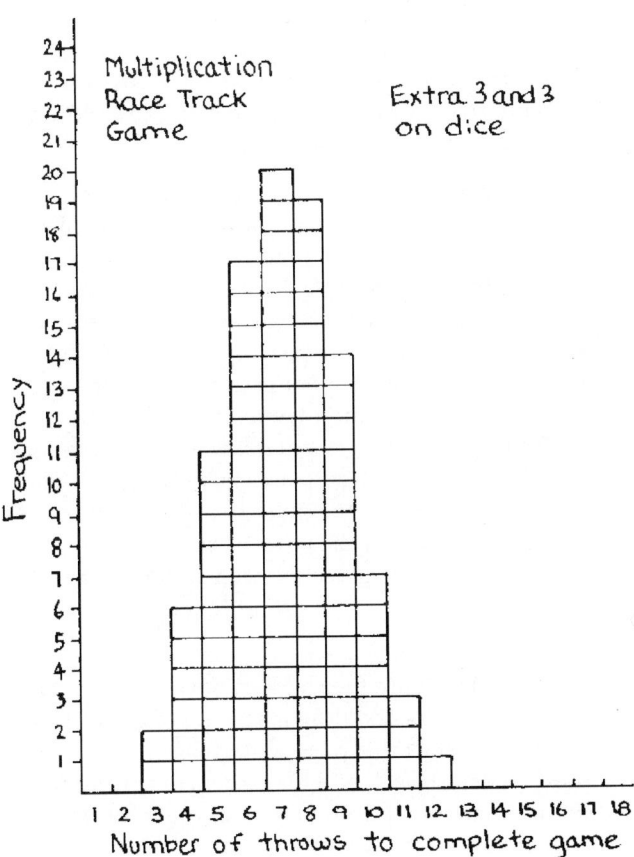

Figure 1.5

The following table gives an indication of the number of throws needed to finish the game using various combinations of dice.

Extra nos. on dice	2–2	2–3	2–4	2–5	3–3	3–4	3–5	4–4	4–5	5–5
Mean	10	9	10	10	7	9	9	9	9	9
Mode	10	9	9	9	7	8	8	9	9	9
Median	10	9	10	9	7	9	8	9	9	9
Range	14	13	14	14	12	13	13	13	12	12
% < 10	40	65	50	50	90	70	70	60	55	60

Page 4 Make it clear to the children that the pictogram illustrates the type of watch preferred and not necessarily the type worn. On the pictogram one watch represents ten people who like that type of watch. Half a watch represents less than ten people. The children should realise that question 2 is easy to answer because the watches shown are all whole. However, in question 3 it is impossible to say precisely just how many adults preferred digital watches as the 'half' watch could represent any number between 1 and 9. The phrases used in question 6 are to help the children realise that they cannot be accurate about the statements they make based on the chart shown. When the children are making their own chart, encourage them to try to be more accurate in their data presentation. The watch pictures on Copymaster 1.1 may be used to help the children produce accurate pictograms.

Page 5 The purpose of this page is to illustrate that pictograms which use scale as the frequency indicator are often inaccurate. Note that Gwen is tracing the outlines of the houses onto squared paper to check how much surface each covers. Provide some tracing paper for the children to trace the house in a similar manner. When the children tackle question 4, encourage them to investigate how they might draw a house covering exactly twice as many squares as the original. They will find this very difficult to do unless they change the shape of the house. Discuss how making one house twice the area of the other might be a better way of presenting the information.

Page 6 Make sure the children have done a survey of letters and drawn a graph of their results before they start this page. Copymaster 1.7 can be used for question 1, and the paper cut up and used to play Scrabble if desired. If someone produces a sheet with too few vowels and then attempts to play the game, he/she will probably discover how difficult it is to form words without them! To tackle question 4, where the activity is repeated using a different language, the children should have done a survey of letters for French, German, Italian, Spanish or whichever language they wish to study.

Page 7 Explain that the letters are represented by a code. Each letter is labelled by its position in the grid by reading the horizontal number first and then the vertical. Thus the label (3, 4) represents a 'w'. The children will need to work out which letters are missing, and their labels in the code. The final paragraph asks the children to make up their own code and write a message for a friend to discover.

Further activities

1. Let the children make their own Multiplication Race Track using Copymaster 1.8. They can write their own choice of numbers on this section of the track and then place it over half the track on pages 2 and 3 of their books. They can then play the game again, using dice marked 2, 3, 4, 5, ☐ and ☐, to see what happens with their own section. Alternatively, you could give the children two copies of the copymaster so that they can join them together to make a full track, on which they can write their own choice of numbers. Have them play the game on their own track and analyse the results.

2. Ask the children to carry out a traffic survey at a busier time or at a busier position than they might have done previously. Have them record their results on a pictogram. The vehicle pictures which are included on Copymaster 1.1 can be used to help them with this. Make sure the children write about their results. (If your school does not have a busy road, why not get some information from another school? If it does have a busy road, why not exchange your results with another school which has a similar amount of traffic, and let the children compare the make-up of the traffic? A school near a major tourist attraction is likely to record a large number of cars and coaches, whereas a school near an industrial estate is likely to record a large number of lorries.)

3. Present the children with some traffic survey graphs. Ask them to interpret the graphs and to say if they can predict where the survey may have been conducted. (See note in parentheses above.) As well as the situations already mentioned, include a graph with a large number of buses where the survey has been carried out, for example, near a bus station. When interpreting the graphs, encourage the children to make probability statements such as 'Our graph shows that 90 out of 100 vehicles passing the school are cars. The next vehicle to go past is very likely, but not certain, to be a car'.

4. Have the children complete Copymasters 1.9–1.11. These supply data collected at different times of the day on the number of vehicles passing a certain place. The children are asked to complete the frequency tables, label the axes and draw bar graphs. They should consider the changes in traffic flow indicated by the three graphs, and comment on the findings. Let them conduct a survey of their own at different times of the day and display their findings. Encourage them to make a picture or collage showing a street scene at two different times of the day.

5. Get the children to use pictograms to display some of the data they collect during school visits or as part of their other studies. The pictures of people on Copymaster 1.1 may be useful, e.g. to display information about the people waiting in queues for different rides at a theme park.

6. Have the children play the 5–10 Multiplication Game, a game for two players. The players take it in turns to spin two spinners with overlays as shown in figure 1.6. The product of the scores is found. Copymaster 1.12 can be used by the players to keep a record of their running total (figure 1.7). They should 'count on', and mark with a point the total after each turn. Make sure the children know how to mark a total with a units digit of 5, as the axis is marked in tens. The first player to cross the target line is the winner. After some experience of the game the children may like to use different coloured pens to mark both their scores on the same chart. They can then compare the paths they take to reach the total.

Ask the children to make a class block graph to record the number of turns required to reach the target (figure 1.8). Encourage the children to work in a logical way to find out all the possible outcomes. They should see that the numbers on the two spinners can be paired, and realise that the areas of the sectors will have an influence on the outcome.

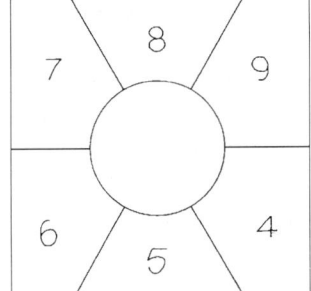

Figure 1.6

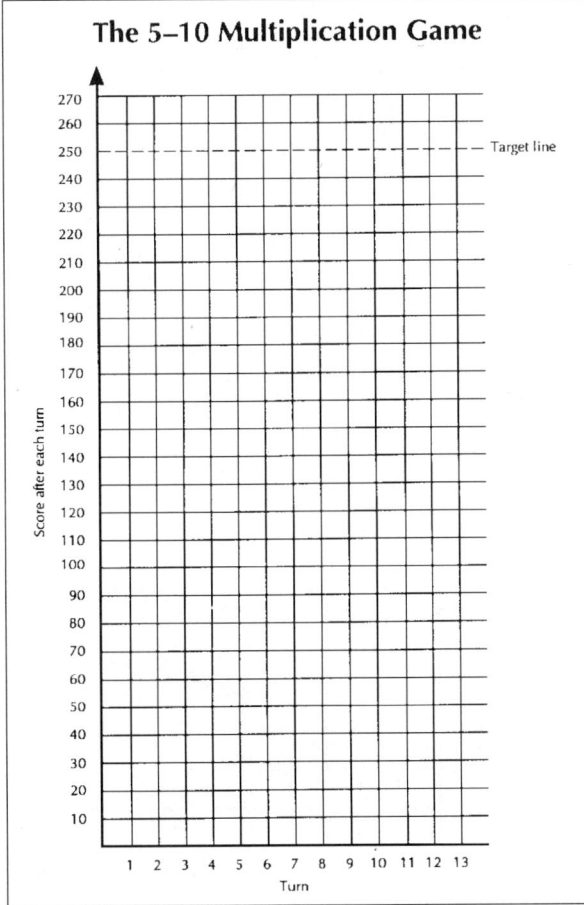

Figure 1.7

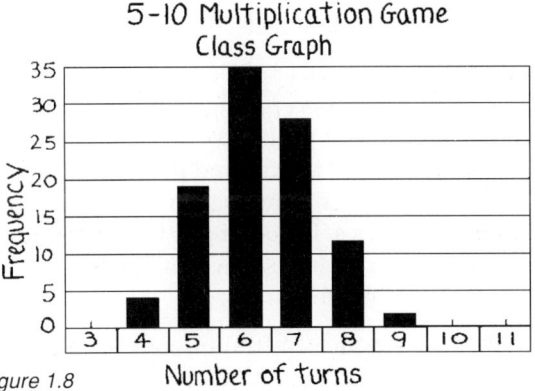

Figure 1.8

7. Ask the children to redesign the 5–10 spinners to make the 5–10 Multiplication Game (see 6 above) take longer to finish. (They will need to decrease the size of the '10' sectors to do this.) Have the children play some games and record, on a class chart, the number of turns to complete the game. Get the children to compare the chart with the one produced in activity 6 above. The children should realise that the possible outcomes in the two cases are the same, but the likelihood of each outcome is different (figure 1.9).

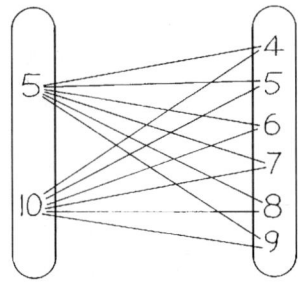

Finding all possible outcomes

×	4	5	6	7	8	9
5	20	25	30	35	40	45
5	20	25	30	35	40	45
10	40	50	60	70	80	90
10	40	50	60	70	80	90
10	40	50	60	70	80	90
10	40	50	60	70	80	90

Figure 1.9

8. Have the children mark a blank dice with 5s and 10s to obtain the same frequency distribution as the original spinner used in the 5–10 Multiplication Game (see 6 above). Let the children devise their own investigation to check if they have succeeded.

9. Ask the children to investigate the frequency of capital letters in passages of print. Do they get the same results as when they looked at letter frequency in Pre-page activity 6?

10. Talk to the children about old methods of printing where each letter had to be set individually. Have the children design a tray, on squared paper, for the typesetter to keep his letters safe and easy to find. Which letters will need the largest space? Which will need the smallest? The children will need to keep the capital and lower case letters separate. If you have a local newspaper office nearby, they may well be able to show you an old tray so that the children can compare their design with the ones actually used. If the children own a printing set of their own, ask them to bring it to school to see what letter distribution they have and how the container is designed.

11. Have each child set a puzzle for their friends. Ask them to choose a passage of print and to transpose some of the letters, for example exchanging a and j, and e and h. They should then complete a tally and bar chart to show the letter frequencies. By looking at the bar charts can the other children say which letters have been interchanged?

12. Make up a simple substitution code such as: a–p, b–z, c–l, d–a, e–j, f–n, g–v, h–e, i–y, etc. Encode a passage of about 100 words. Give the coded message to the children. Using their bar charts from the previous activity, they should be able to find the code for the most commonly occurring letters: e, t and i. When these letters are decoded, a guess can be made of possible words and thus further letters may be decoded. (Note: there are computer programs which will do the encoding for you and which will allow the children to try substitution quickly.)

13. Let the children make up coded messages for their friends to decode.

14. Ask the children to select a number of books of varying difficulty (perhaps at different levels in a reading scheme), and have them tally the number of words with 1, 2, 3, etc., letters. Get them to record their results on a bar chart, and to compare their charts. Can they find differences in the proportions of words of different length?

15. Have the children make a 3-D block graph display with the chips used in a game of Scrabble (figure 1.10). It may be possible to obtain versions in various languages, in which case a display of these chips would prove interesting. Have the children compare their models with the surveys they have done. The following information supplied by the makers of Scrabble may be of interest.

Scrabble letter distribution

English (100 tiles)

A	B	C	D	E	F
9	2	2	4	12	2
G	H	I	J	K	L
3	2	9	1	1	4
M	N	O	P	Q	R
2	6	8	2	1	6
S	T	U	V	W	X
4	6	4	2	2	1
Y	Z	blank			
2	1	2			

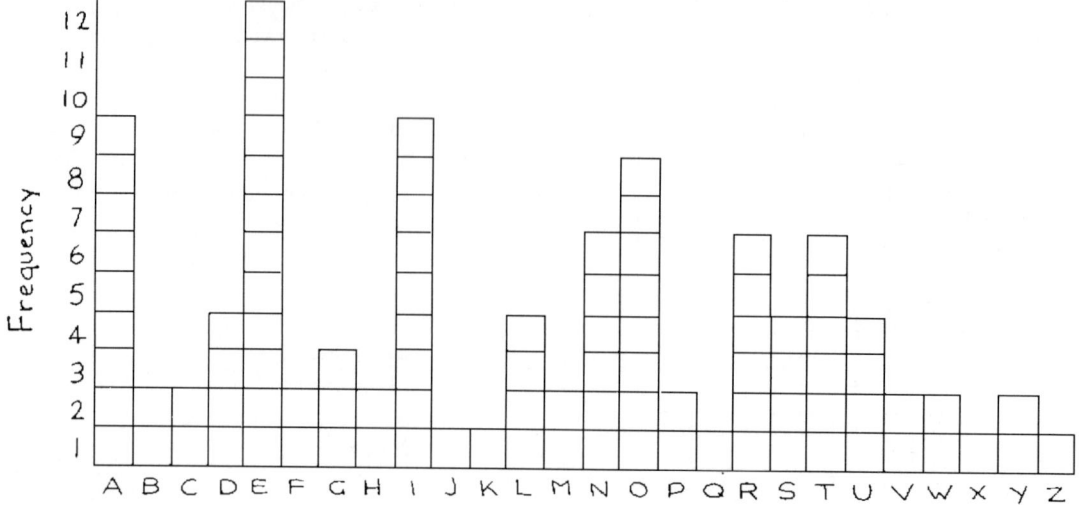

Figure 1.10   Block chart to show the distribution of letters in a game of Scrabble

French (103 tiles)

A	B	C	D	E	F
9	2	2	3	15	2
G	H	I	J	K	L
2	2	8	1	1	5
M	N	O	P	Q	R
3	6	6	2	1	6
S	T	U	V	W	X
6	6	6	2	1	1
Y	Z	blank			
2	1	2			

German (102 tiles)

A	B	C	D	E	F
5	2	2	4	15	2
G	H	I	J	K	L
3	4	6	1	2	3
M	N	O	P	Q	R
4	9	3	1	1	6
S	T	U	V	W	X
7	6	6	1	1	1
Y	Z	blank			
1	1	2			
also	Ä	Ö	Ü		
	1	1	1		

Spanish (101 tiles)

A	B	C	D	E	F
12	2	4	5	12	1
G	H	I	J	K	L
2	2	6	1	–	4
M	N	O	P	Q	R
2	5	9	2	1	5
S	T	U	V	W	X
6	4	5	1	2	1
Y	Z				
2	1				
also	CH	LL	RR	Ñ	
	1	1	1	1	

16. Ask the children to select a passage from a newspaper or magazine and make a tally and then a bar chart of every fifth letter. They should compare their results with the graph on page 6 of the Pupils' Book. This is a form of sampling and should agree reasonably well with the results of the frequency count for all the letters.

Check-ups

1. Can the children read bar graphs and use the mathematical information contained in them?

2. Can the children make statements about the outcomes of random events within their experience?

3. Can the children understand a pictogram when used to illustrate data?

4. Can the children use pictograms to display data?

5. Do the children recognise that all outcomes of certain events may not be equally likely?

6. Can the children make a graph of their results using non-unitary axes?

7. Can the children confidently add, mentally, multiples of 5 and 10?

8. Can the children quickly and accurately find multiples of 2, 3, 4, 5 and 10?

Note It is perhaps worth repeating what was said in the introduction, 'it is recommended that teachers keep a selection of graphs made by different groups, from year to year, so that they can be compared by children performing similar tasks. In this way the children will develop a better understanding of the general nature of these surveys and not be influenced totally by a single activity.'

New Curriculum Mathematics for Schools Key Stage 2

Section 2

AT 1 3a, 3b, 3c. AT 2 3a, 3e.

Pages 8–10   Tens and Units

Page 8   At the Grocer's

Page 9   At the Fruit Shop

Page 10   Sue's Game

Purpose

To review the addition and 'subtraction' of tens and units.
To encourage children to 'experiment' when dealing with tens and units number sentences.

Recommended material

1. 1–6 dice and spinners.
2. **Copymasters 2.1–2.7.**
3. Structural apparatus: Multibase materials (base 10) and interlocking cubes.
4. Cards for games (see Pre-page activities 4 and 9, and Further activities 10 and 12).
5. Calculators.
6. Shopping Triples (**Activity Cards 2.1–2.2**).
7. Dice for Target Golf (see Further activity 3).
8. Items and money for class shop.

Pre-page activities

1. Let the children play Go On, a game for two players. The players take it in turns to throw a 1–6 dice. Players can throw the dice as many times as they wish and they score the sum of the numbers shown on the dice on each series of throws. However, if a 1 is thrown, the scores for that series of throws are not counted. For example, if player A throws 6, 3, 3, 2, 2, and then decides to stop, the score is 16. If player B throws 3, 4, 2, 3, 5, 6, 6, 2, 4, then the score is 35. If player A throws again and gets 6, 5, 5, 3, for a score of 19, A's total so far is now 16 + 19 = 35. If B now throws again and records 6, 3, 2, 4, 1, he/she does not score anything for that turn. The winner is the first player to get a total of 90 or more. A 1–6 spinner may also be used in place of the dice.

2. Have the children consider ways of completing a sentence such as 38 + 27 = ☐ . Let them discuss the algorithms represented in figure 2.1.

Figure 2.1

Figure 2.2

Compare these with other ways of solving the problem (figure 2.2). Give the children some similar sentences to solve and ask them to complete their own 'think bubbles'. Display the range of solutions illustrated by the children. Copymaster 2.1 can be used to help the children compile their own cartoons. They should cut up the sheet, paste the frames onto paper and fill in the 'bubbles' to make their own mathematical cartoon strips. (Note: teachers may like to cut up several copies of Copymaster 2.1 and file them for the children to use, as appropriate, throughout the course.) Get the children to explain their algorithms to you, using apparatus such as base 10 materials.

3. Prepare some workcards involving two-digit addition sentences and ask the children to find the totals. Have them select three of the sentences and solve them again in two different ways. Ask the children to write a story for three of the others. Figure 2.3 shows a sample workcard.

4. Make and play Find the Sum. Make up a set of about 20 cards showing the addition of two two-digit numbers on one side, and the sum on the other side. Shuffle the cards and place them in a pile on the table with the additions face upwards. The first player takes the top card, states the sum and turns the card over. If the sum is correct, the player keeps the card. If the sum is wrong, the card is put at the bottom of the pile. The winner is the player who collects most cards.

5. Ask the children to use their calculators to find the sums of two two-digit numbers in different ways, and to record their findings, e.g. for 48 + 26 = 74:

   $\boxed{4}\boxed{8}\boxed{+}\boxed{2}\boxed{6}\boxed{=}$

   $\boxed{4}\boxed{8}\boxed{+}\boxed{6}\boxed{+}\boxed{1}\boxed{0}\boxed{+}\boxed{1}\boxed{0}\boxed{=}$

   $\boxed{2}\boxed{6}\boxed{+}\boxed{8}\boxed{+}\boxed{1}\boxed{0}\boxed{+}\boxed{1}\boxed{0}\boxed{+}$
   $\boxed{1}\boxed{0}\boxed{+}\boxed{1}\boxed{0}$

   $\boxed{4}\boxed{8}\boxed{M+}\boxed{2}\boxed{6}\boxed{M+}\boxed{MR}$

   $\boxed{4}\boxed{8}\boxed{M+}\boxed{6}\boxed{M+}\boxed{10}\boxed{M+}\boxed{10}\boxed{M+}\boxed{MR}$

6. Have the children explore number patterns as shown below. Get them to continue the sequences, perhaps encountering problems they haven't met before. If so, let them attempt a solution and then ask them to explain, using suitable materials, how they arrived at their result.

   (a) 36   46   56   66
       +27 +27 +27 +27

   (b) 76   66   56   46
       +15 +25 +35 +45

   (c) 24   29   34   39
       +19 +24 +29 +39

   Let the children make up their own patterns for a friend to complete.

7. Have the children consider ways of completing a difference/take away number sentence such as 65 − 36 = ☐. Get them to discuss the algorithms represented in figure 2.4. Compare these with other ways of solving the problem. Give the children some similar sentences to solve and ask them to complete their own 'think bubbles'. Display the range of solutions illustrated by the children. Copymaster 2.1 can again be used, as suggested in activity 2 above. Get the children to explain their algorithms to you, using apparatus such as base 10 materials.

8. Prepare some workcards involving two-digit difference/take away sentences and ask the

---

Solve the following.

```
  37      60      51      57
 +29     +33     +41     +46
 ___     ___     ___     ___

44+36=    40+39=        38+29=


  47      36      45      60
 +19     +18     +47     +35
 ___     ___     ___     ___

66+25=    49+43=        24+39=
```

| Solve three of the number sentences again in two different ways. | Write a story for any three of the above number sentences. |

Figure 2.3

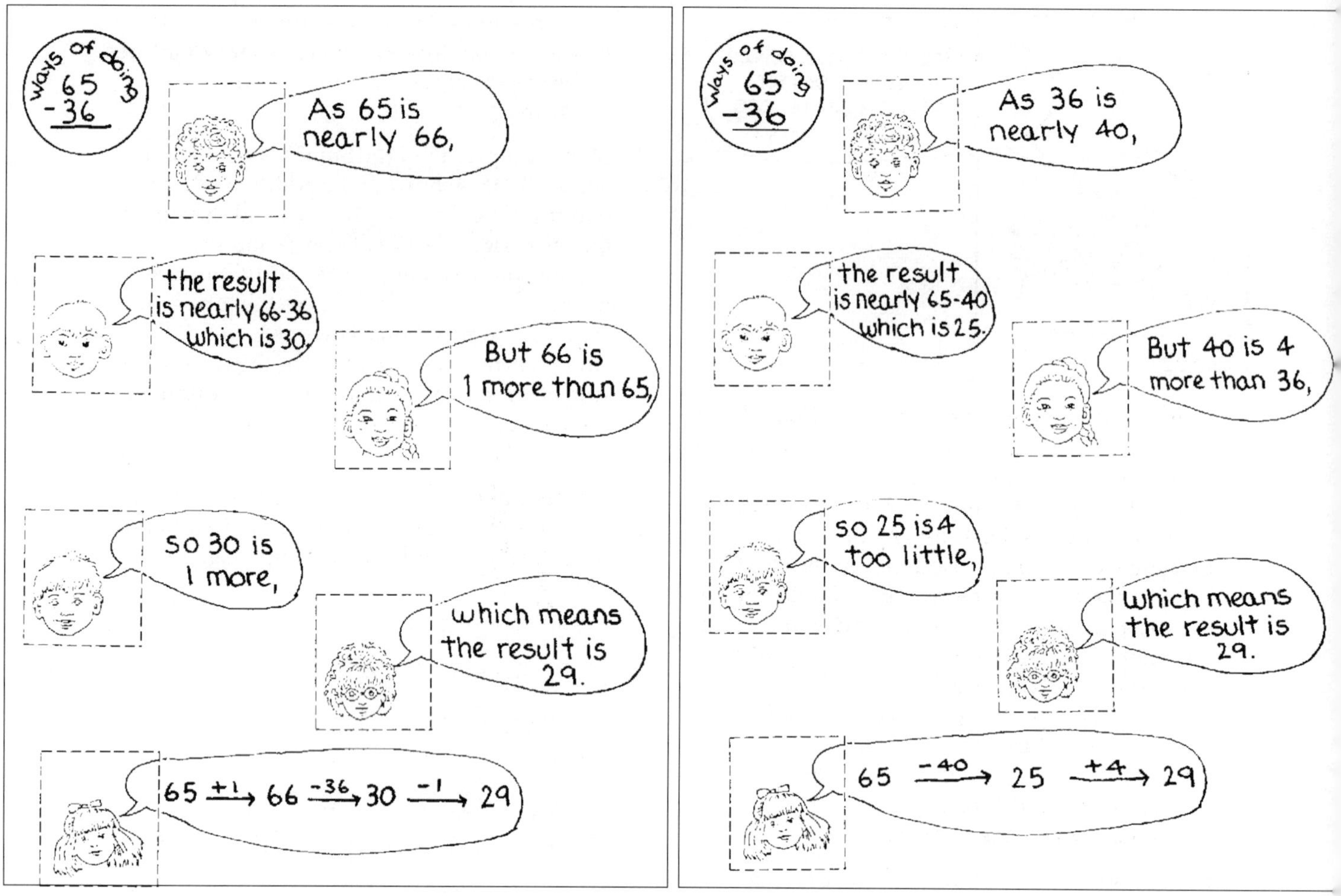

Figure 2.4

Left panel — Ways of doing 65 − 36:
- "As 65 is nearly 66,"
- "the result is nearly 66−36 which is 30,"
- "But 66 is 1 more than 65,"
- "so 30 is 1 more,"
- "which means the result is 29."
- 65 →(+1) 66 →(−36) 30 →(−1) 29

Right panel — Ways of doing 65 − 36:
- "As 36 is nearly 40,"
- "the result is nearly 65−40 which is 25,"
- "But 40 is 4 more than 36,"
- "so 25 is 4 too little,"
- "which means the result is 29."
- 65 →(−40) 25 →(+4) 29

Figure 2.4

---

children to solve them. Have them select three of the sentences and solve them again in two different ways. Ask the children to write a story for three of the others. Figure 2.5 shows a sample workcard.

9. Make and play Find the Difference. Make up a set of about 20 cards showing two-digit number differences on one side, and the solutions on the other side. Play the game as described in activity 4 above.

10. Have the children use their calculators to find the difference of two two-digit numbers in different ways, and ask them to record their findings, e.g. for 74 − 29 = 45:

    | 7 | 4 | − | 2 | 9 | = |
    | 7 | 4 | M+ | 2 | 9 | M− | MR |
    | 7 | 4 | − | 2 | 0 | − | 9 | = |
    | 7 | 4 | − | 9 | − | 2 | 0 | = |
    | 7 | 4 | − | 3 | 0 | + | 1 | = |
    | 7 | 0 | − | 2 | 9 | + | 4 | = |

11. Have the children explore number patterns as in activity 6 above, but this time using

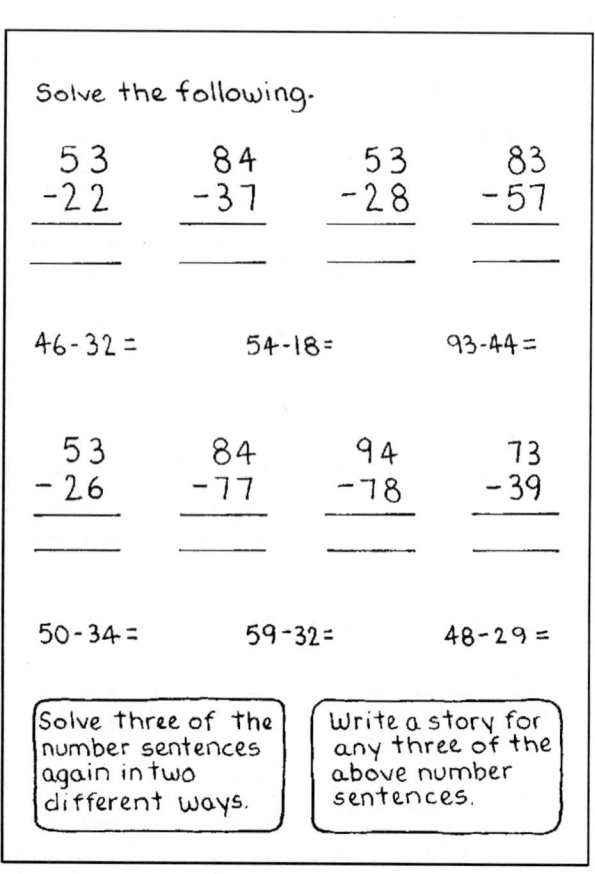

Figure 2.5

difference/take away sentences as shown below.

(a) 96   86   76   66
   −27 −27 −27 −27

(b) 83   73   63   53
   −18 −28 −38 −48

(c) 76   66   56   46
   −58 −48 −38 −28

Let the children again make up their own patterns for a friend to complete.

12. Write sets of three numbers such as 46, 37, 83, on the chalkboard and ask the children to write three related number sentences for each set, e.g. 46 + 37 = 83; 83 − 46 = 37; 83 − 37 = 46. Have them make up a story situation which uses all three sentences.

Key page points

Page 8 This page gives the children practice in the mental addition of two two-digit numbers. Discuss with them the different ways of adding 28p and 37p presented on the page. Try using ten pieces and units, 10p and 1p coins, and a 1–100 number line to illustrate the methods used. Discuss with the children which they think is the 'best' way for them to find a particular sum. How does the way they visualise the operation relate to their choice of method? The children should then complete the page mentally, writing down only the answers. Again, discuss with them the methods they used.

Page 9 This time the children are given practice in finding, mentally, the difference between two two-digit numbers. Ask them to explain the methods shown on the page, using ten pieces and units, 10p and 1p coins, and a 1–100 number line. The children should then complete the page mentally, writing down only the answers. As before, discuss with them the methods they used.

Page 10 Make sure the children understand the rules of the game. Suggest that they make a note of the numbers used. Discuss with them how estimating will help to ensure they collect as many sets of 3 points as possible. Have the children play games 1, 2 and 3 with a friend. The highest scores for games 1, 2 and 3 should be displayed as they are played, and the players should try to beat the record for each game. Copymaster 2.2 is available for further practice, and it includes two scoring systems which can be used for added variety.

Further activities

1. Let the children play Shopping Triples (Activity Cards 2.1 and 2.2). Shuffle the cards and spread them out face down on the table. The children take it in turns to turn over a red card and a blue card. They then turn over a green card. If this green card has the correct sum of the total cost of the two items they have revealed (figure 2.6), then they keep it and turn the other cards over again for another player to use. Play continues in this fashion until all the green cards have been claimed. The winner is the player with most green cards at the end of the game.

Figure 2.6

2. Have the children play the Clay Pigeon Shoot Game using Copymaster 2.3 (figure 2.7). The shooter 'fires' both barrels at once, adding a number from a cartridge on the top row to a

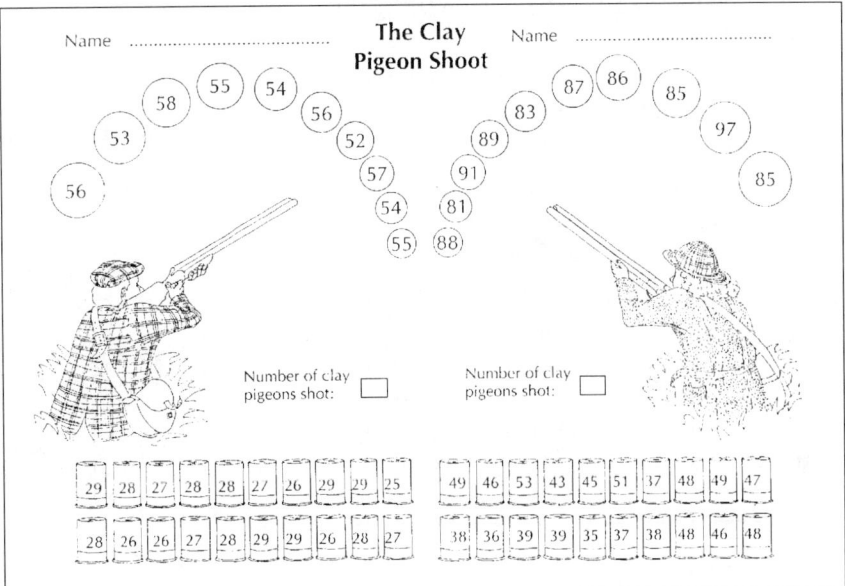

Figure 2.7

number on a cartridge from the bottom row, to match one of the numbers on the clays. Each cartridge can be used only once. The two cartridges used and the clay they 'hit' can be coloured using the same colour to facilitate checking. Calculators can be used to check that the sums are correct before colouring the clay and cartridges. Depending on the cartridges chosen, it is not always possible to hit all the clays, so a mini-competition may be held to find out who is the 'best shot'.

3. Play Target Golf, a game for 2–4 players. Three dice are required: a red one marked 2, 2, 3, 3, 3 and 4; a white one marked 3, 4, 4, 4, 5 and 5; and a blue one marked 4, 4, 5, 5, 5 and 6. The red dice is used on the par 3 holes, the white one on the par 4 holes and the blue on the par 5 holes. Copymaster 2.4 provides the score cards for two famous courses, and the players must first decide which course they will play. Each player should then be given a score card for the course being played. The players throw in turn the appropriate dice for the first hole, determined by its par value, and enter on their score card the number shown on the dice as the score obtained for that hole. Play then moves to the next hole, with the players again throwing the appropriate dice for that hole and recording the scores on their score card. Play continues until all 18 holes have been played, always using the appropriate dice. The players should now total their scores, the winner being the player with the lowest score. Discuss different ways of finding the totals. You could also discuss with the children how their score compares with those of top players playing the same course. For example, Nick Faldo scored 67, 65, 67 and 71 when winning the Open at St Andrews in 1990. In the same championship Ian Woosnam scored 68, 69, 70 and 69, and Sandy Lyle 72, 70, 67 and 72. Provide the children with a card from a local course and have them compare it with St Andrews or Sandwich.

4. Give the children a two-digit number and ask them to find other ways of writing it using addition, 'take away' and difference sentences.

5. Ask the children to list activities which involve addition and finding the difference/'taking away' of two-digit numbers.

6. Have the children go to the class shop with varying amounts of money such as 50p, 80p and 90p. Ask them to buy two items and calculate their change, in each case, by adding on. For example, if they buy items priced at 38p using a 50p coin, they should record:

38p $\xrightarrow{+2p}$ 40p $\xrightarrow{+10p}$ 50p

The change is 12p.

7. Ask the children to go to the class shop and buy three items, making sure that their total cost is less than £1. They should calculate the total cost of the items and the change they will get from £1. Discuss with the children how they found the totals. Let them use a calculator to check their results.

8. Price a number of items in the class shop at between 15p and 45p. Have the children work out how many different purchases they can make and the cost of those choices. Have them say which pair of items costs the most, and which the least.

9. Get the children to carry out some measurement activities involving addition and difference. For example, have them

(a) for addition
(i) draw two straight lines of lengths 18 cm and 37 cm and find the total length;
(ii) put objects or sand into two containers to achieve one mass of 45 g and one of 55 g and then find the total mass;
(iii) draw two shapes on 1 cm squared paper of area 36 square cm and 40 square cm and find the total area;

(b) for difference
(i) draw two straight lines which differ in length by 36 cm;
(ii) put small objects or sand into two containers so that they differ in mass by 32 g;
(iii) draw two shapes on 1 cm squared paper which differ in area by 38 square cm.

10. Make and play Logic Memory Sums, a game for four players. You will need four game mats as shown in figure 2.8, and 21 cards marked:

17 + 15	18 + 17	19 + 17
19 + 18	17 + 14	18 + 14
19 + 14	21 + 16	20 + 16
20 + 15	17 + 17	20 + 13
20 + 12	20 + 11	20 + 17
18 + 18	19 + 15	18 + 15
16 + 15	10 + 15	18 + 16

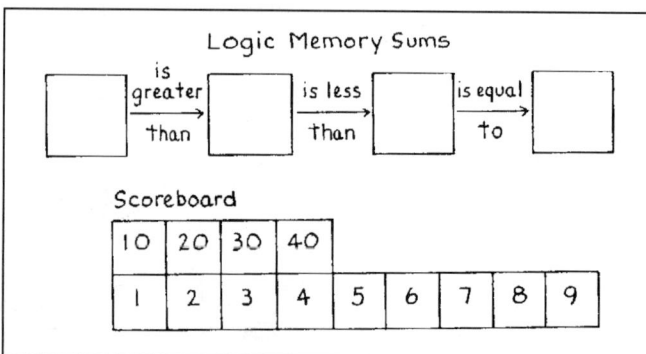

Figure 2.8

Shuffle the cards and spread them face down on the table. Players take it in turns to turn over a card. They may take the card if it can be placed on their mat. If not, it is turned face down on the table again. The aim of the game is to place four cards on the mat so that the logic conditions hold. The first to do so is the winner of that round and gets four points, the second three, the third two and the fourth one. The game ends when a set number of points have been scored or after a set number of games.

11. Copymasters 2.5–2.7 can be used for further practice in two-digit computation.

12. Make and play Tens and Units Happy Families. Prepare 48 cards with the following number sentences displayed on them:

26	27	28	29	78	77	76	75
+27	+26	+25	+24	−25	−24	−23	−22
27	28	29	30	79	78	77	76
+27	+26	+25	+24	−25	−24	−23	−22
28	29	30	31	80	79	78	77
+27	+26	+25	+24	−25	−24	−23	−22
29	30	31	32	81	80	79	78
+27	+26	+25	+24	−25	−24	−23	−22
30	31	32	33	82	81	80	79
+27	+26	+25	+24	−25	−24	−23	−22
31	32	33	34	83	82	81	80
+27	+26	+25	+24	−25	−24	−23	−22

Make four 'wild cards':

The aim of the game is to collect a 'family' which all make the same total. Shuffle the cards well and deal out four to each player, placing the remainder in a pile face down on the table. Take the top card from the pack and place it face up alongside the pack to start the discard pile. Decide on an order of play. The first player, if he/she hasn't been dealt a 'family', takes either the card displayed in the discard pile or a card from the top of the pack. He/she then has to dispose of a card from his/her hand on the discard pile. When players make a family, they must display their hand on the table and state what the family is, e.g. 'I have a family of 56', showing for example:

30	32	81	80
+26	+24	−25	−24

Players with a wild card in their hand must say what two-digit number sentence it represents in order to be included in the family. This number sentence cannot be a repeat of one already held in the hand. Failure to say what the sentence is makes the family invalid, and play passes to the next player. Only one wild card is allowed in a family.

Check-ups

1. Can the children use a variety of methods to complete two-digit addition, difference and take away number sentences?

2. Do the children continue to use an estimate as a 'rough guess' when performing two-digit computation involving addition, difference and take away number sentences?

New Curriculum Mathematics for Schools Key Stage 2

Section 3

AT 1 3c. AT 2 3a, 3c.

Pages 11–14 Position Value (H.T.U.)

Page 11 Choc Ices

Pages 12 and 13 Scoreboard

Page 14 Targets

Purpose

To introduce the position value notation for numbers in the range 101 to 999.
To introduce the children to the pattern, 100, 200, 300, ... 900.
To enable the children to understand the meaning of the hundreds, tens and units digits in recording numbers from 101 to 999, and to write the number words from 101 to 999.
To give the children practice in ordering three-digit numbers.

Recommended material

1. Beads, counters, pebbles, shells, etc., and bags and boxes to put them in.
2. Structural apparatus: Multibase materials (base 10) and interlocking cubes.
3. Straws or sticks and bands for bundling them.
4. Hundreds, tens and units trays (see figure 3.1).
5. 1p, 10p and £1 coins (too many may be required for real ones to be used).
6. Counting boards for hundreds, tens and units.
7. Double Take game (see Pre-page activity 7).
8. Spinners and overlays.
9. **Copymasters 3.1–3.3.**
10. Hundreds, Tens and Units Triples (**Activity Card 3.1**).
11. Cubes for making dice.
12. Envelopes.
13. Calculators.
14. Place Value Strips (**Activity Card 3.2**).
15. Metre rules and tape measures.
16. Balance scales and masses.
17. Cards for games (see Key page points for page 13, and Further activities 1 and 10).
18. Containers with labels showing masses between 100 g and 900 g.
19. Containers with labels showing volumes between 100 ml and 999 ml.
20. Golf scorecards.
21. The 'Nearly' Game (**Activity Cards 3.3–3.4**).

Pre-page activities

1. Ask the children to collect beads, counters, small spheres or pebbles and sort them into plastic bags and boxes, making up bags of ten items and boxes with ten bags in each, so that each box has 100 items in it. For instance, have the children count out 230 items, then make up 23 bags with ten items in each, and then two boxes with ten bags in each. Make sure the children understand that the 230 is made up of two boxes containing 100 each and three bags each containing ten. Give the children cards with three-digit numerals written on them and ask them to model the numbers in a similar manner. Extend the work to include numbers such as 384 and make sure the children realise that:

   384 $\xrightarrow{\text{is made up of}}$ 384 units
   38 tens and 4 units
   3 hundreds, 8 tens and 4 units.

2. Provide the children with a good supply of interlocking cubes, and ask them to make as many strips of ten cubes as they can, and then join ten sets of ten to make a block of 100. Encourage the children to predetermine the number of hundreds they think they can make, and then get them to verify their forecast.

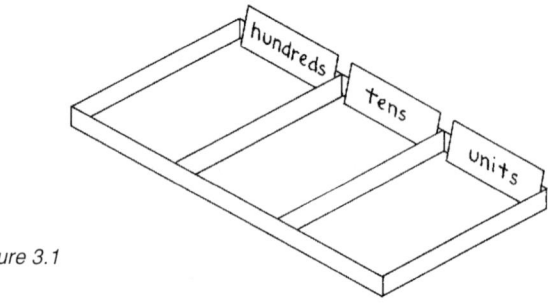

Figure 3.1

3. Ask the children to count straws, 'coins', counters, interlocking cubes, pebbles and other small objects by arranging them in sets of ten and then ten sets of ten, using hundreds, tens and units trays (figure 3.1).

4. Have the children use their interlocking cubes to make shapes with a known number of cubes. Get them to say how many sets of ten they have used, e.g. 'Each of these shapes contains 150 cubes. There are 15 sets of ten in each model.'

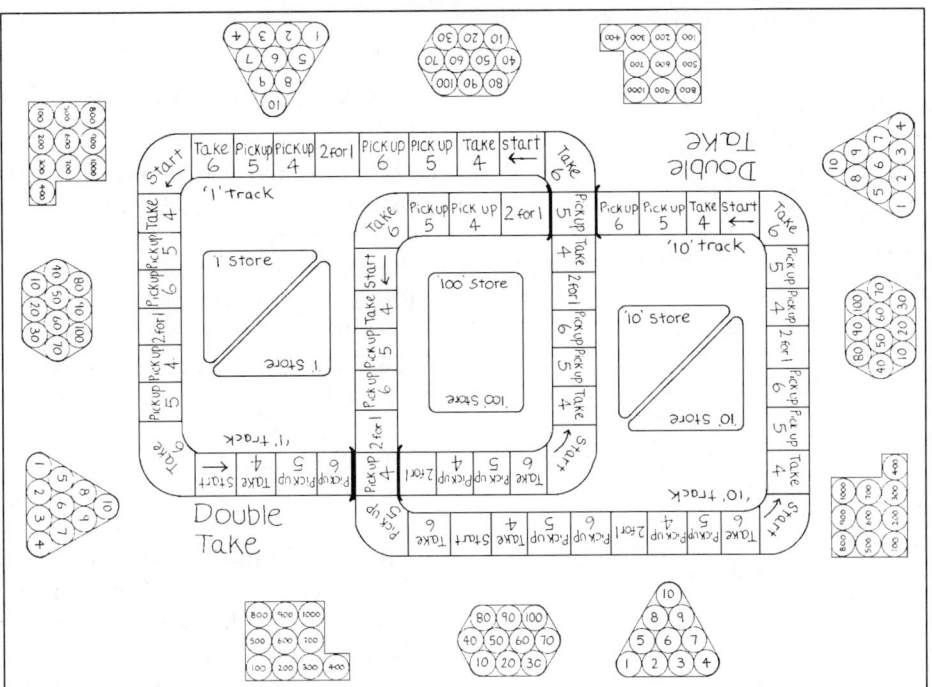

Figure 3.2

5. Play Lucky Grab. Produce a bag with, say, 200 green, red and blue cubes in it. Tell the children that the green cubes are worth ten red cubes, and the red cubes are worth ten blue cubes. The children take it in turns to dip into the bag and grab a handful of cubes. They then sort their cubes into hundreds, tens and units. The player who forms the greatest three-digit number gains a point. The first to reach an agreed number of points wins. The game can be varied to sort for high/low values. You might also like to adjust the proportion of the colours. (*Note*: make sure the cubes used are a reasonable size for young hands, or consider using a scoop.)

6. Let the children count out, say, 145 1p coins (you may prefer to use 'toy' money). Get them then to exchange sets of ten pennies for a single 10p coin, and ten 10p coins for a single £1 coin. Have them record 145p as £1.45. Let the children see that 145p can be made up of 14 ten pence coins and 5 ones, or a 1 pound coin, 4 ten pence coins and 5 ones. Make sure they realise which numbers refer to pounds and which to pence in the decimal notation. Have the children consider amounts such as 160p and note that this is recorded as 16 tens or £1.60, not forgetting the zero. (*Note*: £1.60 is read as 'one pound sixty', although 1.60 in other situations can be read as 'one point six'. As £1.60 will be represented as 1.6 on a calculator, it is vital the children understand that the '6' represents six 10ps.)

7. Make and play Double Take, a game for 2–4 players. The game requires a game board as shown in figure 3.2, a 1–6 dice for each track, fifty '1' counters (red), fifty '10' counters (blue) and forty '100' counters (green). Each player will also require two game pieces to move round the two tracks. The object of the game is to be the first to collect ten '100' counters.

Place a bank of '1' counters (red), '10' counters (blue), '100' counters (green) in the designated regions in the middle of the board. Each player places a game piece on one of the 'start' positions on each track. On each turn a player throws the dice and moves both game pieces forward that number of spaces on the track. There are three possible instructions on each track:

(a) Pick up n, which means a player should pick up n '1' counters and/or n '10' counters from the central bank and place them in his/her collecting stores on the game board. If ten counters of any one kind are obtained, then they must be exchanged for one of a higher value.

(b) Take n, which means a player may take a total of n '1' counters and/or n '10' counters from other players' stores on the game board. The '100' counters cannot be taken by other players. If ten counters of any one kind are obtained, then they must be exchanged for one of the next higher value.

(c) 2 for 1, which means a player may take two new counters for each '1' counter and '10' counter which the player has in his/her collecting stores.

Make sure the children are absolutely clear about this last instruction. It may help to demonstrate a situation before play starts. The 2 for 1 feature will occur about five times per game per player and thus will create a lot of exchanging.

Players are only allowed to keep up to ten counters in their collecting stores. Counters stored in Units and Tens stores can be 'stolen' by other players when they land on 'take' zones. Counters in the Hundreds store are safe and can never be taken by an opponent. Most players will complete the game in less than 23 turns.

New Curriculum Mathematics for Schools Key Stage 2

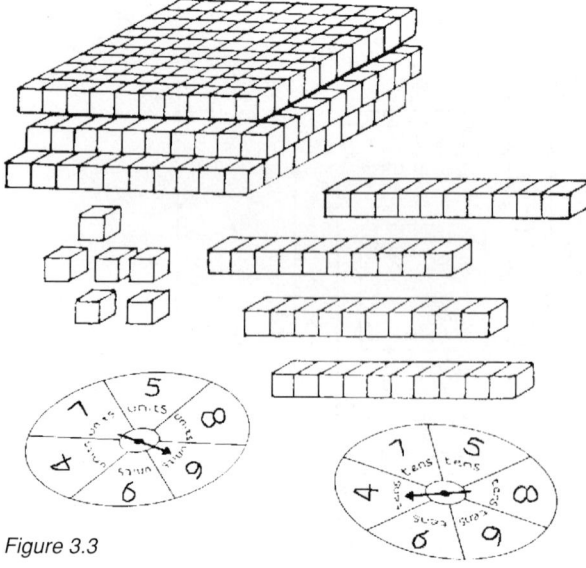

Figure 3.3

8. Play the Exchange Game. The game can be played by 2–4 children. You will require a pool of unit cubes, and cubes connected in tens and hundreds (figure 3.3). (Multibase material will be very useful.) You will also need two spinners with overlays, one marked 4 tens, 5 tens, 6 tens, 7 tens, 8 tens and 9 tens, and the other 4 units, 5 units, 6 units, 7 units, 8 units and 9 units. All the sectors should be equal. The children take it in turns to spin the spinners, and take the appropriate number of unit and ten pieces from the pool. Once a child has collected ten units or ten tens he/she exchanges them for a ten or hundred piece from the central pool. The child who is the first to collect an agreed number of hundreds is the winner. The table below gives an indication of the mean number of 'goes' that it should take to reach, or exceed, certain targets.

Target	400+	500+	600+	700+	800+	900+
Mean 'goes'	6	7	8	10	11	13

Have the children record their number of goes on a class graph. Encourage them to design overlays for their spinners so that they have to exchange more units than before.

9. Play the Counting Board Game. This game is similar to the one above, except that it is played with hundreds, tens and units counting boards and a pool of different coloured counters instead of cubes. It is important that the children have experience of both games since activity 8 above uses size-related materials whilst this activity uses the concept of one counter of a certain colour being worth ten counters of another colour. In setting the target, emphasise the value of the colours, e.g. one red is worth ten blue and one blue is worth ten green.

10. Discuss with the children various ways of writing the numbers they have modelled using structural material or represented on counting boards.

11. Have the children use picture cards of base 10 materials to play Model It, a game for 2–4 players. (Copymaster 3.1 can be used to make the cards if printed on card or 'heavy' paper.) Prepare a set of six target number cards with the following three-digit numbers: 432, 423, 342, 324, 234 and 243. Several copies of Copymaster 3.1 can be cut up to form a pack of base 10 cards. Each player then takes a target number card. This indicates his/her target and should not be disclosed to an opponent. Deal out nine of the base 10 cards to each player. Place the remainder of the base 10 cards in a pile face down on the table. Turn over the top card and place it alongside the main pack. This will be the discard pile. The players decide who is to start. The player selected has a choice of taking the displayed card from the discard pile or a new card from the main pack. He/she then rearranges his/her cards to make up the target number and discards any unwanted card. Play then moves to the next player. The winner is the player who can demonstrate that he/she has collected enough base 10 cards to model his/her target number.

12. Use the base 10 cards from the above activity to play Lucky Numbers. Shuffle the cards and place them in a pile face down on the table. Provide a list of lucky numbers such as:

Lucky Numbers			
7	89	389	790
13	93	472	801
24	123	481	852
26	147	502	852
39	159	520	868
44	172	575	901
56	245	631	921
62	268	693	936
78	364	741	951

The players than take it in turns to take a card from the pile, retaining the cards and continuing until someone can match one of the numbers on the Lucky Number list. Encourage the children to sort the cards in order and to clip sets of ten together with paper clips.

13. Play Hundreds, Tens and Units Triples (Activity Card 3.1). The cards should be shuffled and spread out face down on the table. Players take it in turns to select one card of each colour. If the three match (figure 3.4), then a triple has been formed and the successful

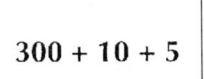 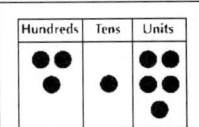

Figure 3.4

player retains the three cards. If a triple is not found, then the cards are placed face down again on the table and play moves to the next player. The player with most triples at the end of the game wins. A game of Pairs can be played in a similar manner if only two out of the three sets are used.

14. Make and play Triple Cubes. As an extension to activity 13 above, mark three (large) cubes as shown in figure 3.5. The children throw the cubes, scoring 2 points if they have a matching pair, and 4 points if they get a triple. The first to get 10 points wins the game. Contrast this activity with the game using cards above. The children should realise that using cubes means that each throw is really a fresh start whereas with the cards each turn reveals crucial information to everyone playing. Most games should be over within 15 throws.

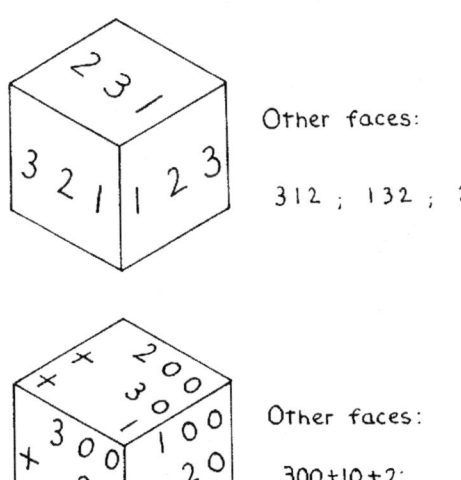

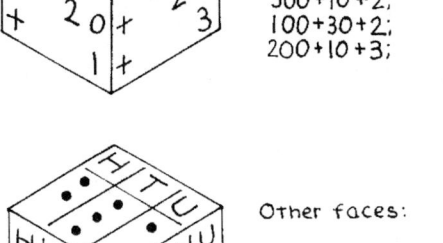

Figure 3.5

15. Play Postman. Take 20 envelopes and write addresses for 20 houses in the same street with three-digit house numbers. Mix the envelopes and ask the children to sort them for delivery from the lowest to the highest numbers.

16. Play 'My Number is …'. Ask the children to think of a number between 100 and 900, and then get them to describe it by saying which number it is close to, e.g. 'My Number is 2 away from 456' or 'My Number is 2 away from 456 and two away from 452'. You may prefer to prepare a series of cards with such clues for the children to solve.

17. Set up a calculator as a '+100' function machine. The calculator can then be used as a check for counting in hundreds by repeatedly pressing the '=' key. Give the children various starting numbers.

18. Set up a calculator as a '+10' function machine. Ask the children to input numbers such as 200, 500, 800, etc., and get them to say what they think the output will be for the next twelve numbers. Have them check using the 'function machine' calculator.

19. Set up a calculator as a '+1' function machine. Now ask the children to input numbers such as 210, 350, 790, etc., and say what they think the output will be for the next twelve numbers, and then to check using the 'function machine' calculator.

20. Use place value strips (Activity Card 3.2) to help children to associate the hundreds, tens and units materials with the positions of the digits when the number is written. The strips are best used with actual apparatus which is size related (figure 3.6). Set out apparatus representing quantities from 1 to 9. Have the children find the relevant place value strip for each number. Repeat the activity to find place value strips for apparatus showing multiples of 10 up to 90. From the sets of tens and units have the children construct numbers with apparatus within the range 11 to 99 and record the number by placing the strips over one another

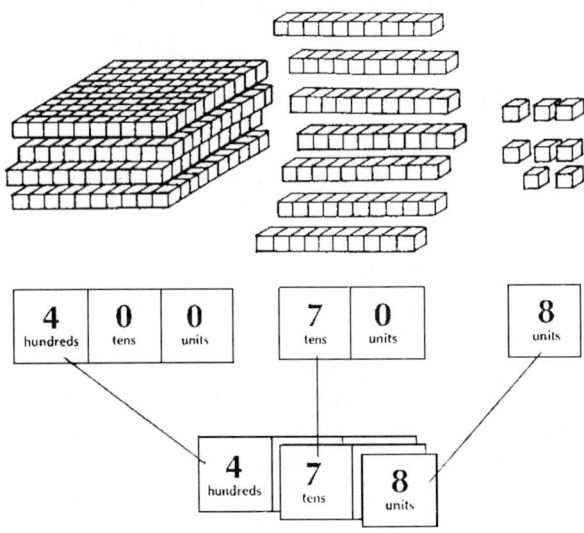

Figure 3.6

(as in figure 3.6). Extend the activity, first using tens and hundreds, then units, tens and hundreds. Continue to use the strips in two ways:

(a) record a number with the strips, then construct the same number with the apparatus;
(b) set out apparatus for a given number, then use the strips to record that number.

21. Replace the apparatus above with metre rules for hundreds, 10 centimetre rods for tens, and centimetre cubes. Tape measures may also be used if the children are able to appreciate the metre and 10 centimetre markings. Have the children measure some lengths in the classroom, then use their place value strips to help make recordings of the lengths in centimetres.

22. Get the children to balance a 125 gram mass with one 100 gram, two 10 gram and one 5 gram masses (figure 3.7). Have them use the place value strips to record the numbers on the marked masses on each scale. Repeat with other masses. *Note*: scales in use in schools are usually only sensitive to about 5 grams, so masses chosen may have to be restricted to multiples of 5.

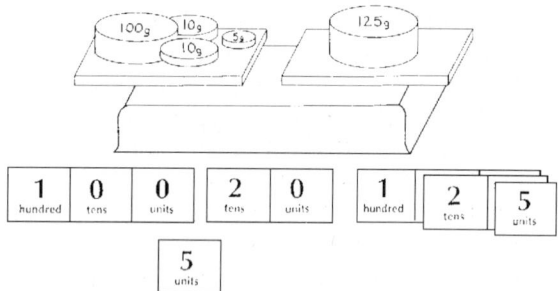

Figure 3.7

Key page points

Page 11 Make sure the children understand that ten choc ices are packed in each carton, and ten cartons are then packed in each box. Get the children to model the situation using size-related structural apparatus.

Page 12 Before starting this page the children should have played the Exchange Game with structural apparatus and on counting boards (see Pre-page activities 8 and 9) so they will be experienced in recording scores. When the page is finished, ask them the quickest way to find the highest and lowest scores to see if they are aware that they should compare the number of hundreds first. If players have the same number of hundreds, then the number of tens should be compared, with the units being compared last, if necessary.

Page 13 Discuss with the children the different ways of recording the numbers represented on the counting boards before they start work on the page. When the page is completed, discuss how the recording shown in question 2 can help when putting tens and hundreds of objects in a box.

To play 'Three out of Five', a set of 36 cards with the following numbers on them is required:

Number   0 1 2 3 4 5 6 7 8 9
Quantity 2 3 3 4 6 6 4 3 3 2

Shuffle the pack well and deal out five cards to each player, who then select three cards to make the highest three-digit number they can. The player with the highest three-digit number scores 7 points, the next scores 5, the next 3 and the last 1. The players then rearrange their five cards to make the lowest three-digit number they can. Again the winner scores 7, the next 5, etc. Play for a number of rounds or to a set number of points. Make a scoreboard for each player to keep their score on.

Page 14 Be sure the children understand the scoring system of the Target game shown in the illustrations.

Further activities

1. Make and play Memory Sequence Bingo. Make a number of bingo mats for the children with three numbers in a sequence missing (figure 3.8). For each mat prepare a series of calling cards. Place all the calling cards face down on the table and let the children take it in turns to reveal a card. If that card fits on the player's mat, he/she places it on the mat in the correct sequence. If it doesn't fit, then the card is placed face down on the table again and play moves to the next player. The first to complete his/her mat wins.

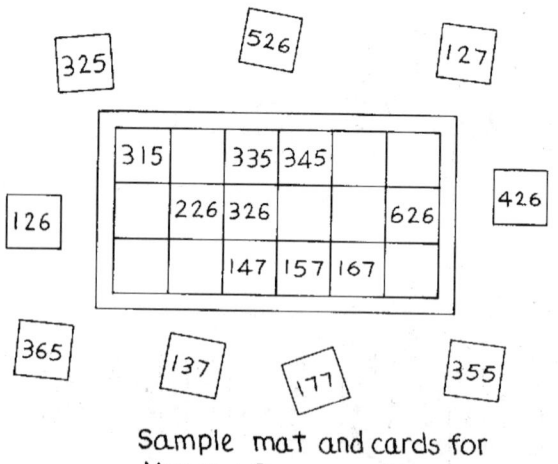

Sample mat and cards for Memory Sequence Bingo

Figure 3.8

2. Take some books with over 100 pages in them. Ask the children to arrange them in order of the number of pages. Get them to describe the position of some of the books in the row, e.g. 'The seventh book from the left has 135 pages in it'.

3. Produce a number of containers with their mass in grams recorded on the labels. Ask the children to arrange the containers in order by mass without looking at the labels. When they have finished, get them to read the labels and to revise the order as necessary. Let them compare the results and display their findings on logic mats (figure 3.9).

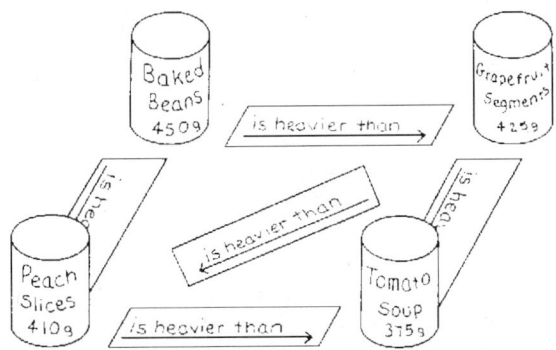

Figure 3.9

4. Repeat activity 3 above with containers which have suitable volumes recorded on their labels.

5. Collect a number of golf scorecards (figure 3.10). Have the children answer questions such as: Which is the longest hole on the course? Which is the shortest hole on the course? How many holes are less than 200 m long? How many holes are longer than 400 m?

NO.	HOLE	METRES	PAR	SCORE	NO.	HOLE	METRES	PAR	SCORE
1	Bay View	390	4		10	Burn	406	4	
2	Short	165	3		11	Valley	493	5	

Figure 3.10

6. Let the children use their calculators to make patterns with three-digit numbers, which they should then record, for example:

316, 326, 336 ... function is +10, next three numbers are ...
218, 227, 236 ... function is +9, next three numbers are ...
155, 166, 177 ... function is +11, next three numbers are ...

Get the children to make some sequences for their friends to continue.

7. Write a three-digit number such as 472 on the chalkboard. Ask the children to input the number into their calculators in different ways, e.g.

(a) [4][7][2]
(b) [4][0][0][+][7][0][+][2]
(c) [2][+][7][0][+][4][0][0]

Repeat for 427, 742, 724, 247 and 274.

Get the children to find other three-digit numbers using the same three digits in different orders, and to say how they can be keyed into their calculators.

8. Let the children play Target Bowls. They will require four balls and a target made up of three concentric circles (figure 3.11). Each player rolls four balls towards the circles and his/her score is recorded. When a ball lies between two regions the lower number is scored. The winner of the round is the player with the highest score. Play a number of rounds to decide an overall winner.

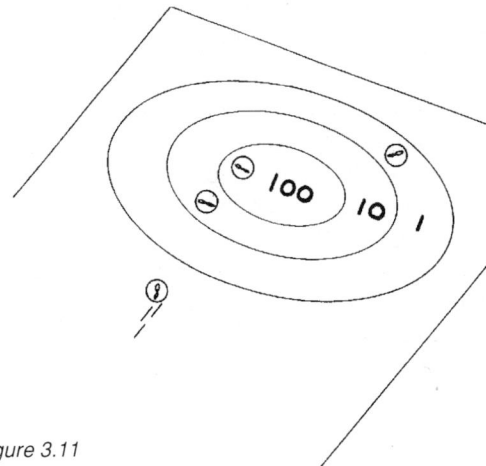

Figure 3.11

9. Have the children make a list of the uses of three-digit numbers in everyday life, for example house numbers, page numbers, etc. Discuss how some hotels, and other large buildings, may use a number like 312 to mean room 12 on the third floor.

10. Make and play Six in Order. Make a set of 36 cards with the following three-digit numbers:

636 437 364 739 247 696 842 666 642
264 258 233 679 854 387 766 837 223
443 831 392 376 646 565 354 553 569
635 688 471 659 760 321 305 695 215

You will also need a game mat for each player (figure 3.12). Shuffle the cards well and place them in a pile on the table. The players take it in turns to take a card from the pile and place it on their game mat. The aim of the game is to take six cards and place them in ascending order on the mat. The first to do so is the winner. If, when a player has taken six cards and placed them on his/her mat and they are not in the correct order, then on his/her turn a player may rearrange any two. On any given turn only

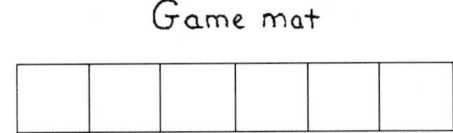

Figure 3.12

New Curriculum Mathematics for Schools Key Stage 2

two cards may be rearranged before play moves to the next player. As a variation the game can be played by putting the numbers in descending order.

11. Play The 'Nearly' Game – a game for four players (Activity Cards 3.3 and 3.4). Shuffle both sets of cards separately. Place the target cards face down on the table. Deal out five of the other cards to the four players. A target card is then turned face up. Players take a card from their hand and place it *face down* on the table. When all have made a selection, the cards are turned face up in order of play. The player closest to the target wins four points (figure 3.13). The player coming second gets two points. If two players tie, then each gets three points each. If three players tie, then they score two points each. If all four players tie, then they all score one point. There is no score for ties in second place. At the end of each round the used cards are put to one side and not used again until the next game. The game is over when all five cards have been used, with a new target card each round, and the winner is the player with most points.

Figure 3.13

12. Play 'Hi-Lo'. Allow one child to select a number between 100 and 900. A partner now has to deduce that number by guessing. The only help he/she can get is when the player who has selected the number responds with 'too high' or 'too low' when the correct number hasn't been selected. Get the children to keep a record of the number of 'guesses' needed to find the mystery number. They should make a graph of the number of their responses and, of course, write about their findings.

13. Have the children complete Copymaster 3.2. The numbers in the hexagons at the centre have been distributed among the outer circles. The three elements of each number and the number itself should be coloured in the same colour. The children should be encouraged to use calculators to confirm that, for example, 900 + 80 + 6 = 986.

14. Make a number of copies of Copymaster 3.3. Write a selection of the numbers below on the players' 'cards' (figure 3.14). Copy these filled-in copies and give them to the children to complete.

2 7 6 1 9	4 6 7 2 1	1 3 8 9 0
4 5 6 9 1	1 2 5 8 9	1 3 5 2 9
1 5 3 8 6	1 5 3 8 3	2 0 9 7 6
2 4 7 0 1	2 0 9 8 4	0 0 9 5 2

4 7 5 1 2	9 1 5 6 4	2 5 3 4 5
8 4 0 1 4	7 7 6 1 0	2 2 4 6 0
6 4 7 8 6	2 4 3 5 3	6 4 1 7 5
4 3 2 5 4	3 0 8 8 5	3 8 9 6 6

0 7 3 5 9	4 7 0 6 8	1 4 5 3 2
1 4 0 3 3	6 2 0 5 3	9 6 8 4 2
9 7 8 6 3	4 3 4 5 6	3 4 5 6 7
4 6 8 1 1	1 8 4 5 7	3 1 5 5 6

You could also give the children an unprepared copy and get them to fill in the numbers for a friend to complete.

15. Have the children contribute to a list of the odd and even numbers in the 1–900 range.

16. Encourage the children to create a number system for themselves using their own hieroglyphics instead of numbers. Have them make a chart showing the relationship between their number system and the numbers 1 to 999. You may like to introduce the children to other bases. If so, make sure the emphasis is on the structure of the system.

Check-ups

1. Can the children recognise numbers in the range 101 to 999?
2. Can the children read and write the numbers and number names in the range 101 to 999?
3. Can the children order three-digit numbers?
4. Can the children state the value of each digit in a three-digit number?
5. Can the children state the number of tens contained in a three-digit number, e.g. that there are 39 tens in 395?
6. Can the children state the number of hundreds contained in a three-digit number?

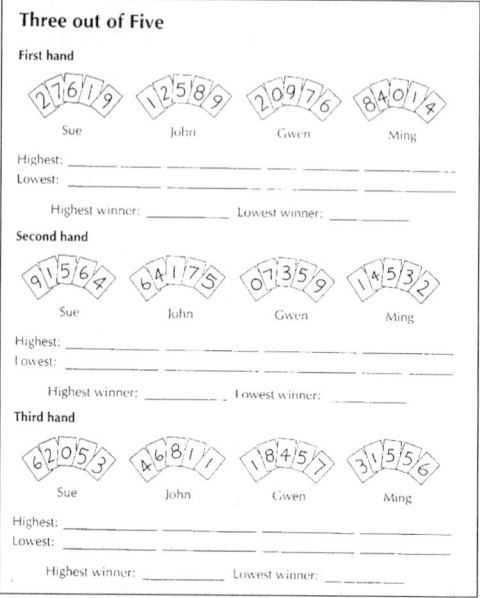

Figure 3.14

Section 4

AT 1 3a, 3b, 3c, 3d. AT 2 3e. AT 5 3a.

Pages 15–19 Time

Page 15   The Watchmaker's Shop Window

Page 16   The Bus Station

Page 17   The Classroom Travel Agent

Pages 18 and 19   Around the World

Purpose

To reinforce the children's understanding of 'am' and 'pm'.
To give the children experience with the 24-hour clock.
To provide further practice in telling the time, in planning the use of time, and in reading and constructing timetables.
To give the children practice in calculations involving time.
To make children aware of GMT and time zones around the world.

Recommended material

1. A calendar and a wall clock, preferable dual analogue/digital.
2. Materials for class display (see Pre-page activity 2).
3. Comic strips for cutting up.
4. Taxi Driver cards (**Activity Card 4.1**).
5. Digital Touch and Say cards (**Activity Card 4.2**).
6. **Copymasters 4.1–4.6**.
7. Simple bus, train and airline timetables.
8. Maps of the world showing time zones, and a globe.
9. World Time Touch and Say Pairs (**Activity Card 4.3**).
10. Cards for games (see Further activity 4).
11. Timers and stopwatches (analogue and digital).
12. The 'Nearly' Time Game (**Activity Cards 4.4–4.5**).
13. Video recorder.
14. TV sections from newspapers, etc.

Pre-page activities

Note   The work in the Pupils' Book now involves the 24-hour clock. As this was an option in Book 1, teachers should confirm with their colleagues just how much 24-hour experience the children have had and plan accordingly. Make sure you have a calendar and a clock (preferably dual analogue/digital) on permanent display in the classroom and refer to them regularly.

1. Have the children make a class birthday graph. Although they will have done this before, they should now be able to extend the analysis, making more use of their computational skills.

2. Organise a class display illustrating changes in design over the years, e.g. a pictorial display of clocks through the ages, fashion through the ages, transport through the ages (with model cars, etc.), old coins, general antiques, etc. Have the children try and date the exhibits and state how old they are.

3. Make sure the children understand that 'am' is an abbreviation of the Latin 'ante-meridiem', which means before noon, while 'pm' is an abbreviation of 'post-meridiem', meaning after noon. Discuss with them the events which commonly take place in their day and when they occur. Ask them to list these activities under the headings 'am' and 'pm', e.g.

am	pm
get out of bed	afternoon lessons
have breakfast	playtime
come to school	go home
morning lessons	teatime
playtime	evening activities (Boys' Brigade/Brownies)
	bedtime

4. Cut up some comic strips and have the children arrange the pictures back into the original sequence. The strips can be cut up to form a jigsaw or a straight sequence. You may feel it wise on some occasions to cut the 'story' into, say, three or four strips containing more than one frame. This technique may give the children more of a clue! Some comic strips have a story box under each picture in addition to the speech bubbles. It may be more of a challenge if the story boxes are separated from the pictures and the children have to put both the pictures and the story boxes in order. You may need to code the pictures in some way to help you with the 'answers'. (*Note*: in *New Curriculum Mathematics for Schools*, making a computational algorithm is regarded as recording a series of 'events'. Pages 20–23 and 56–59 in Book 2 illustrate examples.)

New Curriculum Mathematics for Schools Key Stage 2

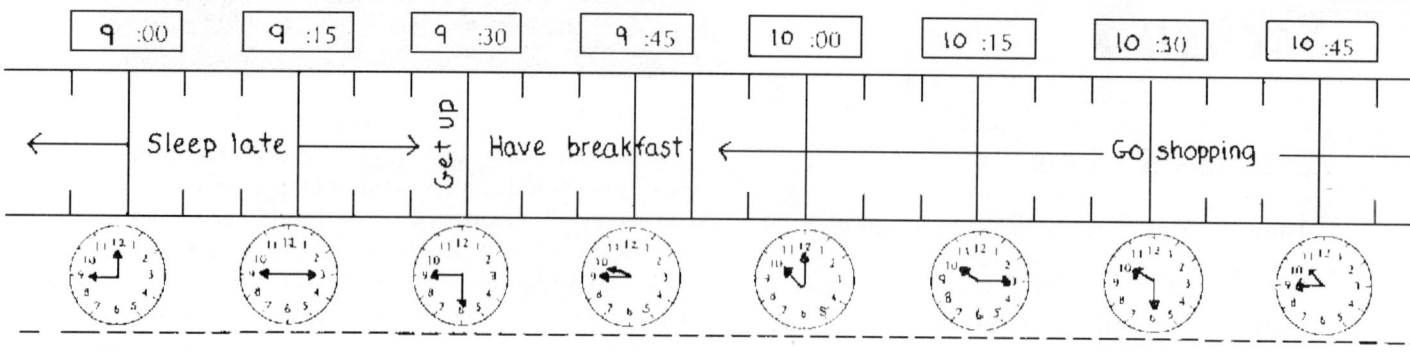

Figure 4.1

5. Discuss the 24-hour clock. Remind the children that the day is split into 24 hours and that the day starts (and ends!) at midnight. Make sure they understand that, as with other measuring devices, zero is regarded as the beginning; so the day begins at zero hour, written as 00:00 (no hours and no minutes!). Show the children a traditional clock face and count round the hours reading, and writing, the time as you go: 'oh, one, oh, oh', written 0100; 'oh, two, oh, oh', written 0200, etc. Take care not to say 'oh, one hundred hours' as this may be confusing at this stage. At 1 pm stress that we are now 13 hours into the day and that this time is recorded as 13:00 ('thirteen, oh, oh'). Continue to count round until the day ends when midnight is reached, i.e. 24:00. Explain that now the time starts again for the new day. Introduce 15-minute intervals, for example 13:15 (thirteen fifteen), 13:30, 13:45, and other subdivisions as appropriate. Tell the children that sometimes they will see 'half past ten in the morning' written as 10:30 on machines (with some displays omitting the first zero in times earlier than 10 o'clock) and sometimes as 1030 in timetables.

6. Ask the children to talk and write about where they have seen digital displays. Airports, railway stations, bus terminals, videotape recorders, time switches and sporting events may be mentioned. Make sure they realise that machines tend to use 24-hour notation as 'they' cannot tell when it is day or night! Personal watches often show 12-hour digital time as the wearer is expected to know when it is day or night! Contrast this with other ways of displaying the time, e.g. on shadow clocks, water clocks, candle clocks, sundials, etc.

7. Have the children order events in flowchart form. Activity Card 4.1 can be used to arrange 'times' in order. The pictures represent the trips made by a taxi driver during one day.

8. Let the children play Digital Touch and Say (Activity Card 4.2). On these cards, reading the analogue watches is complicated since there are no numerals on the faces! The reverse side of each card carries two times, one am and one pm. The children can play with these cards using either am or pm responses or, if so desired, both.

9. Give the children opportunities to plan their weekend activities on a time line. (Copymaster 4.1 can be used.) They should record the times in 24-hour notation (figure 4.1). Have the children compare their plans.

10. Provide the children with a simple airline timetable and show them how to read it. (Note that airline timetables within the UK are very simple – generally they show arrival and departure times, with no intermediate stops!) Take the children through the timetable by following a flight. Set the display clock to the departure time and then turn the hands/digits until the arrival time is found. The time taken for the journey can be calculated by counting on. (Have the children record their counting on.) Examine other flights. Do they all take the same time? Does it take as long to 'come back' as it does to go? Are there any repeating patterns in the timetable, e.g. do the flights go every hour? Have the children extend the timetable by adding in their own extra flights. Some children may well have experience of flying. Discuss with them the airport procedures for checking in and the need to be at the airport a certain time before departure.

11. The huge cost of buying and operating an aircraft means that a carrier needs to keep its aeroplanes flying, and not standing on the tarmac too long. Flight timetables often reflect this fact. Give the children some airline timetables and see if they can discover how many aircraft are needed to fly a route. For example, in the British Midland Diamond Service between Heathrow and Teeside (figure 4.2a), an aeroplane can leave Teeside at 0645 and arrive at Heathrow at 0745. It can then leave Heathrow at 0825 and get back to Teeside at 0925, ready to go out again at 1000 and arriving at Heathrow at 1100, only to leave again at 1140. Continuing this sequence through a day's programme, it will be found

34

that at the end of the day the aeroplane is back at Teeside, ready to repeat the procedure next day. Have the children act out this sequence, with one child being the aeroplane's pilot. Make two destinations in the room and appoint a 'flight controller' for each. At the appointed time have the controller give the pilot a time sheet on which is written the first departure time. The pilot will now take this to the other controller at the other destination and receive a time sheet to enable him/her to make the return trip. By acting out such situations the children will see what happens to the aeroplane and how many are required to fly the route. This particular route only needs one aeroplane as the flight time is quite short. Other routes may need more. The British Midland service from Heathrow to Glasgow (figure 4.2b) shows that two planes will be needed to operate the route. (See also activity 12 below on the number of buses needed to operate a bus timetable.)

Figure 4.2 (a)

HEATHROW TO TEESIDE
Diamond Service

HEATHROW (Terminal 1) → TEESIDE

FLIGHT	FREQUENCY	DEPART	ARRIVE	SERVICE	Off-peak weekday
BD332	Daily	0825	0925	Breakfast	
BD334	Daily	1140	1240	Light meal	*
BD336	Daily ex Sat Sun	1435	1530	Afternoon tea	
BD338	Daily	1740	1840	Dinner	
BD340	Daily ex Sat	2055	2150	Dinner	*

TEESIDE → HEATHROW (Terminal 1)

FLIGHT	FREQUENCY	DEPART	ARRIVE	SERVICE	Off-peak weekday
BD331	Daily	0645	0745	Breakfast	
BD333	Daily	1000	1100	Light meal	*
BD335	Daily ex Sat Sun	1310	1405	Lunch	*
BD337	Daily	1600	1655	Afternoon tea	
BD349	Daily ex Sat	1915	2015	Dinner	

Aircraft type: all flights are DC9 jet.

(b)

HEATHROW TO GLASGOW
Diamond Service

HEATHROW (Terminal 1) → GLASGOW

FLIGHT	FREQUENCY	DEPART	ARRIVE	SERVICE	Off-peak weekday
BD16	Daily ex Sun	0710	0825	Breakfast	
BD2	Daily	0910	1025	Breakfast	*
BD4	Daily	1110	1225	Light meal	*
BD6	Daily	1310	1425	Lunch	*
BD8	Daily	1510	1625	Afternoon tea	
BD10	Daily	1710	1825	Afternoon tea	
BD12	Daily ex Sat	1910	2025	Dinner	
BD14	Daily	2100	2210	Dinner	*

GLASGOW → HEATHROW (Terminal 1)

FLIGHT	FREQUENCY	DEPART	ARRIVE	SERVICE	Off-peak weekday
BD1	Daily	0710	0825	Breakfast	
BD3	Daily	0910	1025	Breakfast	*
BD5	Daily	1110	1225	Light meal	*
BD7	Daily	1310	1425	Lunch	*
BD9	Daily	1510	1625	Afternoon tea	
BD11	Daily ex Sat	1710	1825	Afternoon tea	
BD13	Daily	1910	2025	Dinner	
BD15	Daily ex Sat	2100	2205	Dinner	*

Aircraft type: all flights are by Boeing 737 jet.

12. Discuss with the children how they could make a simple bus timetable, e.g. for an express service between towns, with no intermediate stops shown. Have them decide on a starting time for the first bus, how long the journey takes, e.g. 20 minutes, and how often the buses will run, e.g. every 15 minutes. Encourage the children to notice repeating patterns.

Stoke-on-Trent to Baldwin's Gate
Dep. 0600 *0615* 0630 0645 0700
Arr. 0620 *0635* 0650 0705 0720
Dep. *0715* 0730 0745 0800 *0815*
Arr. *0735* 0750 0805 0820 *0835*

Baldwin's Gate to Stoke-on-Trent
Dep. 0630 *0645* 0700 0715 0730
Arr. 0650 *0705* 0720 0735 0750
Dep. *0745* 0800 0815 0830 *0845*
Arr. *0805* 0820 0835 0850 *0905*

Here the timetable shows that the bus leaves every 15 minutes and the journey takes 20 minutes. The bus waits 10 minutes at each terminus. Let the children see that the first bus at 0600 will get back to Stoke-on-Trent at 0650 in time to go out again as the 0700. Since the 0615 can go out again at 0715, etc., four buses will be used to operate the service. Copymaster 4.2 can be used for further practice.

13. Introduce other bus timetables which have intermediary stopping places, for the children to read and interpret.

14. Provide the children with some airline timetables and let them play at being travel agents. Prepare some questions for them based on the timetables available. Copymaster 4.3 can also be completed, using the flight timetables supplied on Copymaster 4.4.

15. Give the children some flight timetables where planes fly across time zones. For example, Northwest Airlines' timetable from Detroit to Chicago lists the following non-stop flights.

Dep. 0715 0815 0930 1225 1315
Arr. 0715 0820 0934 1226 1316
Dep. 1345 1530 1610 1725 1835
Arr. 1349 1532 1618 1730 1840

Discuss with the children the times taken for a number of the flights. Notice that the 0715 appears to arrive as soon as it departs, the 0815 takes 5 minutes, and the 1315 only 1 minute! Have the children also look at the return times for flights from Chicago to Detroit.

Dep. 0700 0800 0900 1100 1200
Arr. 0843 0959 1103 1255 1359
Dep. 1300 1440 1515 1600 1700
Arr. 1457 1546 1712 1740 1910

The children should notice that the journey time now appears to be 1 hour 43 minutes for the 0700, and 2 hours 3 minutes for the 0900. Take the opportunity to explain to the children about different time zones around the world. Emphasise that time is measured against Greenwich Mean Time, with certain places ahead of Greenwich and others behind. Use the rotation of the globe and illustrations of the earth in orbit round the sun to help the children understand how these differences are the result of the wish to have 'noon', i.e. mid-day, corresponding to the time when, at any particular longitude, the sun is directly overhead at the equator. Show them how the rotation of the earth causes the sun to appear to move from east to west, so that daybreak occurs earlier in places to the east of us and later in places to the west. Point out the 'date line' on the globe and explain how the date has to change as we move across it. If possible, draw on the children's experience of time zones. Some may have been on holiday where they have had to reset their watches. There are often occasions on television where live events taking place in daylight are beamed from other countries when it is night, and dark outside, in this country. Live news reports and major world sporting events such as cricket from the West Indies and/or Australia, World Cup Soccer, the Olympics, World Championship boxing from the USA, all provide illustrations of different times zones. Take the opportunity to discuss with the children the problems which organisers have of timetabling races in the Olympics in Atlanta, Georgia, which are to be seen live on TV in this country at a time when most people are awake and able to watch.

16. Set a classroom clock to show the time in different parts of the world. For example, one day the clock could be set at New York time,

another day it could be at Moscow time. Allow the children to reset the clock each time and make a label to say something like 'The time in New York is now ...' (figure 4.3).

17. Discuss biological problems associated with changing time zones. Some children may have travelled far enough to have experienced 'jet lag'. If not, then have the children try to imagine some of the problems. For instance, if a passenger has breakfast before flying Concorde to New York, departing at 10.30, what meal would they serve on the aeroplane and what meal would they suggest when the aeroplane lands four hours later at 0920 (apparently before departing)?

18. Mention British Summer Time and why we put our clocks forward one hour in spring and back one hour in autumn.

19. Play World Time Touch and Say Pairs (Activity Card 4.3). Shuffle the cards and spread them on the table with the GMT and 'city card' faces showing. The children take it in turns to turn over a city card and must then touch a GMT card and say what the time is in the city shown on the city card when the GMT time is as shown. The GMT card can then be turned over to enable a check to be made (figure 4.4). If the player is correct, he/she keeps the pair. If an incorrect call is made, both cards are turned over again and play moves to the next player.

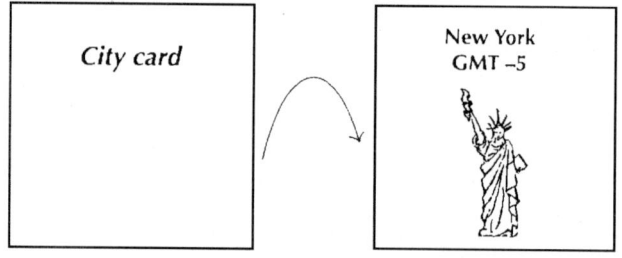

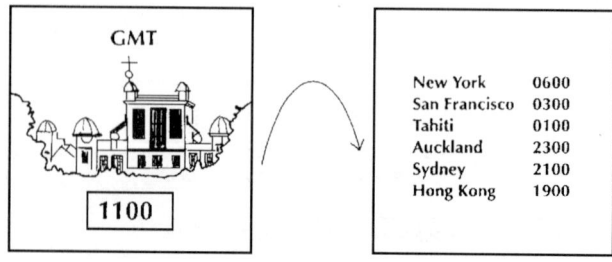

Figure 4.4

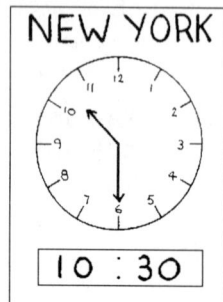

Figure 4.3

Key page points

Page 15 Have the children study the watches shown in the shop window and identify the types mentioned in the text. They can use the table supplied on Copymaster 4.4 to help them answer question 1. In question 2 they are asked to pair analogue and digital times. Not all watches can be paired though! Make sure the children are aware of the correct time when they start question 4.

Page 16 Check that the children understand how to read the timetables on this page. Encourage them to use the timetables they write down for question 6 to work out the answers to questions 7–10.

Page 17 Discuss the London to Paris timetable with the children and have them notice that the flight to Paris takes two hours, whereas coming back the aeroplane appears to arrive as soon as it departs! Make sure they realise that this is because of the one hour time difference between London and Paris. In question 2a, d, e and g the flights are supersonic (Concorde).

Pages 18 and 19 Remind the children that countries to the east of the UK are ahead of us in time, and that countries to the west are behind us. Since the children are asked to put a series of flights in order as an aeroplane flies round the world, make sure they are aware of the various time zones.

Further activities

1. Have the class create an am/pm mural to illustrate a complete day in their lives. The children could be asked to draw a series of pictures to depict events they all experience during the day. Each picture could be overstamped with a clock face to indicate the starting time of the event. The am/pm or night/day effect could be emphasised by the use of suitably coloured backgrounds.

2. Encourage the children to discover ways of telling the time approximately, without using a watch or a clock. During the school day, ask them if they can tell approximately what time it is. What 'signals' help them to know whether it is morning or afternoon? For instance, they know it is (early) morning in school because they have not had their morning break, or it is late afternoon because of the position of the sun shining into the classroom. Listening to sounds around them can also act as 'signals' for the time of the day, e.g. sirens or church bells.

3. Make a series of graphs, for display, of what the children were actually doing on the previous Saturday at, say, 1500 hours, 1700 hours, 1900 hours, 2100 hours and 2300 hours (figure 4.5). Ask them to comment on their graphs. If possible, get children at another school to repeat the survey. Do their graphs look similar to the ones drawn by your class?

4. Make and play Time Clock Patience. Prepare 52 cards with four of each marked as follows: 1300, 1400, 1500, 1600, 1700, 1800, 1900, 2000, 2100, 2200, 2300, 2400; and four depicting two clock hands. Let two children play the game, taking it in turns to try and get it 'out'. The cards are shuffled well and dealt out face down in the positions of the numerals of an analogue clock, with every thirteenth card placed in the 'hands' position in the middle. When all the cards are in position there should be four in each of the 1–12 places on the clock face, and four where the 'hands' should be in the middle (figure 4.6). The children take it in turns to play. As one plays, the other acts as a referee. The first player takes a card from the middle of the 'clock' and turns it over to reveal the 24-hour time. He/she then places it, face up, at the bottom of the pile as indicated on the card, i.e. if 1500 hours is turned over, then the card is placed under the pile at 3 o'clock. The top card of this (3 o'clock) pile is now taken as the new card and should be placed in the correct position on the clock face as before. When a player turns over a 'hands' card, then this card has to go under the pack in the 'hands' position of the clock and a new card taken. The game will end when all four 'hands' cards have been discovered and placed in position. When this

Figure 4.5

Figure 4.6

occurs there will be no more cards to take to distribute. The children should now count how many unused cards are left face down on the table. The individual with the fewest cards left on the table at the end of his/her turn wins. The game can also be played against a timer.

5. Play the 'Nearly' Time Game with four players (Activity Cards 4.4 and 4.5). Shuffle both packs of cards separately. Place the target cards face down in a pile on the table. Deal out five of the other cards to each of the four players. A target card is then turned face up. Players take a card from their hand and place it face down on the table. When all have made a selection, the cards are turned face up in order of play. The player closest to the target wins four points (figure 4.7). The player coming second gets two points. If two players tie, then each gets three points. If three players tie, then they score two points each. If all four players tie, then they all score one point. There is no score for ties in second place. At the end of each round the used cards are put to one side and not used again until the next game. The game is over when each player has played all five cards, with a new target card each time, and the winner is the person with most points.

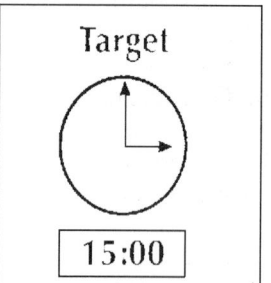 

Figure 4.7

6. Show the children the school video recorder and explain how programmes are timed. You could let the children be responsible for actually setting up the timer for class programmes which may well involve them in converting the 12-hour times given in the TV schedules into 24-hour times.

7. Provide the children with a TV schedule from a newspaper or magazine. Have them choose three programmes which they would like to record on a video recorder, and ask them to note the starting time, the finishing time and the viewing time of each one. Then ask them to work out the total time to spend on recording. Ask the children to design a table for reporting the information.

8. Let the children use Copymaster 4.5 to record programme times on a video recorder. An increasing number of video recorders are used in homes now and the actual way of setting the times may vary from model to model. However, they will all mainly use the 24-hour clock. The copymaster simulates a recorder where both starting and finishing times are required. (In reality, however, some machines ask for a starting time and programme length!) Provide the children with a current copy of the TV listings and ask them to plan a series of programmes which they would like to record, to see later. You could also use this copymaster to set the children specific problems. In this case take a copy of the master, write some programme names in the appropriate places and then copy the copy for the children to complete. If possible, supervise the children, in turn, setting the school's video recorder to record some programmes overnight. These can be checked next day to see if the selections were recorded, without actually viewing them!

9. Copymaster 4.6 provides more work on the 24-hour clock and using time lines.

10. Time and distance can be linked if children can work out how far from school they live and how long it takes them to travel to school. This information could be displayed on two class graphs (how we come to school and how long it takes us to come to school). Have the children find out if the person who lives furthest away from school takes the longest time to travel there. (It may be that he/she travels by car and is therefore quicker than someone who lives nearer but walks.)

11. Repeat the watch survey to see what types of watch are worn by the children. Have the results changed since the last survey was done? Remember, in this series we have said that when conducting a survey the children should say who would find the information useful. The implication of this survey may be that more emphasis should be placed on digital time than analogue, or vice versa!

12. On page 16 of the Pupil's Book the children will have found that four buses are needed to operate the City Centre/Trentham route and four buses are needed to operate the City Centre/Leek route, making a total of eight buses in all. Now let the children investigate what would happen if the two routes were combined. If, when the 0600 City Centre to Trentham bus got back to the Centre, instead of waiting ten minutes to go out again to Trentham, it went out after five minutes as the 0655 to Leek, it would be back in the City Centre at 0745 ready to go out straight away as the 0745 to Trentham. By the same token, if the 0555 bus on the Leek route went out as the 0645 to Trentham, when it got back it could go out as the 0740 to Leek. Continuing these

arrangements, it can be seen that only seven buses will now be used to operate the two routes.

City Centre to Trentham and return		City Centre to Leek and return	
Dep. 0600		Dep. 0555	
Arr. 0625	bus A	Arr. 0615	bus B
Dep. 0630		Dep. 0625	
Arr. 0655		Arr. 0645	
Dep. 0615		Dep. 0610	
Arr. 0640	bus C	Arr. 0630	bus D
Dep. 0645		Dep. 0640	
Arr. 0710		Arr. 0700	
Dep. 0630		Dep. 0625	
Arr. 0655	bus E	Arr. 0645	bus F
Dep. 0700		Dep. 0655	
Arr. 0725		Arr. 0715	
Dep. 0645		Dep. 0640	
Arr. 0710	bus B	Arr. 0700	bus G
Dep. 0715		Dep. 0710	
Arr. 0740		Arr. 0730	
Dep. 0700		Dep. 0655	
Arr. 0740	bus D	Arr. 0715	bus A
Dep. 0730		Dep. 0725	
Arr. 0755		Arr. 0745	
Dep. 0715		Dep. 0710	
Arr. 0740	bus F	Arr. 0730	bus C
Dep. 0745		Dep. 0740	
Arr. 0810		Arr. 0800	
Dep. 0730		Dep. 0725	
Arr. 0750	bus G	Arr. 0745	bus E
Dep. 0800		Dep. 0755	
Arr. 0820		Arr. 0815	

Check-ups

1. Can the children convert am and pm times to 24-hour notation?

2. Can the children work out the interval between two times using the 24-hour clock?

3. Can the children record analogue and 24-hour times correctly?

4. Can the children read a simple timetable?

5. Are the children aware of time zones around the world and can they work out the times in these zones when related to GMT and vice versa?

New Curriculum Mathematics for Schools Key Stage 2

Section 5

AT 1 3b, 3c. AT 2 3a, 3d, 3e, 4a. AT 3 2b. AT 5 3a.

Pages 20–27 Addition (H.T.U.)

Pages 20–23   The Best Kept Village
Page 24   Find the Sum
Page 25   Waste Paper
Page 26   Travel Service
Page 27   Tell Me a Story

Purpose

To promote understanding and proficiency in the addition of three-digit numbers.
To give the children practice in using apparatus to model the addition of three-digit numbers in real situations.
To give children the opportunity of developing an algorithm for the addition of three-digit numbers.

Recommended material

1. Structural apparatus: Multibase materials (base 10) and interlocking cubes.
2. Spinners and overlays.
3. Hundreds, tens and units counting boards and counters.
4. 1p, 10p and £1 coins (toy money).
5. Addition Algorithm cards (**Activity Cards 5.1–5.4**).
6. Balance scales and masses representing numbers 1 to 100.
7. An assortment of items for weighing, e.g. tins of food, etc.
8. Calculators.
9. AA or RAC handbook with distance charts and maps.
10. Three dice for Double Throw (see Further activity 1).
11. Cards for games (see Further activities 2 and 4).
12. 'Nearly' Addition Triples (**Activity Card 5.5**).
13. **Copymasters 5.1–5.3**.

Pre-page activities

Note   As stated in the previous Guide, in this series we use real situations to introduce activities involving computation. We then develop them along the following lines.

(a) Act out the situation if possible, emphasising the numbers and the words, and indicating the kind of computation needed.
(b) Question the intentions of the problem. What is it leading to? What is it asking us to do mathematically? Is it misleading in any way? Does it give us information we don't need?
(c) Model the situation. It may not always be possible to get real objects, so representations of those objects can be used. Structural apparatus is essential.
(d) Model the mathematics by manipulating the materials appropriately.
(e) Record the process.
(f) Develop the algorithm. Standard algorithms are possibly most efficient but the children's understanding of them will be enhanced by allowing them to suggest alternative presentations, and then to modify and improve them. Research has shown that if children can record the mathematics in their own way at the same time as they are manipulating material, they come to understand the underlying algorithm better. In the early stages therefore, this series encourages 'extended notation'.
(g) Test the reasonableness of results. Do they make sense? Are they what was expected? Was it reasonable to add the numbers in the first place?

Our models of addition are built by combining sets, and using the base 10 structure of the number system in exchange experiences. Pupils' Book 2 considers problems involving exchanging tens on page 20, exchanging tens and units on page 21, exchanging units on page 22, and problems with no exchanging on page 23. However, the notes and figures which follow here in the Teacher's Guide are presented in a more traditional format, moving from no exchange to exchanging tens and units. Teachers are strongly recommended to read the section as a whole before planning their programme. Whatever order of presentation is chosen, a variety of materials should be used. In the following activities base 10 materials are used along with counting boards and coins. Teachers will wish to consider the use of other materials as necessary.

1. Give the children further practice in playing the Exchange Game described in Section 3, Pre-page activity 8. Stress that when they have ten unit cubes they must exchange them for one '10' strip, and similarly ten '10' strips must be exchanged for one '100' piece.
2. Suggest a situation where it is necessary to let material represent the items being considered,

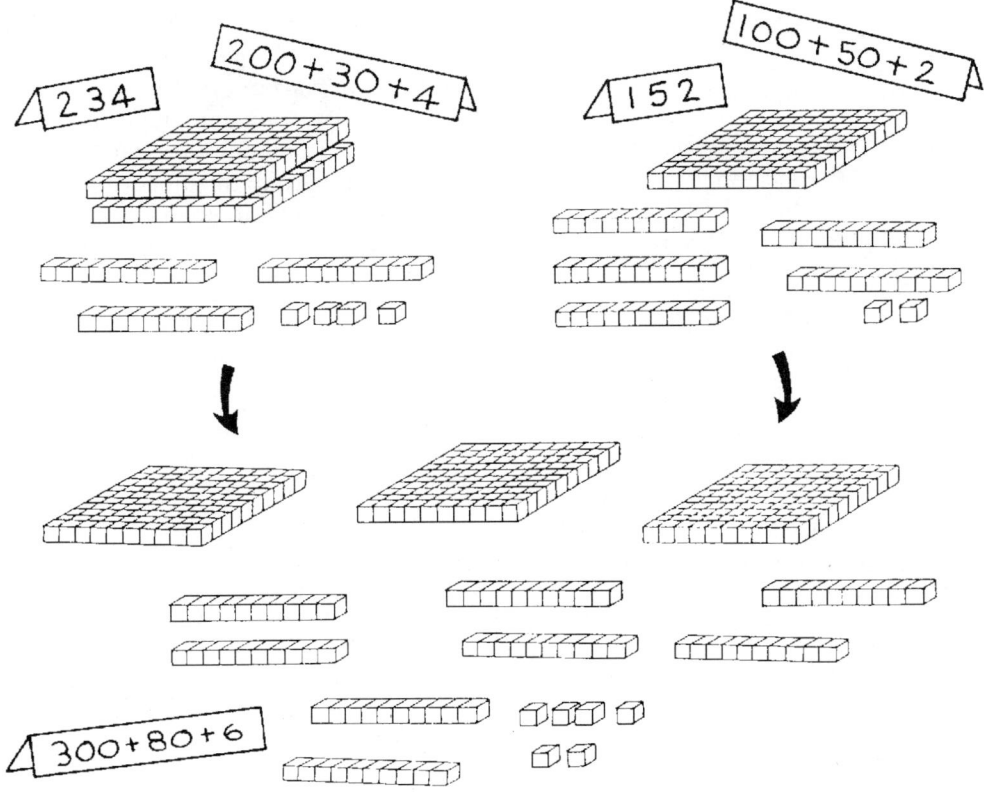

Figure 5.1   '386 people visited the show altogether.'

for example 'If 234 people visited a pet show in the morning, and 152 in the afternoon, how many visited the show altogether?' Discuss with the children how the people can be represented, guiding the discussion towards the introduction of base 10 materials. Have the children model the number of people in the morning with two '100' pieces, three '10' strips and four unit cubes, and the number in the afternoon with one '100' piece, five '10' strips and two unit cubes. They can combine the sets of units, tens and hundreds because they all represent people, and then regroup the material appropriately (figure 5.1).

Get the children to record the mathematics as they go, e.g.

$$\begin{array}{r} 234 \\ + 152 \end{array} \xrightarrow{\text{can be written as}} \begin{array}{r} (200 + 30 + 4) \\ + (100 + 50 + 2) \\ \hline 300 + 80 + 6 \end{array} \longrightarrow 386$$

Make sure the children see that 386 is a reasonable result since 234 is near 250, and 152 is near 150, so the result should be about 400 (250 + 150).

3. Introduce situations where the children need to add, say, 147 to 328 and exchange the units, for example 'If there are 147 boys in the school and 328 girls, how many pupils are there altogether?' Again have the children model the situation, combine the sets and regroup the units into sets of tens (figure 5.2).

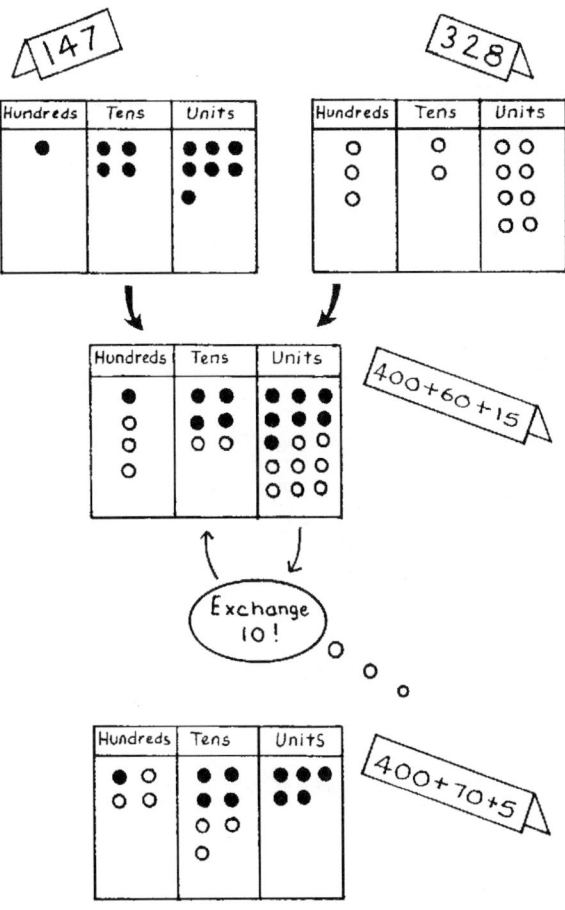

'There are 475 pupils altogether.'

Figure 5.2

147   can be written as   (100 + 40 + 7)
+ 328   + (300 + 20 + 8)
                              ─────────────────
                                400 + 60 + 15
                          ⟶   400 + 60 + (10 + 5)
                          ⟶   400 + (60 + 10) + 5
                          ⟶   400 + 70 + 5
                          ⟶   475

Check that the children realise that 475 is a reasonable result since 147 is near 150, and 328 is near 300 so the result should be about 450.

4. Model a situation such as 'In a one-day international cricket match India scored 283 and the West Indies 362. How many runs did the spectators see scored in the day?' Again have the children combine the sets and regroup the tens, exchanging ten units for a 100 piece where possible (figure 5.3).

283   can be written as   (200 + 80 + 3)
+ 362   + (300 + 60 + 2)
                              ─────────────────
                                500 + 140 + 5
                          ⟶   500 + (100 + 40) + 5
                          ⟶   (500 + 100) + 40 + 5
                          ⟶   600 + 40 + 5
                          ⟶   645

Do the children realise that 645 is a reasonable result since 283 is near 300, and 362 is near 350, so the result should be near 650?

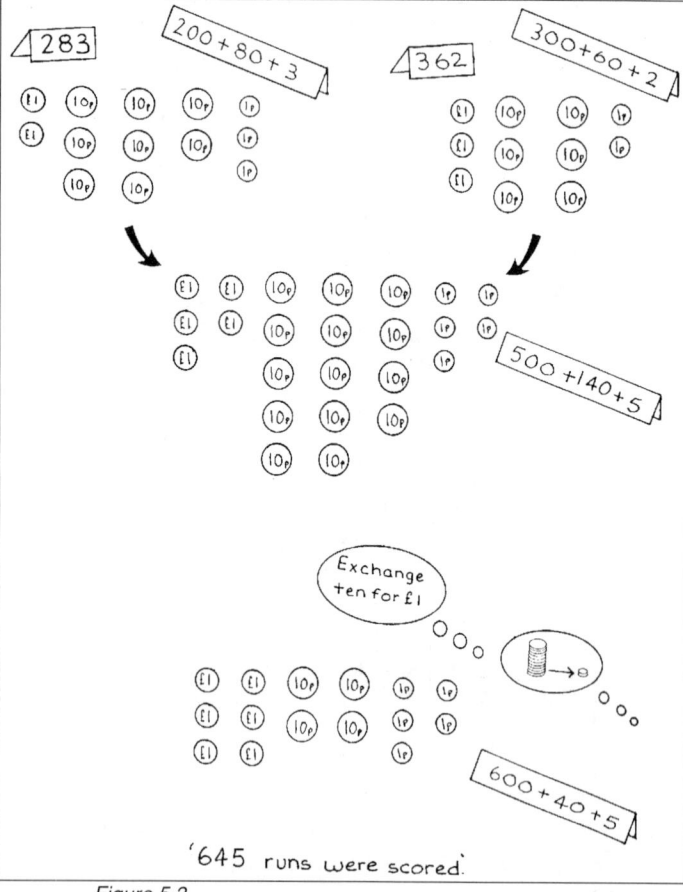

Figure 5.3

5. Introduce exchange situations involving both tens and units, for example 'There are 297 apples in one box and 186 apples in another. How many apples are there altogether?' Have the children model such situations, combine the sets and regroup the units and tens, exchanging where possible (figure 5.4).

Figure 5.4

297   can be written as   (200 + 90 + 7)
+ 186   + (100 + 80 + 6)
                              ─────────────────
                                300 + 170 + 13
                          ⟶   300 + (100 + 70) + (10 + 3)
                          ⟶   (300 + 100) + (70 + 10) + 3
                          ⟶   400 + 80 + 3
                          ⟶   483

6. Have the children discuss the situations on the Addition Algorithm cards (Activity Cards 5.1–5.4). Each set (□, △, ○) depicts a situation and a solution modelled with both base 10 material and counters and a counting board. Get the children to arrange the cards in each set in order (like flowcharts) and have them copy and complete the recordings. Ask them if they

Section 5

can find other ways to perform the operations required to solve the problems on the cards. These cards should not be used until the children have actually modelled similar situations with cubes or counters.

7. Introduce situations where the children have to consider number sentences such as
186 + 217 = ☐
where exchanging their unit cubes creates the need to exchange tens.

8. If masses accurate enough to represent numbers 1 to 100 are available, they may be used to construct physical examples of three-digit numbers and their addition. The additions can be checked by weighing (figure 5.5).

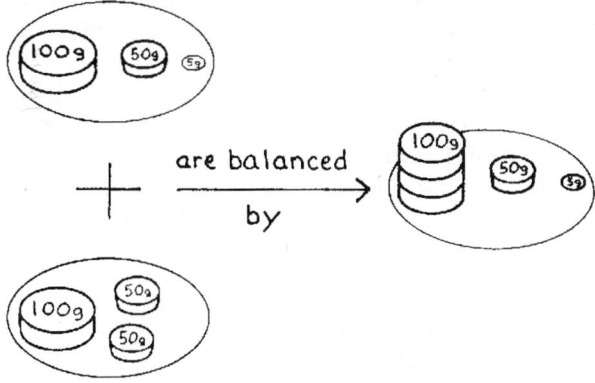

Figure 5.5

9. Get the children to estimate separately the weight of two items, such as a tin of beans and a tub of margarine, and to predict what they think the two will weigh together. Have them check their predictions by weighing. Encourage them to make statements such as 'I think the combined weight of the 450 g tin of beans and the 250 g tub of margarine will be at least 700 g'. Discuss with the children the problem of the weight shown on the label and the weight including the packaging.

10. Write some addition sentences such as
372 + 235 = ☐ on the chalkboard. Ask the children to complete the number sentences and then to write number stories to illustrate them. Have the children read their stories to their friends.

11. Suggest to the children that they find the sum of two numbers such as 436 and 248 by adding on, e.g.

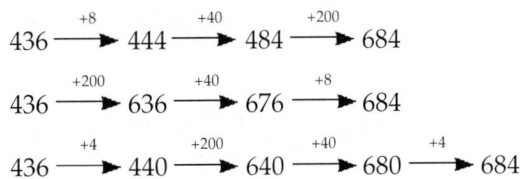

12. Have the children use their calculators to key in sums in different ways, e.g.

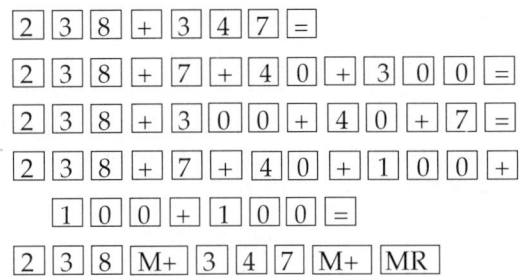

13. Get the children to use their calculators to add three-digit numbers, first getting them to estimate what they expect the answer to be (a) to the nearest 100 and (b) to the nearest 10.

14. Have the children complete 'other ways of writing' three-digit numbers using the addition operation in the first instance (figure 5.6).

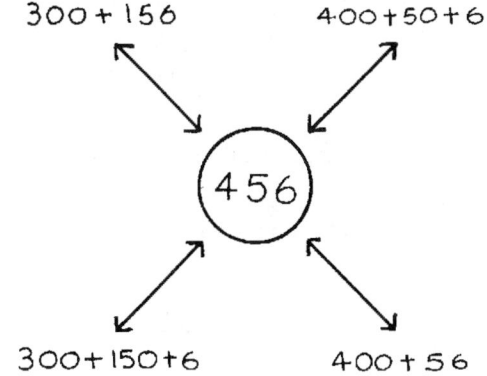

Figure 5.6

15. Write addition sentences such as 321 + 412 = ☐ on the chalkboard and ask the children to estimate the result by saying which multiple of 100 the result is nearest to, i.e. 100, 200, 300, 400, 500, 600, 700, 800 or 900.

16. Remind the children of the 5–10 Multiplication Game they played earlier (Section 1, Further activity 6). Ask the children to investigate how they might exactly reach the target of 250 for different numbers of turns, e.g.
4 turns: 80 + 80 + 60 + 30 = 250;
5 turns: 80 + 60 + 60 + 25 + 25 = 250; etc.
Get them to find the minimum and maximum number of 'turns' possible to reach a total of 250. They should say how likely they feel the various numbers of turns are.

Key page points

Pages 20–23 These pages are each concerned with one idea; we call them single concept discussion pages. Here they are grouped together. You may like to open two Pupils' Books and place pages 22 and 23 alongside pages 20 and 21 to form a four-page spread. Have the children discuss the order of the pictures on the pages and say what they think is happening. On pages 20 and 23 the children should copy and complete the speech bubbles explaining the algorithm. On pages 21 and 22 they are required to place the pictures in sequence. Give the children a selection from the following additions for further practice, either after you have discussed a particular page or after you have discussed the group of pages.

After page 20   Exchange in tens only

493	191	284	322	485	284
+423	+162	+465	+197	+442	+254

281	157	754	295	375	246
+132	+281	+174	+652	+334	+562

After page 21   Exchange in both tens and units

369	448	297	256	169	169
+289	+365	+333	+167	+146	+684

482	735	277	769	153	669
+189	+176	+248	+132	+248	+135

After page 22   Exchange in units only

229	345	129	549	141	117
+543	+317	+757	+336	+739	+725

247	174	356	149	215	649
+416	+618	+128	+119	+146	+248

After page 23   No exchange

474	461	235	338	173	513
+322	+124	+233	+661	+814	+232

475	462	125	434	117	852
+424	+523	+434	+153	+632	+113

Page 24 It is important children use base 10 materials or counters and counting boards for question 1, as modelling the mathematics is as important at this stage as getting the answers. The children should be encouraged to find as many number sentences as they can, within reason, in question 5. They could use their calculators to check the number sentences they have found. If several children are working on this page, have them discuss their results to see if anyone found any unique sentences for question 5.

Page 25 Make sure the children have calculators for question 1. Discuss with them the different ways they found the totals and the merits of the different approaches.

Page 26 Explain to the children that the information on routes and distances is a service that the AA and RAC carry out for their members. Before the children calculate the total distances travelled, get them to estimate the sum first. When the page is completed, let the children examine maps and charts in AA and RAC handbooks which give distances. If possible, obtain a computer printout for a journey which states distances, and in some cases directions, and guidance on selection of roads at intersections.

Page 27 This page consolidates the addition of three-digit numbers. The scenes referred to in question 2 are only there to motivate the children to write stories and it is not intended that the children find, for example, 618 and 271 'things' to add together in any of the pictures. When the page is completed, you may wish to collect the stories and display them.

Further activities

1. Play Double Throw, using three cubes marked as follows: 4, 5, 6, 7, 8, 9; 40, 50, 60, 70, 80, 90; 100, 200, 300, 100, 200, 300. The children take it in turns to throw the cubes twice and write down the total of the two numbers they have thrown, e.g. 279 + 344 = 623. The winner is the player with the greatest total. Let the winner of the round score four points, the second three, and so on. Record the scores on a tens and units scoreboard. After, say, ten rounds the overall winner can be declared.

2. Make and play Between Pairs. You will need a set of, say, eight red cards with addition sentences such as:

123	192	287	223	298	412	538	413
+144	+153	+145	+344	+325	+325	+297	+542

and a set of, say, eight blue cards with the following:

sum between 200 and 300
sum between 300 and 400
sum between 400 and 500
sum between 500 and 600
sum between 600 and 700
sum between 700 and 800
sum between 800 and 900
sum between 900 and 1000

Spread all the cards face down on the table. The children take it in turns to turn over a red 'sum' card and estimate the sum of the two numbers shown. They then turn over a blue 'between' card. If the sum is 'between' the values displayed on the blue card, then a pair is formed (figure 5.7) and that player keeps the

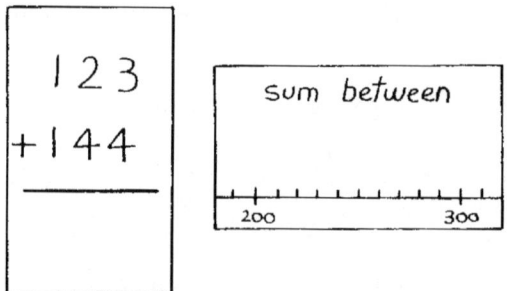

Figure 5.7

cards. The player who collects most pairs wins the game. Have the children read 1000 as 'ten hundreds' as well as 'a thousand'.

3. Play 'Nearly' Addition Triples (Activity Card 5.5). Again the cards should be spread out face down. The children take it in turns to turn over one card of each colour. If the three match (figure 5.8), then the player keeps the triple. If not, then the cards are turned face down again and play moves to the next player. The one with the most triples wins the game.

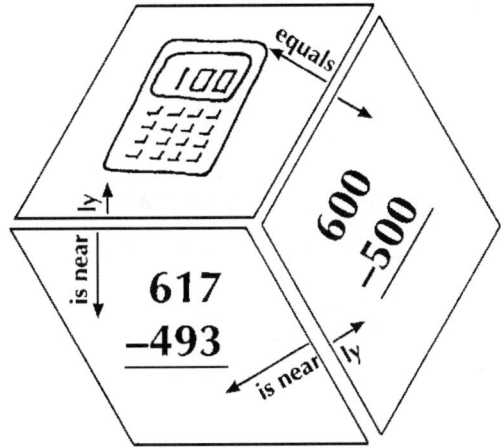

Figure 5.8

4. Make and play Touch and Say Addition. Prepare a series of cards which concentrate on various aspects of hundreds, tens and units additions. Write an appropriate number sentence on the front of each card and the result on the back (figure 5.9). The series could include:

   (a) cards with the addition of two multiples of a hundred, e.g. 400 + 300 = ☐, 200 + 600 = ☐ etc.;

   (b) cards with no exchange in the process, e.g. 543 + 321 = ☐;

   (c) cards with exchange of units, e.g. 548 + 327 = ☐;

   (d) cards with exchange of tens, e.g. 584 + 372 = ☐;

   (e) cards with exchange in both tens and units, e.g. 584 + 378 = ☐;

   (f) cards with a random mixture.

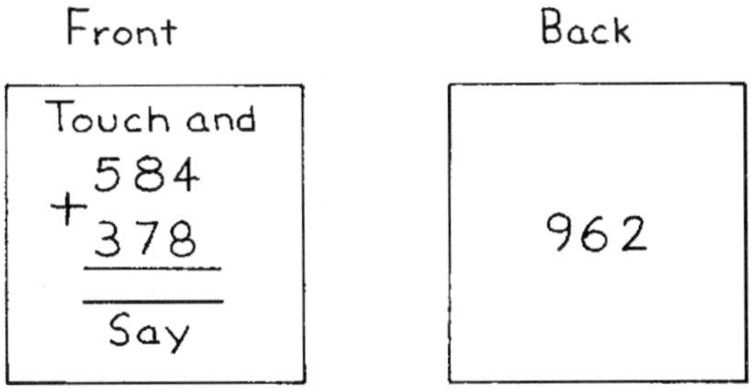

   Front: Touch and 584 + 378 Say
   Back: 962

Figure 5.9

Have the children take it in turns to point to a card and get their neighbour to say what they expect to find on the reverse. If the player calls correctly, he/she keeps the card. If not, the card is turned over again and is left on the table. The player who has just attempted a call then points to another card for his/her neighbour. They should not point to a card they themselves have failed with.

5. Ask the children to continue H.T.U. addition patterns, e.g.

   324 + 145 = ...   198 + 374 = ...
   324 + 155 = ...   298 + 374 = ...
   324 + 165 = ...   398 + 374 = ...
   324 + 175 = ...   498 + 374 = ...

   164 + 435 = ...   173 + 210 = ...
   164 + 440 = ...   173 + 230 = ...
   164 + 445 = ...   173 + 250 = ...
   164 + 450 = ...   173 + 270 = ... etc.

   Get them to create their own sequences.

6. Prepare a series of situations which involve the addition of three-digit numbers for the children to solve.

7. Have the children make up stories involving the addition of three-digit numbers in everyday situations. You could give the children a number sentence and have them write three different stories for each one. To avoid repetition, it may be advisable to suggest some different environments, e.g. in the shopping centre, walking around town, in the factory, etc.

8. Four in a Line can be played to practise addition. Use Copymaster 5.1 to make a game appropriate to the children's needs. To prepare a game sheet, take a copy of the master and write eight different numbers in the spaces in the box at the top of the page. Write the operation to be used in the circle. In the regions in the large square write the results of some of the possible results of combining the numbers in the top box using the chosen operation. Figure 5.10 shows a sheet prepared for the practice of addition of two three-digit numbers. The game is for two players. The children will need one calculator, a game sheet and a coloured pencil each. The object of the game is to capture four squares in a line. The line can be horizontal, vertical or diagonal. The children decide who is to play first. The player decides which square is to be captured. He/she then estimates which two numbers from the box at the top can be used to give the result shown in the square. A number can be used twice. The other player checks the result on the calculator. If the estimate is correct, then the player captures the square and colours it using his/her

New Curriculum Mathematics for Schools Key Stage 2

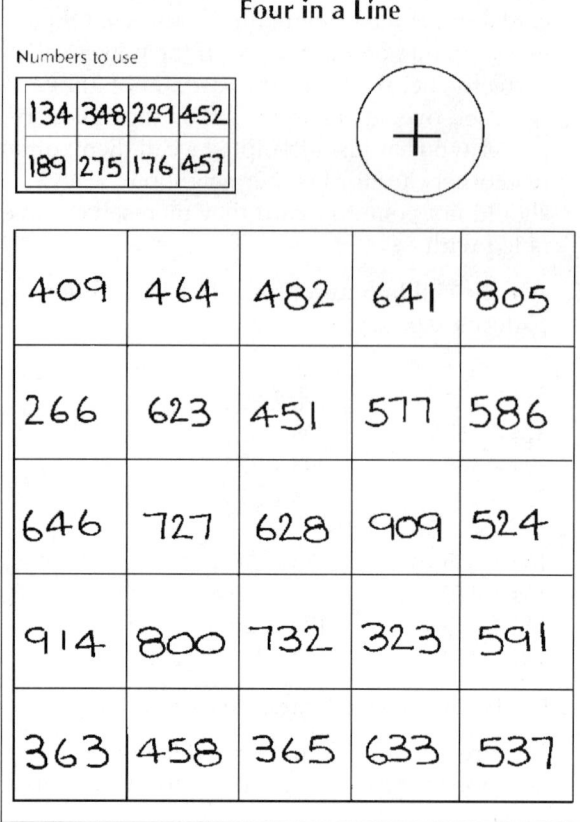

Figure 5.10

colour. The first player to get four squares in a line is the winner.
At the start of the game the players will try to capture the 'easiest' squares but will soon need to estimate results they are not sure of as they try to get a line or to stop their opponent getting a line.

9. Have the children complete Copymaster 5.2. You could let them create a similar situation using pebbles of their own, if wished.

10. Copymaster 5.3 can be used for more practice in the addition of three-digit numbers. The children are also asked for their definition of 'nearly'.

11. When the children are confident with their extended form of recording, discuss with them other more streamlined ways, for example:

```
  485      485      485
 +179     +179     +179
 ----     ----     ----
   14      500      664
  150      150
  500       14
 ----     ----
  664      664
```

Have the children explore other methods of recording such as:

$485 \xrightarrow{+100} 585 \xrightarrow{+70} 655 \xrightarrow{+9} 664.$

Get them to consider the 'best' ways of solving problems such as $345 + 299 = \square$. Encourage solutions such as: $345 \xrightarrow{+300} 645 \xrightarrow{-1} 644.$

Check-ups

1. Can the children recognise an addition situation involving three-digit numbers?

2. Can the children model an addition situation involving three-digit numbers, manipulating appropriate materials and recording the process?

3. Can the children add hundreds, tens and units not involving exchange?

4. Can the children add hundreds, tens and units involving exchange?

Section 6

AT 1 3c, 3d. AT 3 4a. AT 4 2b, 4a, 4b.

Pages 28–31 Shape, Space and Position

Pages 28 and 29 Matchstick Maths
Page 30 Moving a Shape
Page 31 How Do They Look?

Purpose

To introduce the location of points on a lattice using ordered pairs.
To encourage the children to investigate patterns in ordered pairs.
To help children recognise parallel lines as straight lines in the same plane which do not meet.
To encourage awareness of parallel lines in the children's environment.
To introduce simple parallel translations of shapes on a numbered lattice, and to investigate the patterns connecting the corresponding ordered pairs of numbers.
To introduce perpendicular lines as straight lines which meet at right angles.
To introduce the concepts of vertical and horizontal in the environment.
To help children to recognise identical (congruent) plane shapes in fixed positions and in different orientations.

Recommended material

1. Games such as Battleships.
2. **Copymasters 6.1–6.7.**
3. Cards for games (see Pre-page activities 2 and 3, and Further activity 2).
4. Rulers with parallel sides.
5. Metre rules and a ball.
6. Set squares.
7. Geostrips, Meccano strips, strips made from card, etc.
8. An overhead projector and transparency on which a square lattice is drawn.
9. Straws.
10. A computer with a graphics program which has a COPY and MOVE facility to show sliding without rotation.
11. Squared paper.
12. Home-made plumb line.
13. Home-made or commercial spirit level.
14. Dice.
15. A simple clinometer.

Pre-page activities

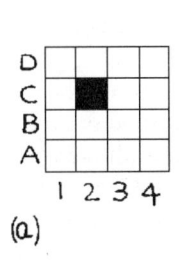 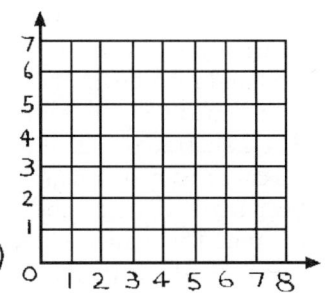

Figure 6.1

Note Our 'grid' completely covers part of a surface, dividing it up into regions, as shown in figure 6.1a. In this case, the 16 regions are 'addressed' with letters and numerals, and the ordered pair for the shaded region is (2, C). Our 'lattice' picks out points on a surface (figure 6.1b). In this case the whole numbers (the set of natural numbers and zero) are used for ordered pairs to 'address' the points of the lattice. Point out the difference to the children as they participate in the following activities. In all the examples on numbered lattices when points, lines and shapes are moved, have the children examine the number pairs for corresponding points on the original and on the final position. Simple cases help the children to see the constant additions connecting the pairs. Examples can then be varied to give further experience.

1. Let the children play the popular game of Battleships. Although this game does not use coordinates in the strictest sense, it does give children practice in giving directions as ordered pairs, albeit in terms of along and up, or letters and numbers. (In Battleships the regions are labelled, whereas for coordinates the lines are labelled.)

2. Have the children play Random Noughts and Crosses. Prepare a series of nine cards as shown in figure 6.2. Copymaster 6.1 will also be required. The object of the game is for a child to play Noughts and Crosses 'against' the pack of cards. The cards should be shuffled and placed face down in a pile on the table. The top card is then turned up, read and placed on the table face up. The ordered pair displayed is now recorded on the scoreboard on Copymaster 6.1 as the 'Pack's' turn and a cross placed in the

New Curriculum Mathematics for Schools Key Stage 2

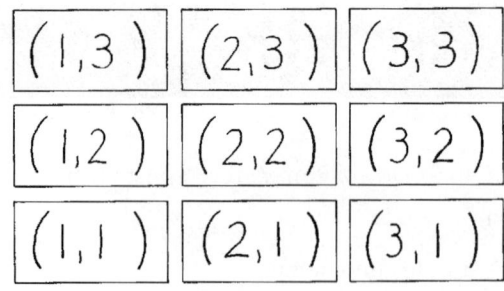

Figure 6.2

appropriate position on the playing grid. The second turn goes to the child. He/she places a 'nought' at a chosen position on the playing grid and records his/her move on the scoreboard. Play then alternates between the 'Pack' and the player. If the card turned over reveals a pair for a region which has already been marked, then another card is drawn from the pile. The game continues until there is a result, i.e. there are three noughts or crosses in a row. A draw is possible. The player should complete the copymaster by filling in the winning line and making a comment about it, e.g. 'The alongs are the same as the ups' or 'The alongs are always 3'.

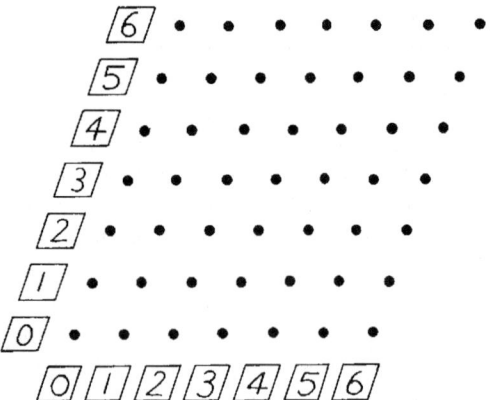

Figure 6.3

3. Mark the points of a lattice on the floor (figure 6.3). Have the children practise moving to positions on the lattice. For example, the ordered pair (4, 3) can be printed on a card which is then given to a pupil, who must take 4 steps 'along' and 3 'up' from 0 to reach the position. He or she should then place the card of the ordered pair on the appropriate point. Let the children repeat the activity with other ordered pairs. When they have become familiar with the idea of 'plotting pairs' in this way, clear the lattice. Now choose a set of ordered pairs which display a relationship, for example (0, 2), (1, 3), (2, 4), (3, 5), and so on, where the second number is more than the first by a fixed number, in this case 2 more. Have the children pace out and 'plot' the points. Other patterns can include: (0, 0), (1, 1), (1, 2), (1, 3), ...; or (0, 1), (1, 1), (2, 1), (3, 1), ...; or (0, 3), (1, 3), (2, 3), 3, 3), ...; or (0, 10), (1, 9), (2, 8), (3, 7),

(4, 6), (5, 5), ... The children can then look for the visual pattern shown by the points plotted on the lattice. Always encourage the children to predict the next pair in the sequence pattern. Have them say what they can about the points plotted on the lattice. Have they noticed the straight line arrangements? The children can then plot their results in the normal way using Copymasters 6.2 and 6.3.

4. Place two metre rules side by side on the ground. Slide one of the rules a small distance away from the other without rotating it. Have the children discuss how the rules are lying, e.g. in terms of direction, distance apart, etc. Introduce the word 'parallel'. Vary the form of the translation and include some non-parallel moves for comparison (figure 6.4).

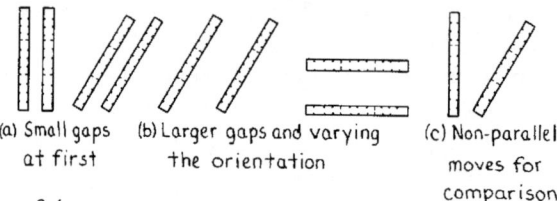

(a) Small gaps at first (b) Larger gaps and varying the orientation (c) Non-parallel moves for comparison

Figure 6.4

5. Provide the children with a ball and two metre rules. Let the ball roll down the inclined rules. Get the children to explain how the rules need to be set. Discuss practical uses of parallel lines, e.g. railway lines.

6. Show the children how to draw parallel lines using a set square and straight edge (figure 6.5).

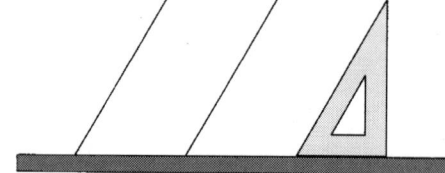

Figure 6.5

Place a set square on the chalkboard; draw a line along one side, then slide the shape along a straight ruler and draw other parallel lines. Have the children practise drawing parallel lines on paper. Encourage them to design some wrapping paper using parallel lines, for example they could draw two sets of lines which cross each other and then colour in the designs. Name the quadrilaterals 'parallelograms'.

7. Make a parallelogram shape using geostrips, or strips of card (figure 6.6). Deform the shape to make various parallelograms. Discuss the shapes and the parallel sides with the children. Have them notice what changes and what stays the same in the various configurations, e.g. what do they notice about the angles. Make sure you consider the position when all the

48

Figure 6.6

angles are equal, and stress that a rectangle is also a parallelogram! Encourage the children to look for examples of parallelograms around them. Show them diagrams such as the one in figure 6.7 and discuss whether the bold lines are parallel or not. Discuss how to test their conclusions.

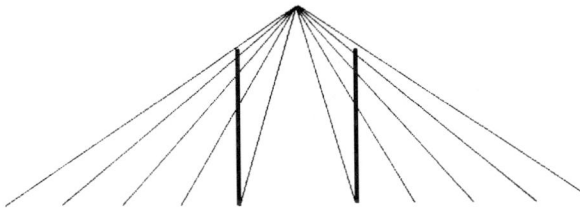

Figure 6.7

8. Get the children to draw parallel lines on Copymaster 6.4. Consider the horizontal and vertical lines first, then the sloping lines. Let the children practise drawing more parallel lines at various inclinations. Have them colour shapes which are similar.

9. Demonstrate sliding without rotation by placing a transparency of a lattice on an overhead projector, then placing two straws side by side on it and moving one without rotation across the lattice. It is useful if the straws are cut so that the ends lie on intersections of the lattice. In this way the number pairs can be read from each end. Have the children draw a straight stick on the lattice on Copymaster 6.3 with one end on the intersection (3, 2) and the other end on (6, 9), and get them to record the ordered pairs at each end. Have them add 4 to the first number of each pair to make two new ordered pairs: (7, 2) and (10, 9). Ask them to draw the new stick between the intersections with these ordered pairs. Discuss the results. Let the children experiment:

(a) adding a fixed number to the second number only;

(b) adding the same number to both numbers of the pair;
(c) adding one fixed number to the first and a different fixed number to the second of each pair, etc.

Let them talk, or write, about their results.

10. Have the children work through Copymaster 6.5 (figure 6.8). Also let the children use any available computer programs which allow them to translate shapes.

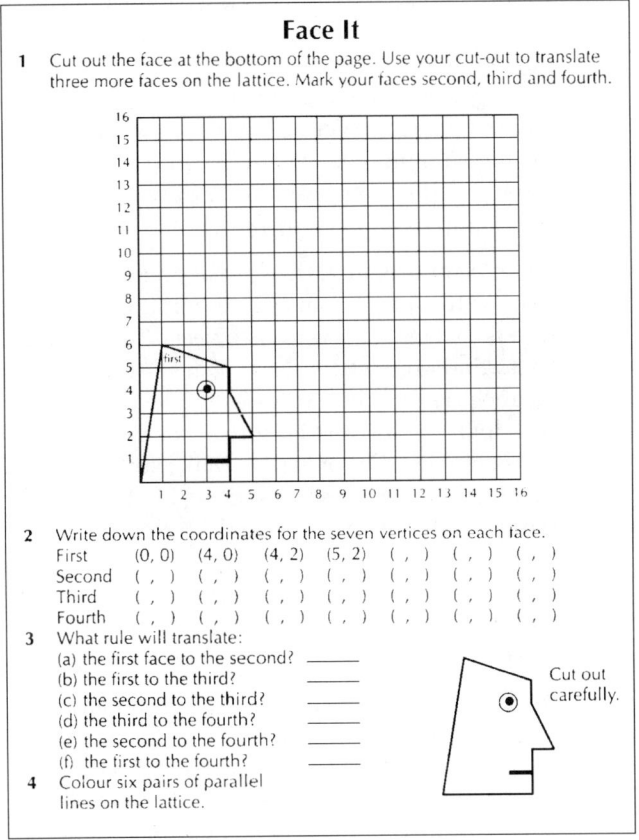

Figure 6.8

11. Let each child make a right angle by folding a piece of paper to make a straight edge, then folding the straight edge onto itself, end to end, making a right angle at the middle point of the edge (figure 6.9). Show the children that a straight edge can also be folded to make a right angle at any point on the edge. Have them label the corner of the fold a right angle. The right angle measures should be kept for other activities.

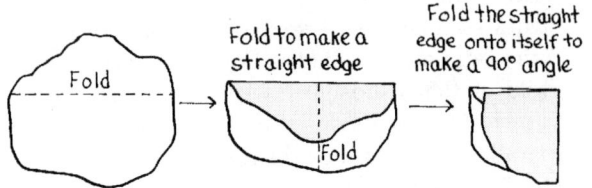

Figure 6.9

12. Choose a convenient rectangular shape, e.g. the chalkboard, a door, or a window, and let some of the children check the right angles with their folded right angles. Introduce the words 'horizontal' and 'vertical' to describe the lie of the sides of the rectangular shape. Introduce the word 'perpendicular', to describe how the horizontal and vertical lines meet at right angles. Have the children find right angles made by horizontal and vertical lines in the room, using their folded angles to check. Encourage them to use the descriptions, 'vertical', 'horizontal', 'right angle' and 'perpendicular lines', when they talk about their findings. You may find it useful to let the children label the vertical, horizontal and inclined alignments which they find in the room. Let them write about, or draw, some of the examples which they find.

13. Tell the children that they are to guess what you are thinking about as you point out some things to look at on various objects. They must try to find other examples which have the same characteristics. Choose, for example, the sides of a door, the top and bottom of the chalkboard, lines between tiles or bricks. Make sure that you include the lines in a writing book, and the parallel sides of a ruler. Use the terms 'parallel', 'vertical' and 'horizontal' in relevant situations. Have the children make lists of places, at school and at home, where they can see examples of these.

14. On Copymaster 6.6, have the children mark horizontal lines blue, vertical lines green, and the enclosed right angles red. Discuss with the children the problem of having horizontal lines in perspective (in the copymaster the roof of the hut, for example, is clearly a rectangular face in reality, although it does not appear so in the drawing). Also talk to the children about representing horizontal and vertical lines on paper. Explain that, although they may be drawing the lines while the page is flat on a table, the line directions are described as though they are on a wall. Have the children draw horizontal and vertical lines on squared paper, using a ruler and pencil on the printed lines of the paper, then extend their experience to drawing lines inclined at 45 degrees.

15. Have the children make a parallelogram with geostrips or Meccano strips so that the joints are quite flexible. Let the children now attach a strut to one of the shorter sides so that it is fixed quite rigid at right angles. Point out to the children that windscreen wipers on many large vehicles (buses, lorries, trains) incorporate a 'parallelogram' in their design. Have the children realise that if one shorter side of the parallelogram is secured in a horizontal

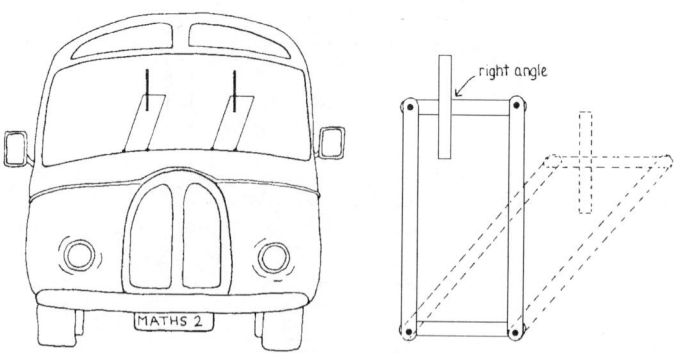

Figure 6.10

position, the opposite side will also be horizontal because it is part of the same parallelogram. The vertical strut will therefore always be vertical to the horizontal and should wipe the window well (figure 6.10). Have the children look out for other 'parallelograms in motion' in everyday life, and explain why the shape is used in each design. For example, a pencil case or toolbox may well have obvious parallelograms, as could a toy forklift truck (figure 6.11).

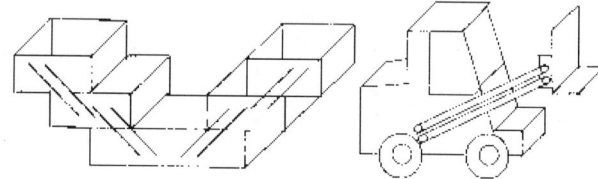

Figure 6.11

16. Allow the children to make a plumb line with a piece of string and a heavy mass such as a metal nut. Ask a child to hold the plumb line so that it hangs freely, and have a partner view the string from the side to see how it behaves. Get the children to compare the line of the string with, say, a known/expected vertical line in the wall. Have them try to find some non-vertical structures in and outside school, and at home. If the wallpaper hanger used a plumb line as a guide, the children may be able to test the accuracy of the work, although some diplomacy may be required if it has been a DIY project at home!

17. Have the children use their plumb line and notice how the string forms an angle with the floor (figure 6.12). Hopefully this will be a right

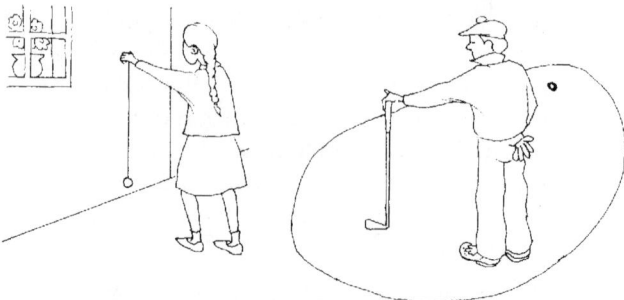

Figure 6.12   Figure 6.13

angle, but the children will have to judge. Also get the children to stand on sloping surfaces and notice the angle the string makes with the surface. (You could mention that golfers sometimes use their putter as a 'plumb line' to judge the slope of the putting green (figure 6.13). Have the children find other sloping surfaces with their plumb line. Can they gauge the amount of slope?

18. Let the children organise a competition to see who can make a 'vehicle' that will roll furthest down an inclined plane. Allow each competitor five runs and measure each. Assign the middle value for each competitor as his/her score. Display the results. Have the children investigate the surfaces around them and find as many inclined surfaces as they can. Let them now roll balls or cylinders on these surfaces.

19. Make a simple spirit level with a large straight-sided, clear plastic bottle. Have the children half fill the bottle with water and mark the horizontal water level with a felt marker. Let them use their 'level' to find different sloping surfaces around the school (figure 6.14). They can mark the water levels on the bottle, and make statements such as 'The ramp is steeper than the drive', etc. As a follow-up let the children use a more accurate commercial spirit level.

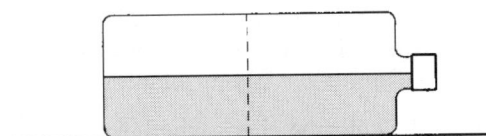

Figure 6.14

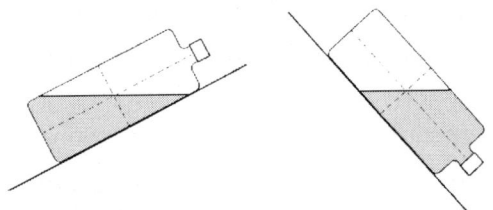

20. Have available a number of rectangular sheets of paper or card of different sizes (figure 6.15). Hold a sheet so that the edges lie horizontally and vertically. Turn the sheet so that the horizontal and vertical edges become inclined. Discuss what has changed and what has remained the same. Repeat with other sheets. Discuss the use of the word 'perpendicular' to

Figure 6.15

describe that adjacent edges remain at right angles as the rectangle is rotated. Have the children draw horizontal and vertical lines on squared paper using ruler and pencil on the printed lines of the paper, then extend their experience to lines inclined at 45 degrees (figure 6.16). Have the children try drawing right angles at other inclinations. Emphasise that the sides of the right angles can be extended as far as they wish without changing the size of the angle.

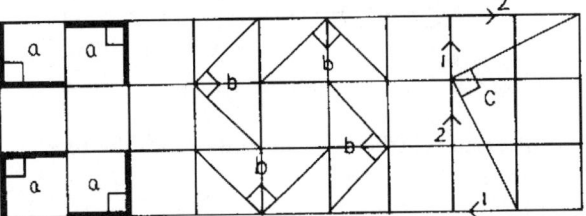

Figure 6.16

21. Prepare large cut-out triangles, not necessarily identical in shape. The children can practise making perpendicular folds at the centre points of the sides, to see that they intersect at one point. They may also make a fold perpendicular to each side which then passes through the opposite vertex. These also intersect at a single point.

Key page points

Page 28 Copymasters 6.2 and 6.3 are available for the children to create their own sets of pairs. Have the children notice not only the relationship which links the points, but also the 'pattern of the lines' formed, i.e. the slope.

Page 29 Encourage the children to notice how the various ordered pairs are linked on each screen.

Page 30 Make sure the children realise that the lengths between corresponding points remain the same in a parallel translation.

Page 31 Have the children draw a house which does *not* have horizontal and vertical alignments!

Further activities

1. Make and play Word Form. Give the children a copy of the lattice shown in figure 6.17 and two dice, one blue and one red. The children roll the dice in turns to form an ordered pair. They read the letter from the lattice corresponding to their pair and 'collect' the letters. On the completion of an agreed number of throws, each child tries to make up a word from the letters collected. One point is scored for each letter correctly used in a word. As a variation, as well as making, say, a five-letter word from five throws, the children could see how many

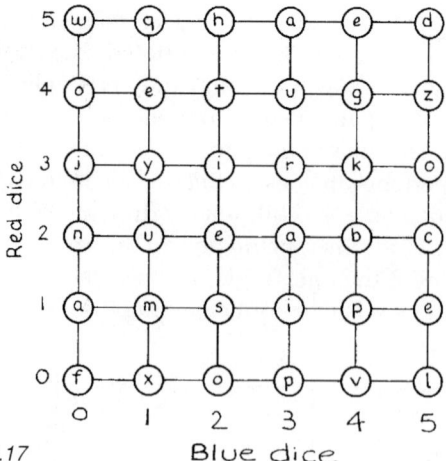

Figure 6.17

different words they can make from the five letters.

2. Make and play Lattice Three in a Row. You will need a set of 36 cards with pairs marked on them as shown below.

(0, 5) (1, 5) (2, 5) (3, 5) (4, 5) (5, 5)
(0, 4) (1, 4) (2, 4) (3, 4) (4, 4) (5, 4)
(0, 3) (1, 3) (2, 3) (3, 3) (4, 3) (5, 3)
(0, 2) (1, 2) (2, 2) (3, 2) (4, 2) (5, 2)
(0, 1) (1, 1) (2, 1) (3, 1) (4, 1) (5, 1)
(0, 0) (1, 0) (2, 0) (3, 0) (4, 0) (5, 0)

Also provide each player with a blank 5 × 5 lattice. Shuffle the cards and place them face down in a pile on the table. The players take it in turns to turn over the top card and mark the point indicated on their lattice. The card is then placed face down at the bottom of the pack and play moves to the next player. The winning player is the first to have three marks on his/her lattice which lie in a row.

3. Have the children complete Copymaster 6.7, for more practice in translating shapes and finding parallel lines.

4. Have the children investigate solid geometrical shapes to see whether they have any parallel edges. Ask them to mark parallel edges on some everyday containers. Let them colour equal angles in the parallelograms found on Copymaster 6.7, and have them write about any pattern they can see in the positions of the equal angles.

5. A simple clinometer may be used to survey the slopes of paths around the school, and to identify distant points which are at eye level, or higher or lower (figure 6.18).

6. Set a group of children the task of erecting a rod (1 or 2 metres in height), using a plumb line, so that it is vertical when viewed from any direction. You may choose to have them place the rod in the classroom or, if you wish to make it more difficult, on a slope outside. Does the plumb line need to be used more than twice?

7. Arrange for a group of children to visit some very young children and ask them to draw a picture of a tree on a hillside! Have them ask some slightly older children to do the same, in order to discover at what age children start to draw trees growing perpendicularly.

Check-ups

1. Can the children say, or write, an ordered pair for any point indicated on a lattice?

2. Can the children identify a simple relationship between the first and second numbers of an ordered pair, e.g. that both numbers are the same or the second number is three more than or twice the first?

3. Can the children recognise from the pattern of the associated ordered pairs that the points on a lattice lie in a straight line?

4. Can the children identify parallel lines and edges on common objects and on geometrical shapes?

5. Can the children draw parallel lines?

6. Can the children find the number pattern relating the ordered pairs for the corresponding points in two parallel lines drawn on squared paper?

7. Can the children identify parallel lines and determine the pattern, as in check-up 2, when a shape is moved without rotation?

8. Can the children check whether two lines meet at right angles?

9. Can the children use the word 'perpendicular' correctly:

   (a) when horizontal and vertical lines meet?

   (b) when the lines are not horizontal or vertical?

10. Can the children recognise simple cases of perpendicular edges in their environment?

11. Can the children point out lines, or edges, about them which are horizontal or vertical?

12. Can the children point approximately in horizontal and vertical directions?

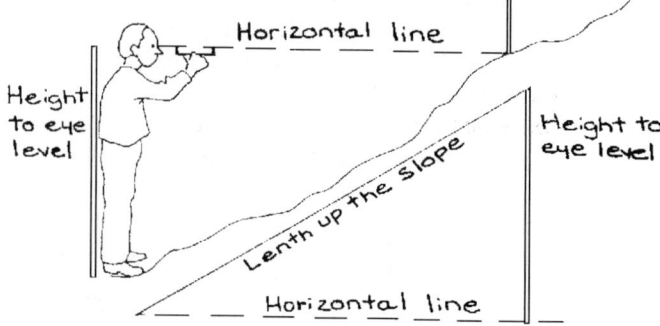

Figure 6.18

Section 7

AT 1 3a, 3c, 3d. AT 2 3e. AT 3 2b. AT 5 3a.

Pages 32–34 Negative Numbers

Pages 32 and 33 World Weather: The USA

Page 34 Everybody Counts

Purpose

To give children practice in reading temperatures which are below zero on a thermometer.
To enable children to identify negative numbers as points on the number line.
To introduce numbers such as ⁺5 (positive five) and ⁻5 (negative five) as movements in opposite directions on a number scale.
To make children aware of the way a calculator displays a negative number.

Recommended material

1. Thermometers.
2. **Copymasters 7.1–7.7.**
3. Calculators.
4. Cards for games (see Pre-page activity 6, and Further activities 6 and 7).
5. World weather chart from a newspaper.
6. Temperature Touch and Say (**Activity Card 7.1**).
7. Dice marked ⁻3, ⁺/⁻2, ⁻1, ⁺1, ⁺/⁻2, ⁺3, and counters.
8. Squared paper.
9. Negative Number Dominoes (**Activity Cards 7.2–7.3**).
10. Watch Your Step! (**Activity Cards 7.4–7.5**).

Pre-page activities

Note Formal addition and subtraction of positive and negative numbers is not dealt with at this stage, although a beginning is made when comparisons are considered. Teachers may feel that some children can express such situations in terms of 'difference' sentences, and links with addition are encouraged. Steps taken upwards, or to the right, are described by positive numbers, steps taken downwards, or to the left are described by negative numbers. Often children will hear ⁻5 verbalised as 'minus five'. In this series we recommend that phrases such as 'negative five' are used, we will refer to 'minus' as part of the subtraction operation.

1. Draw a vertical thermometer scale on the chalkboard showing positive and negative numbers and zero as points on the scale (figure 7.1). Describe zero degrees Celsius as being the freezing point of water. Move your finger up the scale as the children count, saying 'positive one, positive two,' etc., to describe the temperature rising. Then, starting from zero again, have the children count 'negative one, negative two,' etc., to describe the temperature falling. Move your finger to the points below zero in order as they count.

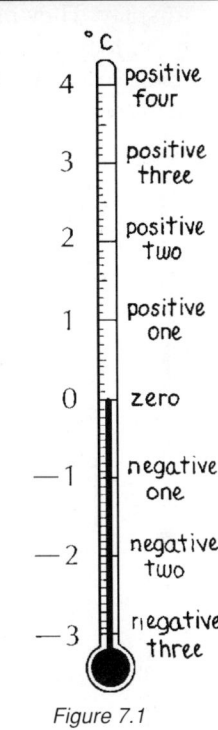

Figure 7.1

2. Have the children continue to collect weather data by taking the temperature each day. As the temperatures fall, take the opportunity to follow the pattern and hopefully, as far as mathematics is concerned, the sequence will fall below zero and provide the opportunity to extend the number line below zero.
Figure 7.2, which shows the lowest temperatures recorded across Britain, may be of interest. Let the children compare the findings they have recorded with other places in the

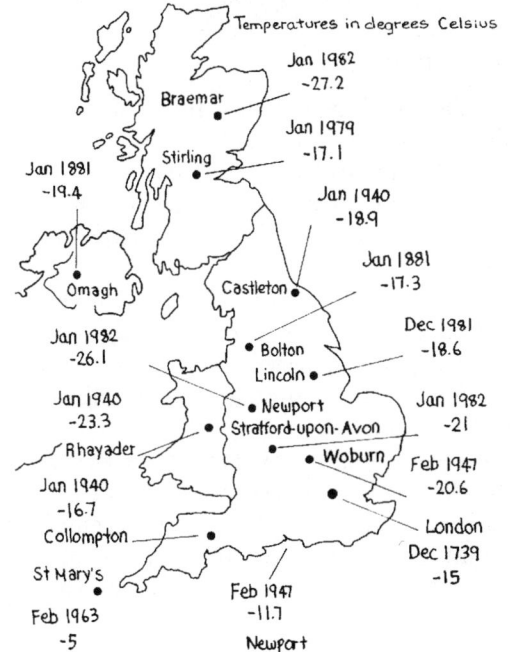

Figure 7.2

world (figure 7.3). Have them illustrate the hottest and coldest temperatures they can find in world weather records on a thermometer for display. They may like to compare these with their local recordings. When writing comparison number sentences, remind the children that '–' means 'find the difference'.

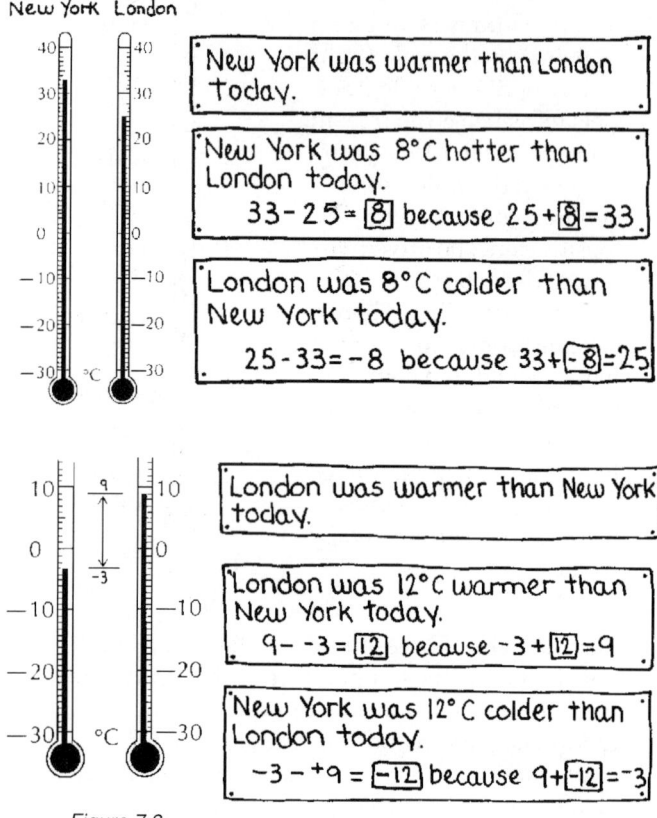

Figure 7.3

3. Discuss with the children the idea of zero as a starting point in various situations. Combine this with the idea of describing a movement in one direction by a positive number, and a movement in the opposite direction as a negative number. Examples of zeros as starting points include:

(a) the freezing point of water on a thermometer (degrees colder than zero);
(b) the surface of water, e.g. the sea, a swimming bath, a tank or bowl of water in the classroom (metres/centimetres below the surface);
(c) the ground floor of a hotel or other building with a lift (floors below the ground floor);
(d) the ground surface at the top of a mine (metres below the ground when going down into the mine);
(e) the starting line for a race (metres behind the starting line to handicap the fast runners);
(f) having no points at the start of a game (points may be lost so that a score below zero is reached – any points gained have then to be used to get back to zero);
(g) having no money (borrowing money which has to be paid back);

(h) the position on a map or grid prior to moving north or south, or east or west (north and east on a graph are, by convention, accepted as the positive directions, and south and west as the negative directions);
(i) the beginning of a timed event (time before the beginning of an event, such as the countdown to a rocket launch, may be in negative numbers), or giving someone a 3 seconds start in a sporting event is like starting them at negative 3 seconds.
(j) the beginning of a tape measure or rule;
(k) the start of a trip meter on a car.

Copymasters 7.1 and 7.2 provide work related to examples (b) and (c) above.

4. Encourage the children to extend some 'difference' number patterns as far as they can:

$8 - 1 = \ldots$ $9 - 2 = \ldots$ $10 - 3 = \ldots$
$8 - 2 = \ldots$ $9 - 3 = \ldots$ $10 - 4 = \ldots$
$8 - 3 = \ldots$ $9 - 4 = \ldots$ $10 - 5 = \ldots$ etc.

Eventually they will come to $8 - 8 = 0, 9 - 9 = 0, 10 - 10 = 0$, and then $8 - 9 = \boxed{?}, 9 - 10 = \boxed{?}, 10 - 11 = \boxed{?}$. Suggest they consider taking the patterns further. (See also Further activity 9.).

5. Make sure the children understand that the set of 'counting numbers' is (1, 2, 3, 4, 5, 6, 7, ...). If zero is included, then the set is known as the set of whole numbers (0, 1, 2, 3, 4, 5, ...), and when negative numbers are introduced the set is known as the set of integers (... ⁻4, ⁻3, ⁻2, ⁻1, 0, 1, 2, 3, 4, ...). Show this information on a wall display.

6. Prepare some logic number chains (see figure 7.4). Make some outline mats, some relationship arrows and some cards with

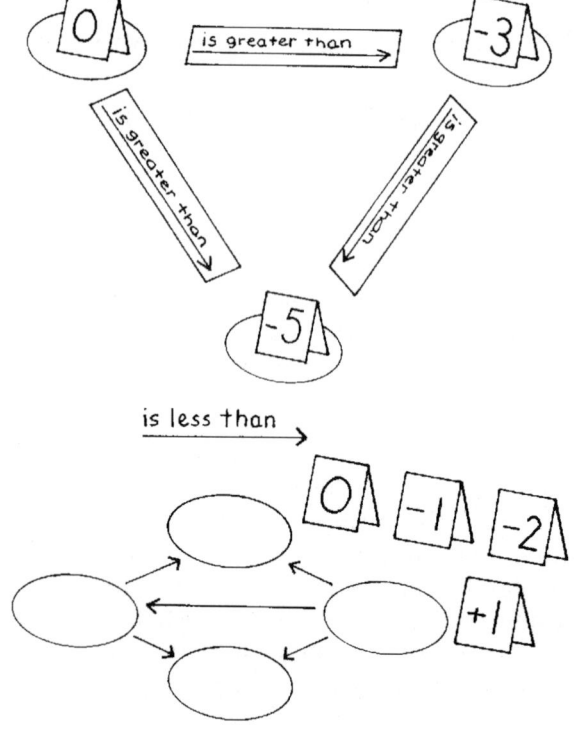

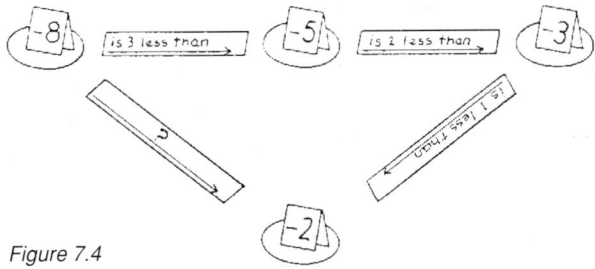

Figure 7.4

numbers on them. Lay out a simple logic chain and invite the children to place the number cards in the correct place. Discuss with the children the relationship between the first number and the last number in the chain. Can they spot a pattern? Copymasters 7.3 and 7.4 can be used for further practice.

7. Have the children repeatedly add ⁻1s into the cleared memory of a calculator, i.e. [1] [−] [M+]. Ask them to count out loud as they do this, then press [MR] to see if the calculator now displays the number they have reached in their counting. Have the children repeat the activity by pressing [1] [M−] a number of times. Again [MR] can be pressed to verify their counting.

Key page points

Pages 32 and 33 Thermometer charts are supplied on Copymaster 7.5 to help the children record the temperatures in question 3. Teachers have the option of encouraging children to write 'comparison' number sentences to go with the thermometer models; e.g. for Minneapolis: ⁺24 − ⁻24 = 48. You will need to provide the children with a press cutting of world temperatures in order for them to complete question 6. The information in figure 7.5 could be used if necessary. Have the children find the day's maximum and minimum temperatures for the UK from a newspaper.

Page 34 Make sure the children understand that the numbers in the set (1, 2, 3, 4, 5, ...) are called counting, or natural, numbers. When zero is included it becomes the set of whole numbers, and when the negative numbers are included it is the set of integers. These names will be investigated later in the series. However, the experiences on the page highlight the development which will be formalised later.

Further activities.

1. Play Temperature Touch and Say (Activity Card 7.1).

2. Let the children try the Crazy Holiday Game on Copymaster 7.6. This game may be used to illustrate movements in a positive or negative direction. Zero is the starting point, and the children should play in pairs. A dice marked ⁻3, ⁻/+2, ⁻1, ⁺1, ⁺/−2, ⁺3 is rolled and a counter moved in a positive or a negative direction, according to the number shown on the dice. If, however, ⁺/−2 is thrown, then the player may choose either ⁺2 or ⁻2. The winner is the one who reaches either of his/her posts first. Have the children keep a tally of the number of turns taken for each game and test Hannah's prediction.

3. A code which uses positive and negative coordinates to denote letters of the alphabet may be used in competitive games. Remind the children of the horizontal and vertical axes on the lattices in Section 6, and point out the position of negative numbers on the axes. You may need to start with some oral practice, giving the number pairs for selected letters. Draw axes on the chalkboard with letters placed at various points. The coordinates may be introduced as a guessing game. Write a word, or a name, on the board and say that you will write it in code. Write the coordinates on the board for the first letter and ask if anyone can see how the code is 'broken' or 'solved'. Tell the children that you do not want them to explain the code, that you will know if they have broken it if they can give the coordinates for the next letter. Repeat for each letter at a time until you can see that the rule is generally understood. The code on Copymaster 7.7 may be given to the children for them to solve. They might like to make up their own messages for their friends to decode.

4. Play a code game similar to 3 above in which players have to make up, say, a six-letter word and state the code coordinates. The first to do so wins. Repeat with other words of different lengths.

World Weather Today

t=thunder; d=drizzle; fg=fog; s=sun; sl=sleet; sn=snow; f=fair; c=cloud; r=rain

	°C			°C			°C	
Ajaccio	19	f	Gibraltar	22	f	Paris	18	s
Akrotiri	25	s	Helsinki	11	f	Peking	28	c
Alexandria	32	s	Hong Kong	30	s	Perth	18	s
Algiers	21	c	Innsbruck	22	s	Prague	15	s
Amsterdam	14	s	Istanbul	21	s	Reykjavik	14	s
Athens	22	s	Jeddah	33	s	Rhodes	23	s
Bahrain	32	s	Johannesburg	17	f	Rio de Janeiro	25	s
Bangkok	29	f	Karachi	30	s	Rome	21	f
Barbados	30	f	Las Palmas	20	c	Salzburg	19	s
Barcelona	20	s	Lerwick	7	c	San Francisco	18	s
Belgrade	25	f	Lisbon	20	c	Santiago	11	c
Berlin	15	f	Locarno	21	c	Seoul	27	c
Bermuda	26	c	London	12	f	Singapore	31	f
Biarritz	17	c	Los Angeles	18	s	Stockholm	10	c
Bordeaux	21	c	Madrid	22	f	Strasbourg	21	s
Brussels	15	s	Majorca	19	c	Sydney	22	f
Budapest	22	s	Malaga	21	f	Tangier	21	c
Cairo	35	s	Malta	19	r	Tel Aviv	22	s
CapeTown	21	s	Melbourne	13	r	Tenerife	21	s
Chicago	27	s	Mexico City	27	s	Tokyo	22	r
Christchurch	9	s	Miami	34	f	Toronto	24	f
Cologne	17	f	Milan	23	s	Tunis	18	c
Copenhagen	14	s	Montreal	24	s	Valencia	22	f
Corfu	24	s	Moscow	16	c	Vancouver	12	c
Dublin	12	c	Munich	19	s	Venice	21	c
Dubrovnik	21	s	Nairobi	22	c	Vienna	18	s
Faro	21	f	Naples	25	s	Warsaw	13	f
Florence	24	s	New Delhi	36	s	Washington	28	f
Frankfurt	18	s	New York	28	s	Wellington	10	f
Funchal	19	f	Nice	21	s	Zurich	21	s
Geneva	23	s	Oslo	13	f			

Figure 7.5

New Curriculum Mathematics for Schools Key Stage 2

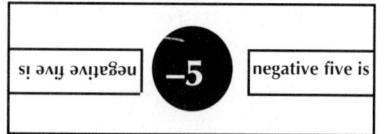
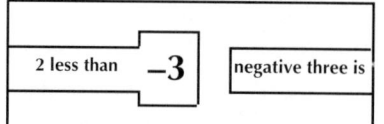
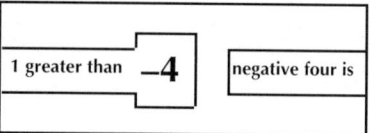

Figure 7.6

5. Play Negative Number Dominoes (Activity Cards 7.2–7.3). Select any Domino starter card and place it on the table. Share out the other dominoes so the children playing have five each. The remaining dominoes should be placed face down in a pile on the table. The players take it in turns to place a domino which will complete the sentence (figure 7.6). If the player cannot go, then he/she takes another domino from the pile left on the table, if there are any left. The winner is the first to play all his/her cards. Both ends of the starter domino may be used.

6. Make and play the Integer Memory Game. Prepare a pack of 44 cards showing four of each of the numbers within the range ⁻5 to ⁺5, i.e. four of ⁻5, four of ⁻4, four of ⁻3, etc. Prepare also four game mats (one for each player) with 11 spaces for the cards (figure 7.7). The aim of the game is to collect the 11 cards which complete the sequence from ⁻5 to ⁺5.

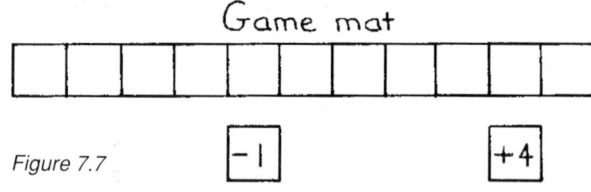

Figure 7.7

The cards should be shuffled well and spread out face down on the table. Players take it in turns to turn over a card and try to place it on their mat in the correct position within the sequence. When the first card is taken, players must take care to place it in the correct position. Subsequent cards can only be selected if they are immediately next to a card already displayed. Thus, if the first card a player selects is ⁻1, then the next card must be either ⁻2 or 0. If a player is not able to place the exposed card on his/her mat, then the card is turned face down again and play moves to the next player. In memory games of this type, you may decide to allow a successful selection to be followed by another turn. This should be made clear at the start of the game.

7. Make and play Integer Sequence Bingo, a game for four players. Prepare four game mats as shown in figure 7.8 and 21 cards individually marked with the numbers from ⁻10 to ⁺10. Spread the cards face down on the table. The players take it in turns to turn over a card to see if it will fit in a place on their mat, following the logic of the < > signs, e.g. 4 > 3, ⁻4 < ⁻3, etc. If it does, the card is placed in position. If not, then the card is turned face down on the table again and play moves to the next player. The winner is the first player to complete his/her mat. Repeat the game, allowing the children to exchange the mats and play with different conditions.

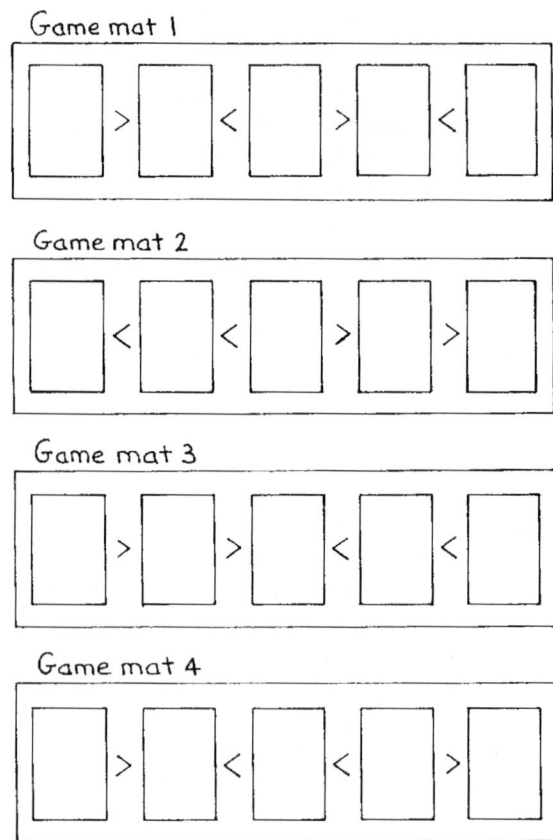

Figure 7.8

8. Play Watch Your Step! (Activity Cards 7.4 and 7.5). Activity Card 7.4 should be cut and folded to form the puzzle maker's board. The puzzle solver's board, the score strip and the colour cards should be cut out from Activity Card 7.5. A small counter will be required for use on the score strip. Two players take it in turns to be the puzzle maker and the puzzle solver. The puzzle maker takes one yellow, two red, three blue and four green tiles and places them on the puzzle maker's board so that the other player cannot see them. The tiles must be placed according to these rules.

(a) All the tiles must be used.
(b) The red, blue and green tiles must be grouped together by colour so that the sides touch (figure 7.9).

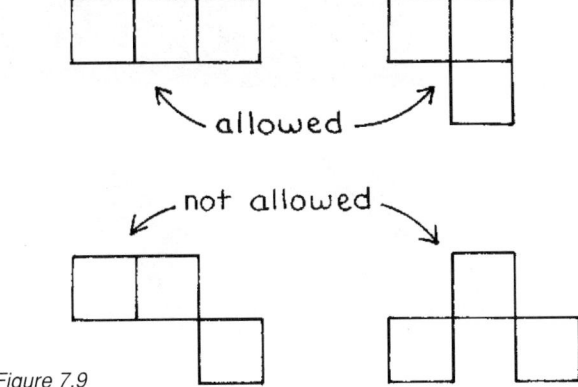

Figure 7.9

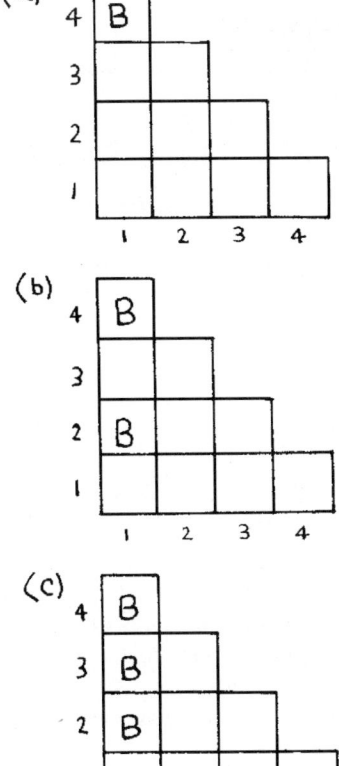

Figure 7.10

The puzzle solver's task is to match the puzzle maker's board. In trying to do so, he/she may do one of the following.

(a) Ask what colour tile belongs on a given square. Such a move will cost the player one point.
(b) Guess the colour of a square. If the guess is correct, the player earns two points. However, if the guess is incorrect the player loses two points.

The scores are recorded by the puzzle maker on the score strip by moving the counter left (negative) one or two places for a request or wrong guess, and two places to the right (positive) for a correct guess. A sample play could proceed as follows.
Puzzle Solver: 'May I please know the colour of the tile on square (1, 4)?'
Puzzle Maker: 'That tile is blue.'
The puzzle solver places a blue tile on square (1, 4) on his/her board, as shown in figure 7.10a, and the puzzle maker moves the counter to $^-1$ on the score strip. The puzzle solver could now say 'May I please know the colour of the tile on square (1, 2)?', to which the puzzle maker may say 'That tile is blue.' The puzzle solver will now cover (1, 2) with a blue tile (figure 7.10b) and the puzzle maker will move the counter to $^-2$ on the score strip. The puzzle solver should now say 'I think that (1, 3) is blue because there are three blue tiles and they must all touch.' If the logic is right, the puzzle maker should agree. The puzzle solver will now place a blue tile at (1, 3) as shown in figure 7.10c, and the puzzle maker should move the counter two places to the right to 0 on the score strip. The puzzle solver may now say 'I think that the square at (1, 1) is yellow', and the puzzle maker may reply 'No, you are incorrect' as he/she moves the counter to $^-2$ on the score strip. It is hoped that the puzzle solver will now remember that (1, 1) is not yellow. Play continues in this way until the puzzle solver has reproduced the puzzle maker's board. The solver makes a note of his/her score. They should now change their roles and at the end of the game the two players should compare their scores. The player with the higher score wins. Have the children play a number of rounds.

9. Encourage the children to explore an extension of the patterns suggested in Pre-page activity 4, now attempting sentences such as $10 - {}^-1 = \square$ after following a pattern the 'other way', e.g.
$10 - 5 = \square$, $10 - 4 = \square$, $10 - 3 = \square$,
$10 - 2 = \square$, $10 - 1 = \square$, $10 - 0 = \square$,
$10 - {}^-1 = \square$, ...

Check-ups

1. Can the children explain that $^-4$ °C, say, indicates a position which is four degrees below zero?

2. Do the children understand that $^-3$ is greater than $^-4$?

3. Can the children work out that $^-3$ is 2 greater than $^-5$?

4. Can the children relate negative numbers to meanings in more than one physical situation?

5. Do the children understand that directions such as up/down and left/right can be referred to in terms of 'negative' and 'positive'?

New Curriculum Mathematics for Schools Key Stage 2

Section 8

AT 1 3b, 3c, 3d. AT 4 2a, 3a

Pages 35–37 Shape, Space and Position

Page 35 The Solid Shape Quiz
Page 36 Boxes
Page 37 Quick Fit

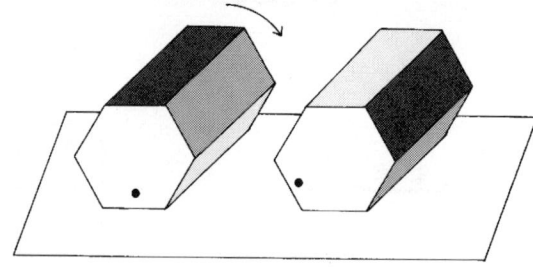

Figure 8.1

Purpose

To encourage the children to discover similarities between solid shapes based on properties introduced in Section 6, e.g. parallel edges, edges at right angles to each other, identical (congruent) shapes, number of faces, edges or vertices.
To enable children to recognise common plane shapes as faces of three-dimensional shapes.
To introduce the rotational symmetry of some plane shapes.
To introduce children to the properties of some common plane shapes.

Recommended material

1. Models of simple solid shapes in different sizes: cubes; cuboids; square, triangular, pentagonal and hexagonal prisms; square and triangular pyramids; cones and cylinders. Logibeads (NES/Arnold SY411/4) and Logishapes (NES/Arnold SY486/2) will be useful in this context.

2. Everyday containers and packets, such as Easter egg boxes, chocolate boxes, cosmetic packages, etc., in a variety of shapes and sizes.

3. Collections of sorting objects, e.g. buttons, shells, old keys, lids, hairclips, etc.

4. Blank cards to make sorting labels.

5. Wool or string loops, for set rings.

6. **Copymasters 8.1–8.3**.

7. Pictures of regular and irregular plane shapes drawn on (post)cards.

8. Tracing paper.

9. Squared paper.

10. Solid shape construction materials.

Pre-page activities

1. Recall characteristics previously encountered in the sorting of shapes. These have included:

    (a) what solid shapes can, or cannot, do, e.g. roll, slide, rock, stack, appear the same when turned over, appear the same after a number of rotations (figure 8.1);

    (b) recognition of shape types, e.g. cubes, square prisms, cuboids and other prisms with various end faces; pyramids; cones and spheres;

    (c) what can, or cannot, be observed in the shape, e.g. identical end faces and cross-sections, and plane faces such as squares, rectangles, triangles, pentagons and hexagons.

2. Have the children investigate ways in which three-dimensional shapes are alike. Compare the shapes of some or all of the faces, the forms of the angles found on the faces and around the vertices of the shape, the number of edges, and faces, positioned around each vertex. Find packages of commercial products which are

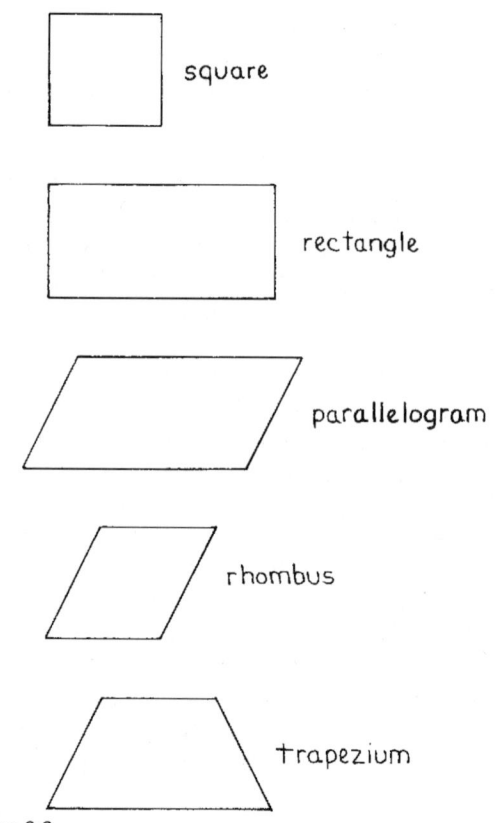

Figure 8.2

made in simple shapes. The children can cut out the faces and sort them to find identical shapes, or shapes of a similar type. The cut-out shapes may be set out as a wall display showing the solid and its faces. It would be difficult to predict all the shapes the children are likely to find in their collections but figure 8.2 shows a range. Children will see that many of these shapes have similar properties, e.g. all sides equal, all angles equal, opposite angles equal, opposite sides parallel, etc. (See also Further activity 7.)

3. Provide the children with a collection of similar objects, not necessarily geometric shapes, e.g., buttons, shells, old keys, etc. Have them select one attribute to sort a handful of objects from the given collection. Get them to write out label cards to describe their work. For example, using a selection of buttons and sorting for colour, they may make a series of cards as shown in figure 8.3a. The written labels should then be placed to one side in a pile. (In this and other logic activities, use language appropriate to the children and the mathematics.) The objects are mixed up and sorted again on a different attribute, e.g. shape of button (figure 8.3b), number of holes, etc. The children should be encouraged to be as flexible in their thinking as possible, generating as many different ways to sort the given collection as possible, but always on a single attribute. Keep the accumulated label cards with the given collection of objects as they can then be used in activities 4, 6 and 8 below.

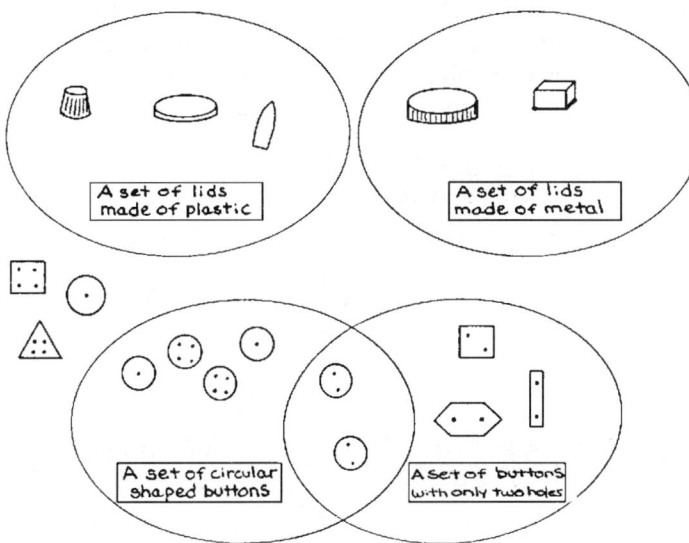

Figure 8.4

4. Have the children shuffle the attribute labels made in activity 3 above and pick out two labels at random. Ask them to sort a handful of objects from a given collection according to the labels (figure 8.4). Have them use the set rings and labels to discuss their work. Get the children to repeat the above activity with two different labels from this or a different collection. Challenge the children to select three attribute labels at random from the pile and sort a handful of objects from the collection accordingly (figure 8.5).

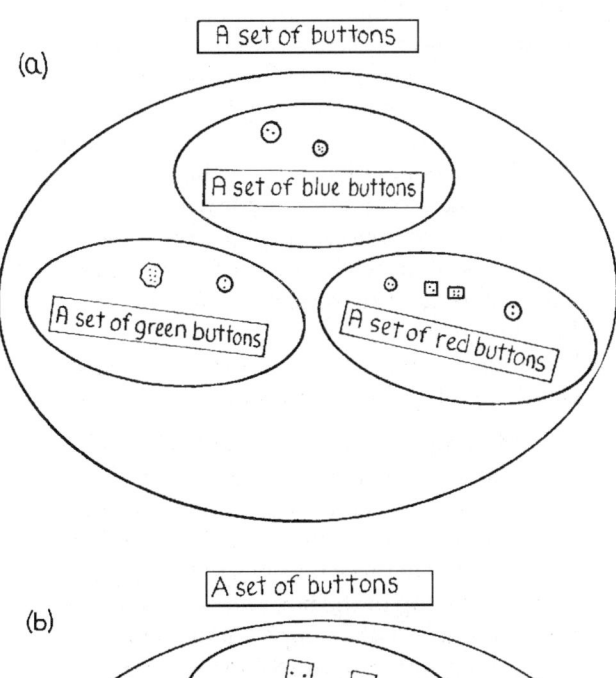

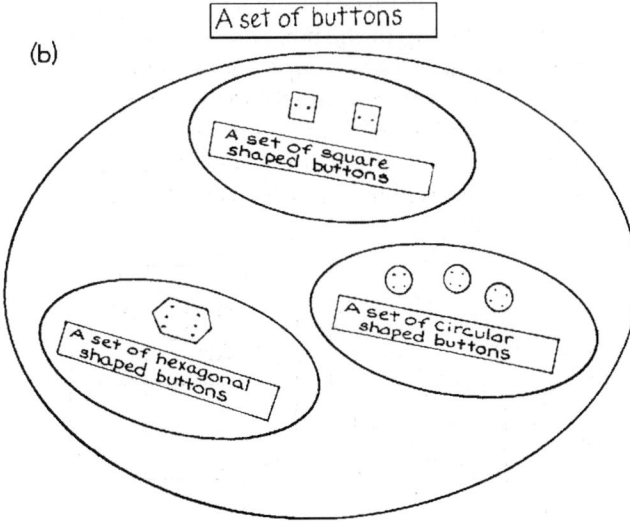

Figure 8.3

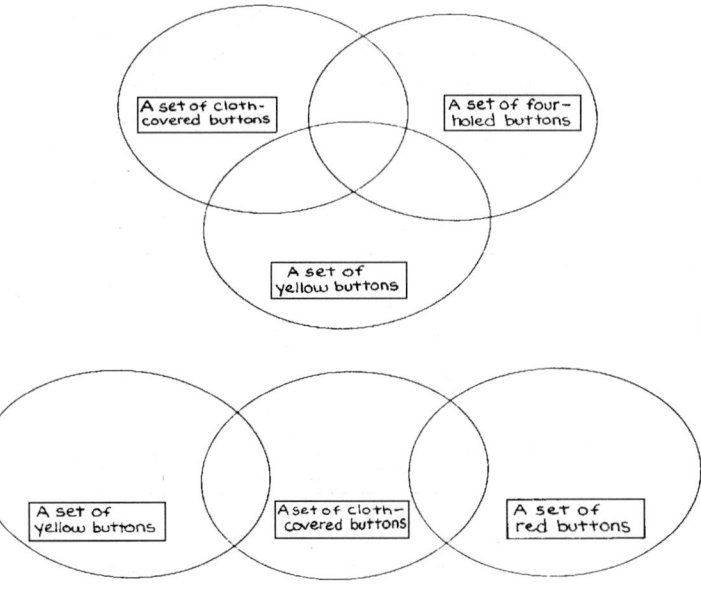

Figure 8.5

5. Make a set of label cards for a set of shapes (Logibeads and Logishapes), placing one of the following attributes on each card: 'a set of large solid shapes', 'a set of small solid shapes', 'a set of red solid shapes', etc. Include yellow, blue, green, cube, cuboid, triangular, prism, pyramid, cone, circular base, triangular base, square base, rectangular base, hexagonal base, etc., in the set descriptions. Shuffle these cards and have children draw two or three cards from the pile at random. Have them use the label cards to sort the shapes appropriately, using set rings to display the final groups (figure 8.6).

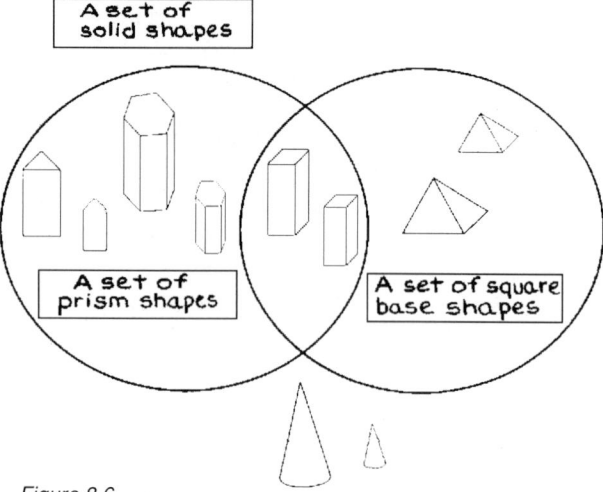

Figure 8.6

6. Select two attribute labels made in activity 3 above, without showing them to the children. Arrange the set rings appropriately and turn the labels face down within the set rings (figure 8.7). Challenge the children to correctly identify the attributes hidden on the labels. Have them take it in turns to place one object from the collection in a section of the sorting space. Tell each child whether or not an object belongs where it was placed. An object is removed if it does not belong in the given sorting space. Children should be encouraged to discuss what they learn from each attempt to place an object on the sorting space and a written record could be kept. Later the children can take it in turns at being the 'teacher', playing the role of the person who responds to objects that are placed in the sorting space. As the children become proficient at sorting two attributes, the activity should be repeated with three sorting labels (and three set rings).

7. Repeat activity 6 above using a set of solid geometric shapes and corresponding labels made in activity 5 above.

8. From a collection of objects select one, e.g. a specific lid from a collection of varied lids, and write a selection of 'clue cards' for the mystery object, e.g.
   (a) is circular on top,
   (b) twists on and off,
   (c) is clean on the inside,
   (d) has ridges around the outside surface,
   (e) is one colour,
   (f) has writing on it.

   Read one clue at a time slowly, allowing children to sort possible lids from those that can be eliminated. Repeat with other clue cards, the last clue should then clearly identify the 'mystery' object. Discuss with the children which clues were most helpful and which were least helpful. Get them to say how the clues could be rewritten to use fewer clues to identify the same mystery object. Have the children work in pairs to identify their own mystery object from the collection, then write a set of clue cards, all of which are needed by other children to identify the specific object. Encourage them to work together to 'streamline' the clues, i.e. write fewer clues to clearly identify the specific object.

9. Collect some everyday containers which have lids or liners which fit inside them, e.g. chocolate boxes. Have the children record how many different ways the lid can be placed on the 'box'. Relate these findings to the actual shape of the top of the box and see why there are differences. For example, in the two octagonal boxes in figure 8.8 the regular 'Turkish Delight' box lid will fit in eight different ways, but the irregular octagonal 'Cookies' tin will only fit two ways. Discuss

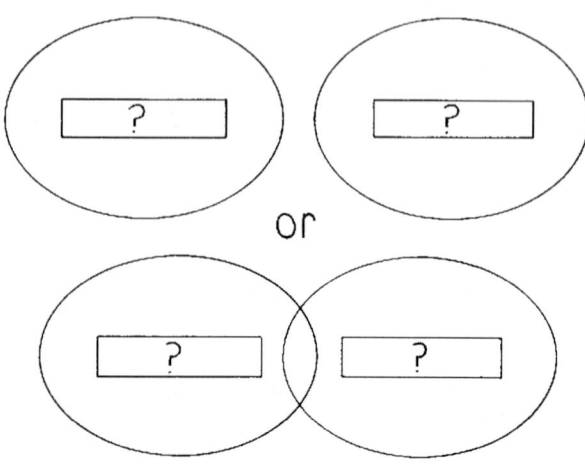

Figure 8.7

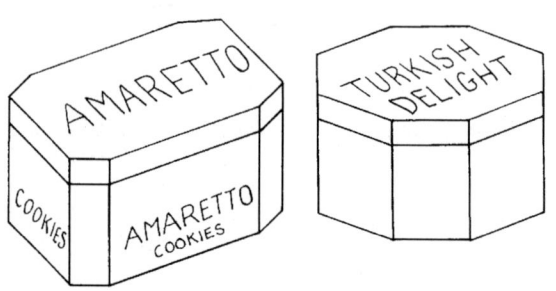

Figure 8.8

with the children the reasons why they feel this is so, after all both are octagonal prisms. Encourage the children to see which sides and angles match each other. Repeat with other packages. You may be able to find some biscuit tins which appear to be square shaped but on trying to fit the lid on one discovers that it will only fit two ways, when if the tin had been square it would have fitted four ways! Some shapes are more obvious than others. Have the children look out for, and bring to school, unusual types of containers such as (empty!) Easter egg boxes. Consider also how many ways a cylindrical jar lid can be fitted.

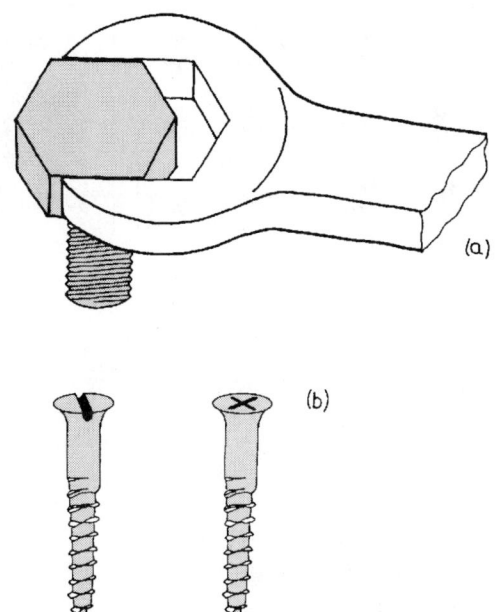

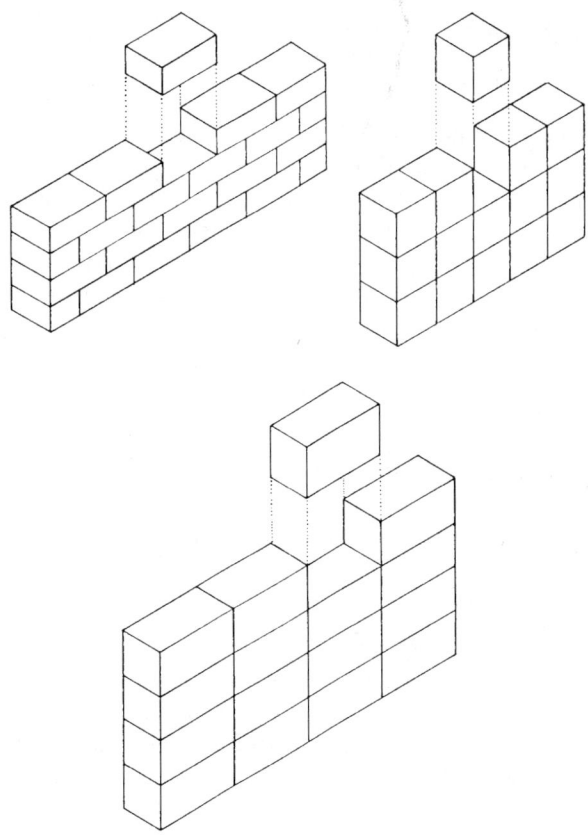

Figure 8.9

Figure 8.10

10. Discuss with the children the design of various containers and have them say why they feel many kitchen containers are circular and the lids are 'easy on, easy off' types. Let the children see how the design of some objects involves symmetry to help their function. For example, a teapot may have a circular lid which, although aesthetically pleasing, could easily fall off. However, a lip may well change the symmetry which means the lid will only fit one way and by turning will become secure. Have the children consider the design of a spanner and see how the hexagonal shape provides a number of 'easy on' positions, at the same time supplying enough 'grip' (figure 8.9a). The two types of popular screwdrivers in everyday use also have rotational symmetry built into their design as they easily fit their respective screws (figure 8.9b). Have the children consider the design of some inefficient objects such as a spanner that will only fit a nut one way or a saucepan with a lid that only fits one way!

11. Have the children make model walls with cubes, cuboids and square prisms (figure 8.10).

How many ways can each each brick be placed in a space in the wall?

12. Encourage the children to recall other situations where rotational symmetry can be seen in the environment (clue: fitting panes of glass in windows). Have them illustrate their findings in some way.

Key page points

Page 35 You may wish to let some of the children use solid shapes when doing this page. Allow the children to work in pairs to make up their own questions. When they have created, say, ten question cards, including the answers, have the pairs challenge each other. In this way a 'Class Shape Quiz' can be held, either on a league or knock-out basis. Offer two points for a correct answer and a penalty of three points if the question setter makes an error. Copymaster 8.1 can be used with this page.

Page 36 Have the children define the faces of the containers in a variety of ways. Encourage them to use the term quadrilateral and to include the words square, parallelogram, rectangle, trapezium, etc., as appropriate. Discuss with the children which containers have edges that are parallel, perpendicular, and perhaps vertical when placed on a horizontal surface. If the children can find the relationship between the vertices, faces and edges of the shapes ($v + f = e + 2$) have them verify their findings by making or collecting other shapes within the classroom. Copymaster 8.1 can also be used with this page.

Page 37 Make sure the children have the necessary materials to make some shapes in question 2, e.g. Plasticine, card, glue, etc. Note that they have to make *two* shapes which just fit into each hole! You may care to provide the children with a hole template which matches the plans on the page so that they can test their models.

Further activities

1. Give the children some plane shape outlines which are 'footprints' of common solid shapes. Have the children record how many different ways they can fit the solid shape onto its 'footprint'.

2. Discuss Copymaster 8.2 with the children. Have them cut out the four shapes on the left, and colour the vertices/corners of all the shapes as indicated. Ensure that they colour the back of each vertex/corner using the same colour, and that they write 'front' and 'back' on the cut-out shapes. Have them fit the shapes on the outlines on the right of the sheet using rotation only at first. Rotation and reflecting/turning may be used for the second part of the activity. Copymaster 8.3 may be used for further practice.

3. Let the children make card shapes which can rotate to fit into their own outlines for display in the classroom. They should also make drawings of their outlines on paper. The card shape can be fitted onto its outline and both pinned to a board so that the card shape can be rotated over the outline. The pin has to be placed at the centre of symmetry. The models can form a display showing the number of times each shape fits onto its outline in a complete turn.

Figure 8.11

4. Organise a 'Draw a Plane Shape Freehand' competition. Have the children draw a number of different plane shapes freehand. Have them use tracing paper to trace their sketches and then judge each one for its expected symmetrical properties. (*Note*: try testing the two 'squares' in figure 8.11.) Experiment with a variety of regular and non-regular shapes.

5. Have the children examine the rotational symmetry of a traditional pack of playing cards (figure 8.12). How could they make, for example, the six of spades or the eight of clubs more symmetrical?

Figure 8.12

6. Have the children use tracing paper to examine the rotational symmetry of crossword puzzle outlines (figure 8.13). Give the children a 10 × 10 matrix of squared paper and have them create a variety of symmetrical designs.

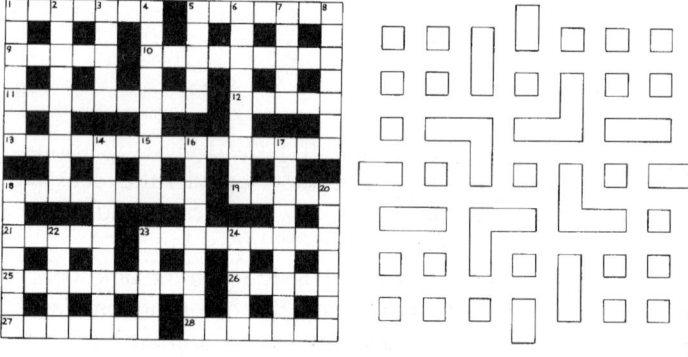

Figure 8.13

7. Repeat some of the Pre-page activities (e.g. 5–8), this time using plane shapes. Give the children a series of (post)cards with a plane shape drawn on each. Have the children sort the shapes for one attribute and then make a label for their sorting. Have them repeat the activity, making a series of labels as they do so. Encourage the children to describe their shapes using features involving the sides and angles, e.g. opposite sides parallel (figure 8.14), and then opposite sides parallel and opposite angles which are right angles (figure 8.15). Have the children make statements about their Venn diagrams, e.g. from figure 8.15 'all rectangles are parallelograms' but 'all parallelograms are not rectangles'. Encourage the children to make

Section 8

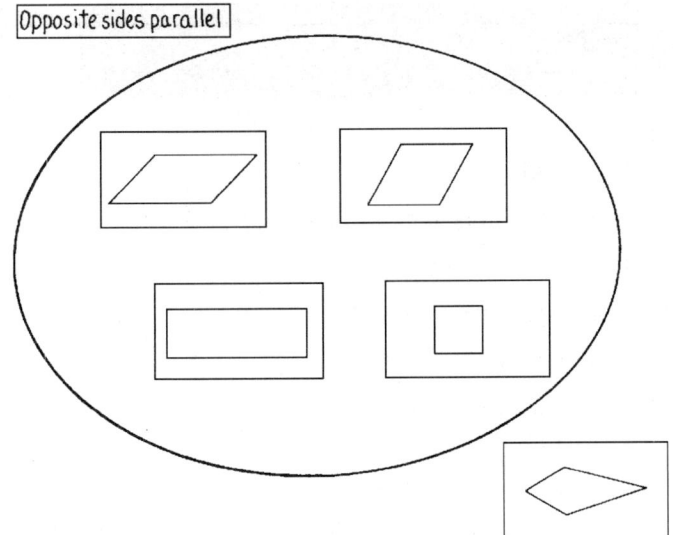

Figure 8.14

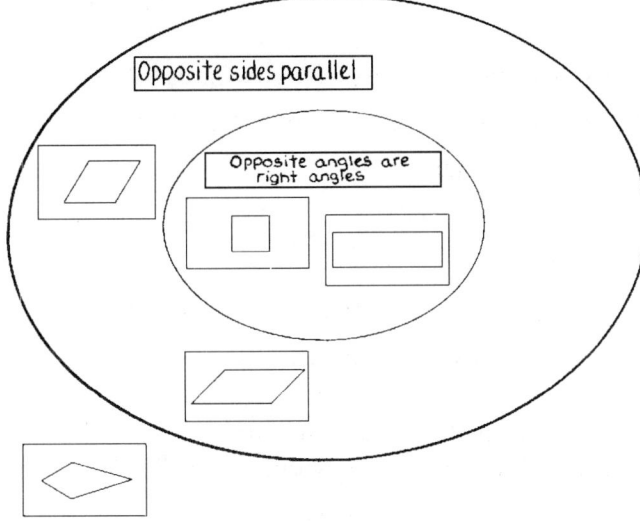

Figure 8.15

replaced in one way only? Yours faithfully, …' Have the children make a box to satisfy the letter writer.

10. The potter's wheel is a symmetry model. If possible allow the children to experience throwing a pot!

11. Let the children make their own spinning disc as shown in figure 8.16. By colouring part of the disc and then 'winding up' the string, the disc should rotate producing a continuous pattern.

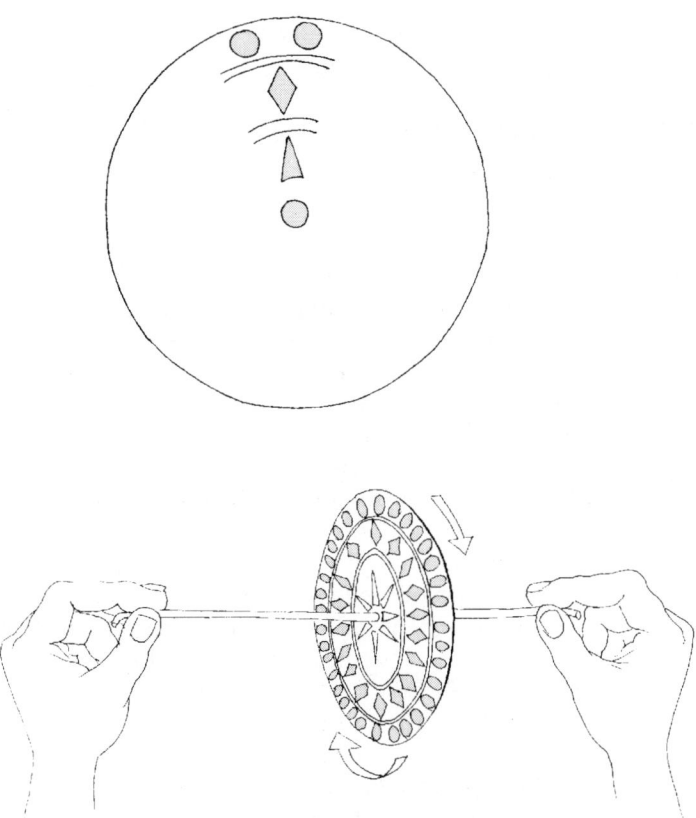

Figure 8.16

Check-ups

1. Can the children:
   (a) name the faces of common three-dimensional shapes?
   (b) identify faces, edges and vertices (or corners) of shapes?
   (c) identify parallel edges of shapes?
   (d) identify right angles at corners of shapes?

2. Can the children identify the symmetrical properties of everyday shapes?

3. Do the children know that a square is a rectangle, but that a rectangle is not necessarily a square?

4. Do the children realise that the set of cuboids contains a subset of square prisms and a subset of cubes?

other statements through Venn diagram displays, e.g. sorting for opposite angles which are right angles and all sides equal in length will show that 'squares are rectangles'. Keep the accumulated cards as they can be used for a plane shape version of Pre-page activity 6.

8. Sort some solid shapes in a similar manner to the plane shapes in activity 7. Create a Venn diagram which sorts 'shapes where all faces are rectangles', 'shapes where two faces are square' and 'shapes where four faces are square'. Have the children sort for other properties and make statements about their findings.

9. The following letter appeared in *The Times* newspaper: 'Sir, Prompted by yet again opening a box of matches upside down with the usual results, I wonder if the time has come for manufacturers to provide us with a box clearly marked "top" and the drawer asymmetrically designed so that it can be

New Curriculum Mathematics for Schools Key Stage 2

Section 9

AT 1 3a, 3b, 3c, 3d. AT 2 3b, 3c. AT 3 2b, 3a.

Pages 38–46 Multiplication

Pages 38 and **39** Party Time
Page 40 Situations
Page 41 Have a Go
Page 42 At the Baker's
Page 43 At the Toy shop
Page 44 Tiles
Page 45 Grow it Yourself
Page 46 Bingo

Purpose

To introduce the children to the concept of Cartesian products, i.e. to understand how, in practical terms, we can pair each member of one set with each member of another set in a given order, so as to obtain a set containing all the possible 'ordered pairs'.
To have the children review their understanding of the multiplication process and the terms factor, product and multiple.
To have the children revise the multiplication facts they have experienced with the 5×5 multiplication matrix, and also in the 2, 5 and 10 multiplication tables.
To enable children to apply their knowledge of multiplication to create the full range of multiplication 'tables', i.e. from 0×0 to 10×10.
To enable children to recognise multiplication situations as they arise in context.
To give the children further exposure to the commutative and distributive properties of multiplication.
To give the children further practice in finding products using a calculator.
To help children to see patterns in the multiplication process.
To encourage the children to commit the full range of multiplication 'tables' to memory and to recall them whenever needed.

Recommended material

1. The school lunch menu and other simple menus.
2. A selection of clothing such as hats and scarves, shirts and shorts.
3. Rulers marked in centimetre units, and rods of lengths 1 to 10 centimetres.
4. Squared paper.
5. Interlocking cubes.
6. Beads, counters, etc., and bags to put them in.
7. Pegboards and pegs.
8. **Copymasters 5.1 and 9.1–9.13**.
9. Calculators.
10. Multiplication Touch and Say cards (**Activity Card 9.1**)
11. Balance scales and 10 gram masses.
12. Sand and bags to put it in.
13. Coins and goods for sale in a class shop.
14. Cards for games (see Further activities 6, 10, 13, 19 and 26).
15. Party Time Flowcharts (**Activity Cards 9.2–9.3**).
16. 'Tell Me a Story' cards (**Activity Card 9.4**).
17. A tape recorder.
18. Spinners and overlays.
19. Cubes for making dice.
20. Go for Goal game (**Activity Cards 9.5–9.8**).
21. Safari Park game board (**Activity Cards 9.9–9.10**).
22. Two ten-sided dice marked 1–10 (e.g. Taskmaster Polyhedron Number Dice: T685).
23. World Series Golf game (supplied by Taskmaster).
24. Jump Off game (supplied by NES/EJ Arnold, ref: SY416/9).
25. Multiplication Dominoes (**Activity Cards 9.11–9.14**).
26. Factor Dominoes (**Activity Card 9.15**).
27. Cross the Board (**Activity Cards 9.16–9.21**).
28. A selection of solid shapes and string or plastic hoops for making set rings.

Pre-page activities

Note Throughout this section the terms 'product', 'multiple' and 'factor' should be used when appropriate. It is recommended that in activities 1 to 3 the selections you ask the children to make fall within the product range considered in Pupils' Book 1, i.e. within the 5×5 matrix and the 2, 5 and 10 multiplication tables.

1. Discuss the school lunch menu with the children and let them make some choices. Ask them to find out how many different meals they

could have from the courses on the menu. You may need to simplify the menu if there are too many choices, for example you could include only the main dishes, all with standard vegetables, and a dessert. When the children have made some random choices get them to put their selections in some order (figure 9.1).

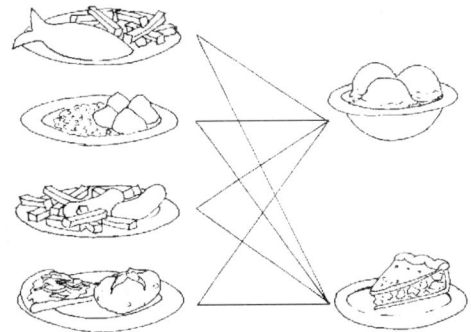

Figure 9.1

The choices can also be displayed in tabular form:

	Ice-cream	Apple pie
Fish and chips Mince and potatoes Sausage and chips Pizza and jacket potato		

Discuss with the children how many meals have ice-cream as the dessert, and how many have apple pie. Ask them how many different fish and chips meals there are, etc. Have the children see these choices in terms of 'sets of' (figure 9.2). Discuss with them how the introduction of another dessert would affect the choices, for now there would be another four choices available. If instead of an extra dessert another main course was introduced, two further choices would be available, one with ice-cream and one with apple pie.

2. Have the children make up a menu for their own café. Encourage them to make a poster to say how many different meals the menu can supply, e.g. '12 different delicious menus'. Make other menus, varying the number of choices. Some restaurants now prepare their bills to include all the items on offer. Have the children make some bills for the meals available at their restaurant.

3. Put three different hats and four different scarves on a table. Ask the children to find out the number of different 'outfits' that can be worn. Have them illustrate their findings (figure 9.3). Again consider how the choices would change if another item was introduced.

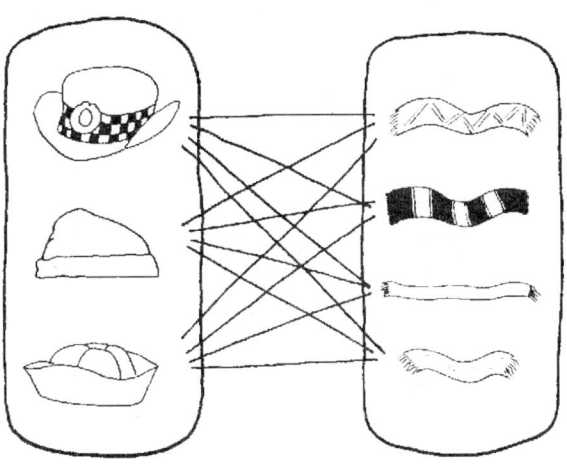

Figure 9.3

4. There are times when postponements and replays delay the normal course of sporting events. In a knock-out cup competition the following fixture backlog may occur.

    Norwich   Nottingham Forest
or Manchester United   v   or Newcastle
                                   or Southampton

Have the children work out how many different possible variations there can be.

5. Review multiplication sentences such as $4 \times 5 = \square$ which were considered in Key Stage 2, Book 1. Encourage the children to read these sentences and understand their meaning, seeing them individually, not just as part of a 'table'. They should be able to model the sentences, and make up situations to illustrate them.

I have sorted the meals by dessert

Set of meals with ice-cream

Fish and chips	Ice-cream
Mince and potatoes	Ice-cream
Sausage and chips	Ice-cream
Pizza and jacket potato	Ice-cream

Set of meals with apple pie

Fish and chips	Apple pie
Mince and potatoes	Apple pie
Sausage and chips	Apple pie
Pizza and jacket potato	Apple pie

2 sets of 4 = 8
4 × 2 = 8

.... and by main course

Set of fish and chip meals

| Fish and chips | Ice-cream |
| Fish and chips | Apple pie |

Set of mince and potato meals

| Mince and potatoes | Ice-cream |
| Mince and potatoes | Apple pie |

Set of sausage and chip meals

| Sausage and chips | Ice-cream |
| Sausage and chips | Apple pie |

Set of pizza and jacket potato meals

| Pizza and jacket potato | Ice-cream |
| Pizza and jacket potato | Apple pie |

4 sets of 2 = 8
2 × 4 = 8

If there was another dessert, I could make another set of 4. If there was another main course, I could make another set of 2.

Figure 9.2

6. Let the children experiment with centimetre rods to find the total lengths formed when, say, four rods of 6 cm are compared with six rods of 4 cm, the rods in both cases being placed end to end along a ruler starting at zero (figure 9.4). Have the children challenge each other to find other pairs, completing the number sentences each time.

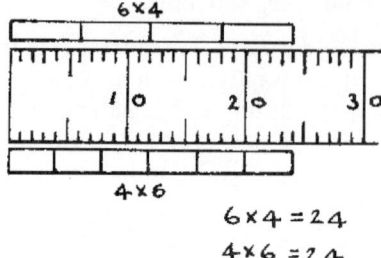

$6 \times 4 = 24$
$4 \times 6 = 24$

Figure 9.4

7. Provide the children with a number of squares cut from squared paper. Have them make larger rectangles with their cut-outs (figure 9.5).

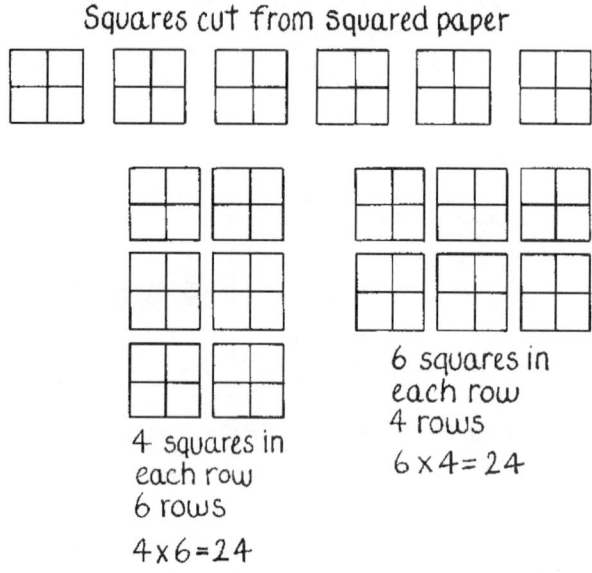

Figure 9.5

8. Have the children make a cuboid of 36 cubes made in four layers of nine cubes. Let them record their result, and then reassemble the 36 cubes to form a cuboid with nine layers of four cubes. The cuboids will not have the same shape (figure 9.6) so the equivalence has to be seen in the number of cubes used in each. Ask the children to make other pairs of 'different' cuboids, each with the same number of cubes.

9. Ask the children to make up three bags with one bead in each, then three bags with two beads in each, then three bags with three beads in each, and then continue the pattern. They should then use their experiences to complete the pattern:

$1 \times 3 =$
$2 \times 3 =$
$3 \times 3 =$
...
$10 \times 3 =$

Repeat the activity for six bags and then nine bags. Have the children complete the patterns:

$1 \times 6 =$ $1 \times 9 =$
$2 \times 6 =$ $2 \times 9 =$
$3 \times 6 =$ $3 \times 9 =$
...   ...
$10 \times 6 =$ $10 \times 9 =$

Note that these tables may also be written as:

$3 \times 1 = 3$
$3 \times 2 = 6$
$3 \times 3 = 9$
$3 \times 4 = 12$ etc.

In this case you may like to model the situations with three beads in one bag, three beads in two bags, etc.

10. Have the children make arrays on their peg boards. Ask them to complete number sentences for their arrays. Make sure they link the number of rows and the number in each row with the multiplication sentence.

11. Get the children to illustrate sentences such as $9 \times 1 = 9$, $9 \times 2 = 18$ and $9 \times 3 = 27$ on separate sheets of paper, and then display the sheets as a file in the mathematics display area (see figure 9.7).

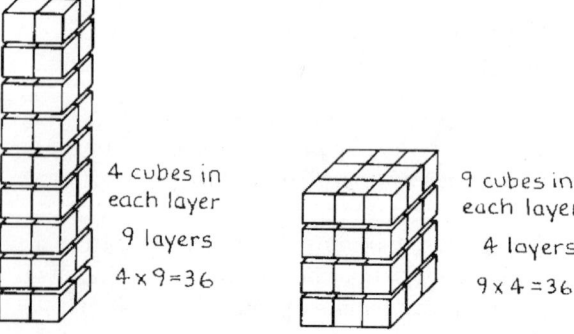

Figure 9.6

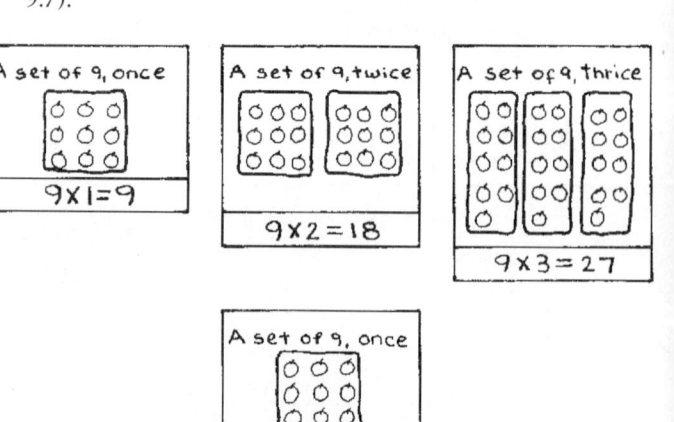

Figure 9.7

12. Use the children's knowledge of the meaning of multiplication to illustrate what number sentences including zero, such as $8 \times 0 = \square$ and $0 \times 8 = \square$, could mean. You may prefer to use the set notation in this activity, i.e. $8(0) = \square$ and $0(8) = \square$, but don't ignore the '×' symbol altogether.

13. Give the children a 10×10 multiplication matrix to complete.

```
× | 0 1 2 3 4 5 6 7 8 9 10
0 |
1 |
2 |
3 |
4 |
5 |
6 |
7 |
8 |
9 |
10|
```

Ask them to write about any patterns they see. Can they explain the symmetry of the numbers about the '\' diagonal? Which number(s) did they write most often, and which least often? Have them list the numbers in order of most to least 'written'. Get the children to complete another row and another column by studying the patterns. Ask them to model the new results as number sentences using unit material.

14. Let the children display on a 1–100 square (Copymaster 9.1 can be used) the multiples for the 2, 4 and 8 tables. Discuss the patterns with them, e.g. are all the multiples of 8 also multiples of 2, and are multiples of 2 also multiples of 8? Ask the children to find the next three numbers in each sequence beyond the 100 on the square. Have the children make a Venn diagram of their multiples (figure 9.8). Repeat for other multiples, e.g. the multiples for the 3, 6 and 9 tables. Notice the difference when multiples of 3, 5 and 7 are considered. Copymaster 9.2 provides more work on the classifying of various multiples.

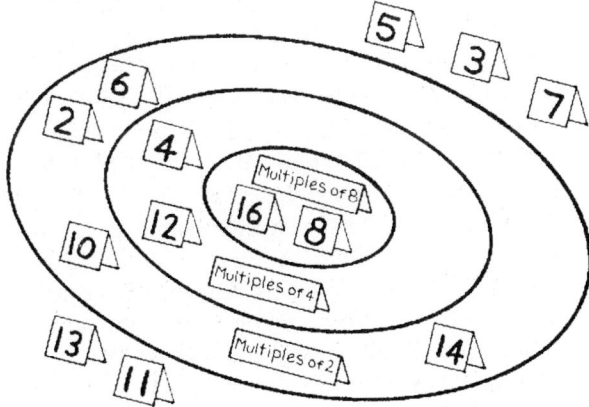

Figure 9.8

15. Write some multiplication sentences such as $8 \times 9 = \square$ and $9 \times 8 = \square$ on the chalkboard. Ask the children to write number stories for the sentences. Copymaster 9.3 can be used for further practice. Take a copy of the master and write in appropriate number sentences for the children to use (figure 9.9).

> Write a story where
> $\boxed{4} \times \boxed{5} = \square$
> is seen ... at home,
>   at school,
>   anywhere else in the world!

> Write a story where
> $\boxed{5} \times \boxed{5} = \square$
> is seen ... at home,
>   at school,

Figure 9.9

16. Give the children further practice in finding multiplication facts using a calculator. They should be encouraged to find, say, $6 \times 7 = 42$, and then use the constant function to get the same result by adding 6 seven times (figure 9.10). Get the children to record their sentences using both multiplication and repeated addition sentences.

Figure 9.10

17. Let the children cut rectangular pieces of squared paper, to make identical smaller pieces, then repeat the process until they cannot proceed any further (figure 9.11). Get them to make an exhibition of their findings. Stress that 1, 2, 3, 4, 6, 8, 12, 16, 24 and 48 are factors of 48. Let the children find the factors of other numbers. Have them make a display of the

factors they find for various numbers. Include some prime numbers such as 7, 11, 13, ..., whose only factors are themselves and 1.

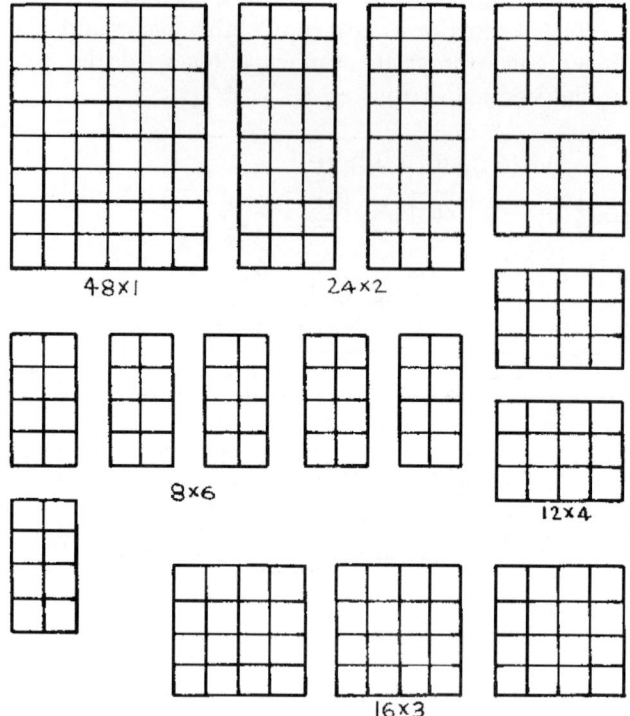

Figure 9.11

18. Give the children a rectangular sheet of paper showing, say, an array of 36 squares displayed as nine rows of four. Let the children cut the sheet into two with a single horizontal cut, e.g. to make (4 × 4) and (4 × 5). Get them to write a multiplication number sentence about the two pieces and link the number sentences. See if the children can recognise that
(4 × 4) + (4 × 5) = 4 × (4 + 5) = 4 × 9 = 36.
They should find as many other ways of cutting a similar array as they can. Repeat with other arrays.

19. From squared paper cut out two rectangles with the same lengths but different widths (figure 9.12). Make sure that the children can express the total number of squares in each rectangle as a multiplication number sentence. Ask them how the rectangles can be placed together to make one larger rectangle, then discuss the connection between the lengths and widths of the two original shapes and the newly constructed shape. Have them record the combination of the two multiplications:

(6 × 2) + (6 × 4) = (6 × 6)
12 + 24 = 36

Repeat using other suitable rectangles, including some squares, and others in which the two rectangles involved are identical.

20. Have the children place five rods, each of length 7 cm, end to end along a ruler to measure how far they reach. Get them to record the number sentence as 7 × 5 = 35. Let them repeat the operation with three rods of length 7 cm and record 7 × 3 = 21 (figure 9.13). Have them add the numbers representing the two total lengths, then record the multiplications and the additions together and discuss them as a distributive pattern:

7 × 5 = 35
7 × 3 = 21
7 × 8 = 56

Have them check their calculations by placing all of the rods end to end to find the total length practically. Repeat with other lengths of rod but ensure that the children appreciate that for the pattern to work in this activity, the rods in each of the two sets used must all be of the same length. Discuss the results to establish confidence. Have the children interpret number sentences such as 6 × 9 = ☐ in terms of two other sentences, e.g. as 6 × 6 = ☐ and 6 × 3 = ☐.

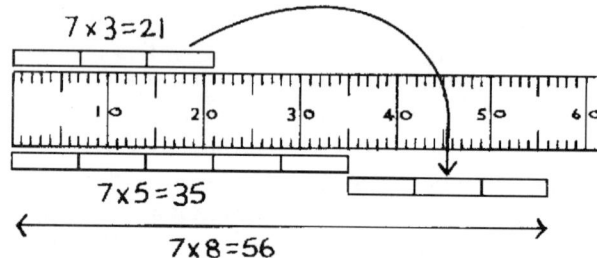

Figure 9.13

21. Give the children copies of Copymaster 9.4 and get them to cut out multiplication strips with the multiplier displayed at the beginning of each strip. Discuss the numbers on each strip to check that the children relate them to multiplication and multiples. Have the children place two of the strips one below the other, and add the corresponding numbers on the strips. Let them compare the results with other strips to see which strip matches (figure 9.14). Discuss the results to see if the children can express the relationship in words. Write their attempts on the chalkboard. Emphasise that the idea is to see if they can predict which strip will result when they are given two other strips to add. The blank strips at the foot of the sheet can be used by the children to make their own strips.

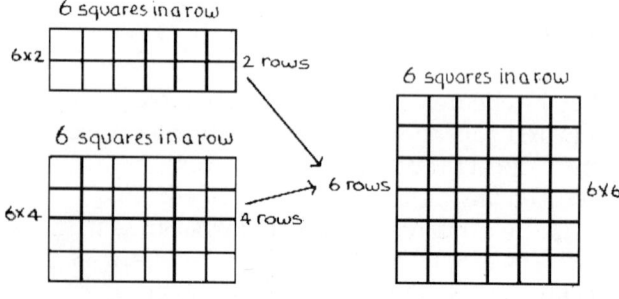

Figure 9.12

×5	5	10	15	20	25	30	35	40	45	50
×2	2	4	6	8	10	12	14	16	18	20
×7	7	14	21	28	35	42	49	56	63	70

Figure 9.14

Copymaster 9.5 can also be used for further practice.

22. Get the children to add two multiples from the set of multiples of 7, to notice that the sum is still a member of that set (figure 9.15). This activity may be linked with the distributive pattern, e.g. two sevens and three sevens together make five sevens. Let the children explore other pairs and display their findings. Repeat with other multiples.

23. Let the children use interlocking cubes to build towers one layer at a time (figure 9.16). Making each layer different in colour will help the children's observations. As each tower is built, ask the children how many cubes there are in each layer, how many layers there are and how many cubes there are in the total. Record the numbers under headings so the children can distinguish between the numbers representing the cubes in each layer from the numbers representing the layers.

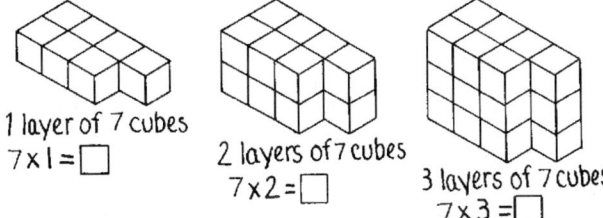

Figure 9.16

24. Have the children find the multiples for 3, 4, 6, 7, 8 and 9, building up the multiplication facts for those numbers (figure 9.17). Copies of Copymaster 9.6 can be cut up to provide support.

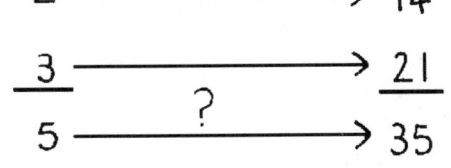

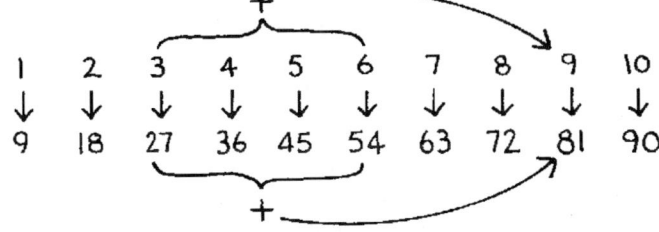

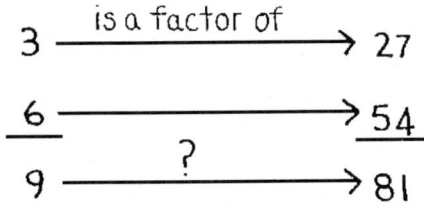

1	2	3	4	5	6	7
8	9	10	11	12	13	14
15	16	17	18	19	20	21
22	23	24	25	26	27	28
29	30	31	32	33	34	35
36	37	38	39	40	41	42
43	44	45	46	47	48	49
50	51	52	53	54	55	56
57	58	59	60	61	62	63
64	65	66	67	68	69	70

1	2	3	4	5	6	7	8
9	10	11	12	13	14	15	16
17	18	19	20	21	22	23	24
25	26	27	28	29	30	31	32
33	34	35	36	37	38	39	40
41	41	43	44	45	46	47	48
49	50	51	52	53	54	55	56
57	58	59	60	61	62	63	64
65	66	67	68	69	70	71	72
73	74	75	76	77	78	79	80

Figure 9.17

25. Play Multiplication Touch and Say (Activity Card 9.1), which covers key products within the 6, 7, 8 and 9 tables.

26. Have the children make a set of dominoes which use the full range of multiplication facts

Figure 9.15

studied to date. Have them express the products as Cartesian products (see figure 9.18). Encourage the children to take their game home to play with their parents.

(As A and B will be different, no repeats should occur.)

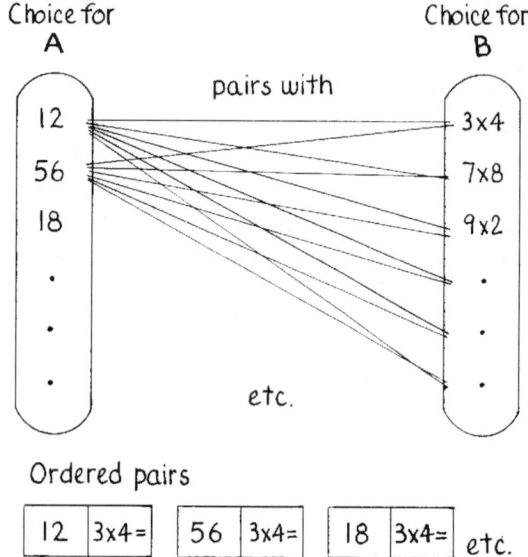

Figure 9.18

27. Give the children numbers and ask them to write them in other ways using multiplication facts (figure 9.19). Encourage the children to include other operations as well.

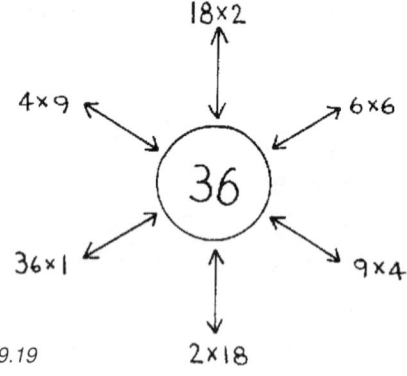

Figure 9.19

Key page points

Pages 38 and 39 Encourage the children to work systematically as they solve the problems on these pages. The situations can be used to create flowcharts (see Further activity 7).

Page 40 This page illustrates situations where Cartesian products are used in everyday life. Encourage the children to be aware of such situations when writing stories for multiplication number sentences.

Page 41 Make sure the children can follow what Sue and John are doing in the illustrations. Discuss with them the two different methods the children have used. Question 2 asks the children to solve some number sentences in different ways. Encourage the children to find more than one way for each number sentence. There are two sentences in this set which are outside the range of products considered so far. Let the children 'have a go' and not claim that they 'haven't done that yet'.

Pages 42 and 43 These pages encourage the children to make their own 'tables'. Have the children look for patterns within their sequences. Can they compare, say, the 4 table they make with the 8 table, and the 3 table with the 6 and 9 tables? Be sure to emphasise the commutative property as illustrated in questions 6 and 7 on page 43, i.e. $9 \times 5 = 5 \times 9$.

Page 44 This page emphasises the commutative property of multiplication in practical situations, as Hannah makes rectangular patterns with her tiles. Give the children more tiles so that they can extend Hannah's puzzle in question 2.

Page 45 Let the children use the strips made from Copymaster 9.4 to complete the activities on the page. Make sure they understand that $(5 \times 5 = 25) + (5 \times 4 = 20) = (5 \times 9 = 45)$.

Page 46 This page asks the children to make four bingo mats to cover facts within the 6, 7, 8 and 9 multiplication tables. Make sure the children realise that they can put the products on their mats in any way they wish. They must then read the calling cards printed on the page and mark off the products on their mats. Stress that they can start at either end of any row of the calling cards, but that they must go along the chosen row and down to the next. At the end of the bottom row they must then go to the top row and continue in the same direction. The activity ends when the first of their mats is full, i.e. all the products marked on the mat have been 'called'. Copymaster 9.7 can be used to help prepare the mats. See also Further activity 10.

Further activities

1. Have some children make bags of sand so that each bag balances with eight equal masses, while others make bags which balance with five of the equal masses. (10 g masses are convenient as the equal masses but each 10 g should be regarded as one unit. Any objects of equal weight could, of course, be used and considered as a unit.) Each bag should be marked with the equivalent number of balancing masses. Get the children to place five of the 8 unit bags, one at a time, on one pan of the balance, and then place the 5 unit bags on the other pan to try and find a balancing combination, e.g. five of the 8 unit bags will

balance with eight of the 5 unit bags. Encourage them to find other balancing combinations.

2. Ask the children to find the cost of eight articles at 10p each from the class shop, setting out the coins required. Now ask them to find the cost of ten articles at 8p each, again by setting out the coins. Have the children exchange both sets of coins for 10p pieces to show the equivalence of the values. Have the children repeat the activity with other amounts.

3. Use a calculator as a function machine. Tell the children that the calculator is a function machine and that they have to decide what the function is. Set it to multiply by 3, 4, 6, 7, 8 or 9. For example, to multiply by 9 repeatedly, key in $\boxed{9}\boxed{\times}\boxed{0}\boxed{=}$. Zero will now be displayed. Have the children key in a series of numbers to see if they can identify the function from the results they obtain. Some calculators have a different procedure to input a constant. You may have to consult the instructions.

4. Have the children investigate the different ways in which they can produce multiples of 6 using a calculator.

    (a) Keying in $\boxed{6}\boxed{+}\boxed{=}\boxed{=}\boxed{=}$ ... produces 6, 12, 18, 24 .... (You may have to use $\boxed{6}\boxed{+}\boxed{+}\boxed{=}$, depending on the type of calculator.)

    (b) Keying in $\boxed{6}\boxed{M+}\boxed{MR}\boxed{+}\boxed{MR}\boxed{+}\boxed{MR}\boxed{+}\boxed{MR}$ ... also produces 6, 12, 18, 24 ....

    (c) Keying in $\boxed{6}\boxed{\times}\boxed{\times}\boxed{1}\boxed{=}$, then $\boxed{2}\boxed{=}\boxed{3}\boxed{=}\boxed{4}\boxed{=}$ ... is another way of producing 6, 12, 18, 24 ....

Get the children to record the outputs on a 1–100 square, encouraging them to notice that each sequence of key presses results in the same number sequence. Repeat to obtain multiples of 3, 7, 8 and 9.

5. Copymaster 9.8 can be used to illustrate repeated addition. The children select a function, such as 'add 6' and then shade in multiples on all the rectangular grids on the sheet (figure 9.20). The children should repeat the activity on another sheet using a different function. Have the children discuss the patterns with you.

6. Play the calculator versus memory game – a game for three children. Make up 30 cards with multiplication facts written on them from the 3, 4, 6, 7, 8 and 9 multiplication tables, but excluding the facts in the 5×5 multiplication matrix. One child acts as the umpire and holds the cards. The second child has a calculator. The umpire draws a card from the pack and shows it to the other children. The second child has to obtain the product on the calculator and the third child has to give the product from memory. The first to supply the correct product receives a point. The winner is the first to get ten points. The roles of the players are then changed.

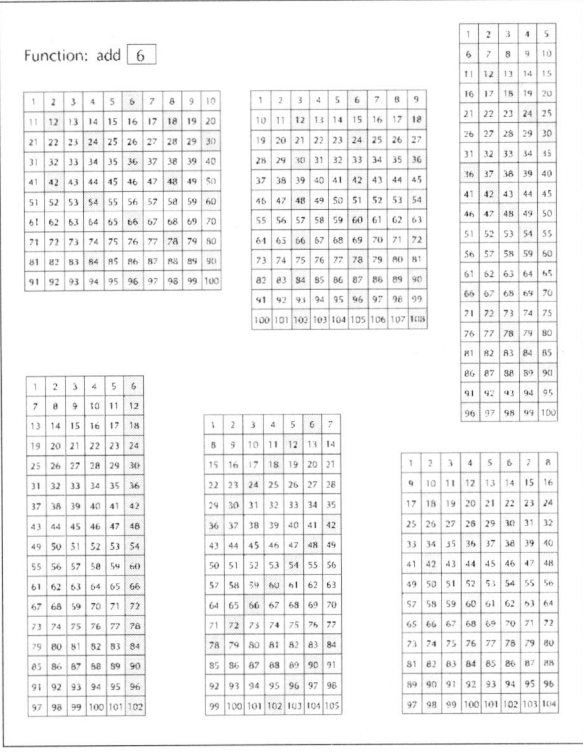

Figure 9.20

7. Let the children use the Party Time Flowcharts (Activity Cards 9.2–9.3), arranging the cards to show the stages for (a) getting dressed for the party (figure 9.21) and (b) selecting a meal from

Figure 9.21

New Curriculum Mathematics for Schools Key Stage 2

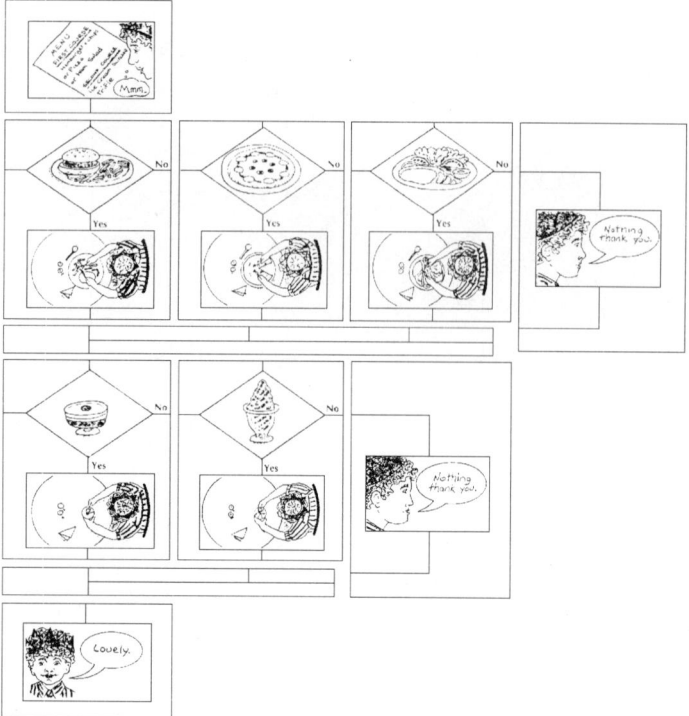

Figure 9.22

Figure 9.23

Figure 9.24

the menu (figure 9.22). Discuss with the children all the different routes through the flowcharts. Let them find other ways of arranging the cards (figures 9.23 and 9.24). In the menu cards it is possible to decide not to have anything after all. However, in the dressing flowchart it is desirable that something is worn. Make sure the children notice this difference in the two flowcharts. Get them to draw a flowchart from the cards (the words on the reverse of the cards should help them). As an extension, have the children create their own flowcharts when an extra sweater and/or skirt is included in the wardrobe, or when an extra main course or dessert is added to the menu. A selection of drinks could even be added to increase the choice. Discuss with the children the links which these selections have with their multiplication experiences.

8. Get the children to list situations where people such as shop assistants, gardeners, builders and joiners will use their multiplication facts to find numbers of objects. Also have the children play 'Tell Me a Story' (Activity Card 9.4). Shuffle the two sets of cards well and place them face down in two piles on the table. The children take it in turns to turn over one of each type of card and then tell a story about the number sentence as it could relate to the scene depicted on the picture card. 'Tell Me a Story' is not a memory game. Encourage the children to invent situations illustrating Cartesian products as well as repeated addition.

9. Have the children use a tape-recorder to record a tape of multiplication questions. Each question should be followed by a 15-second interval before the product is recorded. When 30 facts have been recorded and the tape rewound, let the children listen to the questions and try to give the product before the tape recorder. A point can be awarded for each correct product given in time.

10. Make and play Multiplication Memory Bingo. Prepare a series of calling cards based on products within the 6, 7, 8 and 9 multiplication tables. (See Pupils' Book page 46.) Also prepare some bingo mats with the products on them (Copymaster 9.7 can be used). Give each child a mat. Spread the calling cards face down on the table, making sure they are well mixed up. The children take it in turns to turn over a card. If the product is on their mat, they place the card in position and have another turn. If not, then it is turned face down on the table again and play moves to the next player. The first to cover all the numbers on his/her mat is the winner.

11. Play Double Spin, a game for two players. Prepare overlays for two spinners with the numbers 3, 4, 6, 7, 8 and 9 on each (figure 9.25).

Section 9

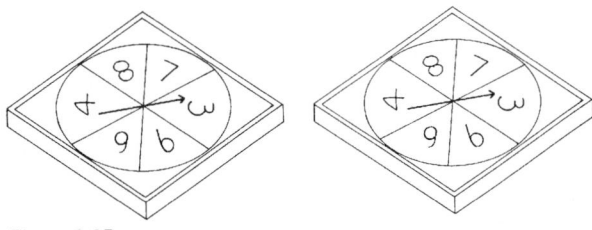

Figure 9.25

The children take it in turns to spin the spinners and state the product of the numbers shown. A calculator can be used to check this, if necessary. The player with the largest number wins a point, and the first to reach an agreed target wins the game.

Double Spin can also be played by giving the players a target such as 500 to reach. Instead of gaining a point each time, the players find the cumulative total after each spin. The first to reach 500 wins. A target of 500 should be reached by most players in 16 spins or less. To help children with their addition, allow them to use a hundreds, tens and units scoreboard as shown in figure 9.26.

Hundreds, tens and units scoreboard		
900	90	9
800	80	8
700	70	7
600	60	6
500	50	5
400	40	4
300	30	3
200	20	2
100	10	1
0	0	0

Figure 9.26

12. Give the children two dice, both marked with the numbers as in Double Spin above. Get them to throw the dice a number of times and make a class graph of their results, i.e. everybody should contribute to the same graph, each child recording his/her results in a different identifiable colour. The children should write about the class graph as they record their results. As the graph grows, have a class discussion on how it is changing. Get the children to say whether the graph is as expected or not (figure 9.27).

13. Make a series of Multiplication Pairs games to cover the tables featured in this section. For example, on red cards print the number sentences:

$0 \times 9 =$ $1 \times 9 =$ $2 \times 9 =$ $3 \times 9 =$
$4 \times 9 =$ $5 \times 9 =$ $6 \times 9 =$ $7 \times 9 =$
$8 \times 9 =$ $9 \times 9 =$ $10 \times 9 =$

and on blue cards write the products:

0 9 18 27 36 45 54 63 72 81 90

Shuffle the cards and spread them face down on the table. The children take it in turns to turn over a red card and then a blue card. If the cards match, then the player keeps the pair. If not, the cards are turned face down again on the table and play moves to the next player. As a variation, have the winner tell a story, putting the number sentence and the product in a context.

14. Show the children a map such as the one in figure 9.28 where there are two roads between Weston and Middleton, and three roads between Middleton and Easton. Ask the

Class Chart of Products for Double Spin

I expected to get more 24s

because 3 × 8 = 24
8 × 3 = 24
4 × 6 = 24
6 × 4 = 24

You can only get 81 with 9×9.

Figure 9.27

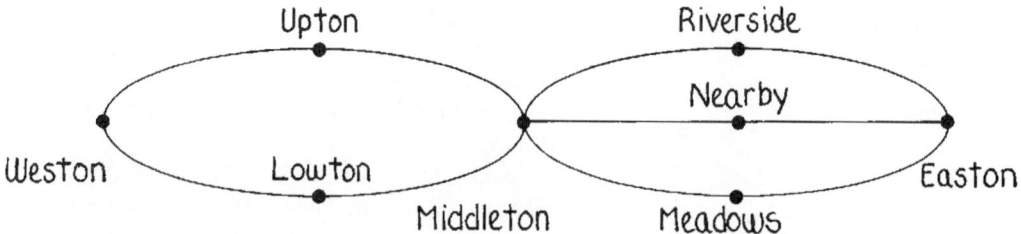

Figure 9.28

children to find how many different ways it is possible to travel from Weston to Easton. Get the children to make up their own maps connecting three towns, varying the number of roads between each town. Again they must find the number of different ways it is possible to travel from the first town through the second to the third. They should write about the patterns they find. Let the children create more of their own maps, listing all the possible routes between towns.

15. Give the children multiplication sentences to complete and then ask them to use them to complete a third sentence, for example:

   $4 \times 2 =$ $8 \times 4 =$ $7 \times 9 =$
   $4 \times 10 =$ $8 \times 10 =$ $7 \times 10 =$
   So $4 \times \boxed{12} =$ So $8 \times \square =$ So $7 \times \square =$

   $6 \times 10 =$ $8 \times 10 =$ $7 \times 10 =$
   $6 \times 10 =$ $6 \times 10 =$ $7 \times 10 =$
   So $6 \times \square =$ So $6 \times \square =$ So $7 \times \square =$

   Get the children to check their results with a calculator.

16. Give the children some more multiplication sentences and again ask them to derive other sentences from them, for example:

   $8 \times 8 =$ $7 \times 6 =$ $6 \times 6 =$
   $16 \times 4 =$ $14 \times 3 =$ $12 \times 6 =$
   $32 \times 2 =$ $28 \times 3 =$ $24 \times 6 =$

   Have the children check their results with a calculator.

17. Let the children use cubes (or counters) to investigate the rectangular arrays which can be made with any given number. (The numbers should be mostly greater than 25.) For example 36 shapes can form rectangles 1×36, 4×9, 6×6 and 12×3. Discuss the (prime) numbers which form one row of shapes only. Have the children list the arrays which are square shaped.

18. Play the game of Buzz. A set of multiples is chosen. The children then start a count round the class, each child saying a number in turn. When a child has a multiple to say, he/she says 'buzz' in place of the multiple. For example, a game where multiples of 7 have been chosen would go 'one, two, three, four, five, six, buzz, eight, nine, ten, eleven, twelve, thirteen, buzz, fifteen, sixteen,' etc.

19. Make and play Product Winners, a game for two players. Prepare a pack of 40 cards as follows:

    Number on card   0 1 2 3 4 5 6 7 8 9 10
    Number of each   2 2 2 3 3 2 6 6 6 6 2

    Shuffle the cards. Each player takes two cards and states the product (figure 9.29). The player with the higher product takes all four cards. The game continues until all the cards are collected, when the winner is the player with most cards.

Figure 9.29

20. Make and play Score 100. On two, say, blue cubes write the numbers 5, 6, 7, 8, 9 and 10, and on two, say, red cubes write the numbers 2, 2, 3, 3, 4, 4 and 1, 2, 3, 4, 5, 6 respectively. The players take it in turns to throw the two blue dice and record the product. Each player must then decide whether to stop or go on, choosing to throw either the blue dice again or to throw the red dice. If a player goes on, the two products are added. (In each turn a player may roll the blue dice only, or the blue dice and then the red dice.) The winner is the player with a score of 100 or the highest score below 100. If a score is above 100 it is disallowed. A player scores one point for each win and the first to score 20 wins the game.

21. Have the children play a game based on the addition of multiples, where one child places two counters on two numbers in one of the columns, or one of the rows, of a multiplication square. The second child has to place a third counter on the sum of the two numbers in the same row, or column (figure 9.30). Copymaster 9.4 can be used. The children can compare it with their multiplication strips by placing them in the same order. Let the children experiment with a multiplication square for multiples up to 100.

x10	10	20	30	40	50	60	70	80	90	100
x9	9	18	27	36	45	54	63	72	81	90
x8	8	16	24	(32)	40	48	56	64	72	80
x7	7	14	21	28	35	42	49	56	63	70
x6	6	12	18	24	30	36	42	48	54	60
x5	5	10	15	(20)	25	30	35	40	45	50
x4	4	8	12	16	20	24	28	32	36	40
x3	3	6	9	(12)	15	18	21	24	27	30
x2	2	4	6	8	10	12	14	16	18	20
x1	1	2	3	4	5	6	7	8	9	10

Figure 9.30

22. Give the children several rods, or strips, in two different lengths. Emphasise that they are going to see if they can find a pattern when they take the same number of each length and make them into a 'train' along a ruler. Ask the children to arrange all the same lengths together, as shown above the ruler in figure 9.31. Have them now rearrange the strips so that the rods are in pairs as shown below the ruler. Discuss the need for there to be the same number of each length. An area model can also be used (figure 9.32).

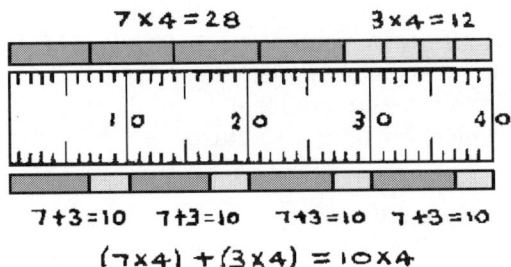

Figure 9.31

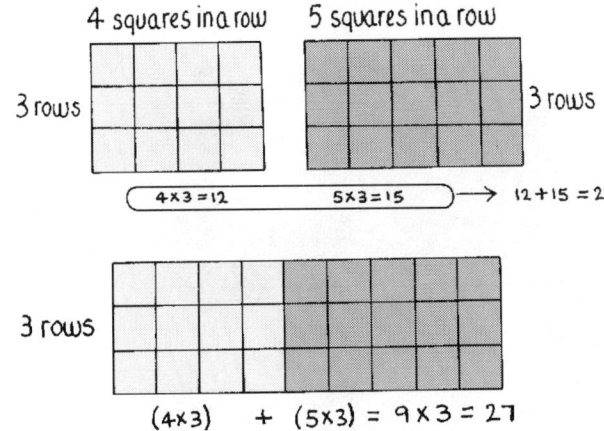

Figure 9.32

Have the children experiment to find other examples. Encourage them to make appropriate multiplication sentences.

23. The children can use calculators to investigate multiplication by numbers greater than 10, e.g.

$5 \times 13 = (5 \times 7) + (5 \times 6) = \square + \square = 65$
$ = (5 \times 8) + (5 \times 5) = \square + \square = 65$
$ = (5 \times 9) + (5 \times 4) = \square + \square = 65$
$ = (5 \times 10) + (5 \times 3) = \square + \square = 65$

24. Play Go for Goal (Activity Cards 9.5–9.8). The game is played on a game board made from Activity Cards 9.5 and 9.6 (figure 9.33). Two players can play, or four can act as two two-a-side teams. The playing cards are supplied on Activity Cards 9.7 and 9.8. A counter is required to act as the ball. Before the game starts, the players decide who is to play Green and who is to play Yellow. Green defends the green goal and attacks the yellow goal. Yellow defends the yellow goal and attacks the green goal. The cards are well shuffled and the pack is placed alongside the playing area, with the sentences showing. If a black card is on view, then it is removed and placed in the middle of the pack. The 'ball' is placed on the centre spot. If a green card is showing, then the Green player must answer. If he/she gets the answer wrong and the opponent challenges the response with a correct call, then the opponent passes the ball. The product can be checked by

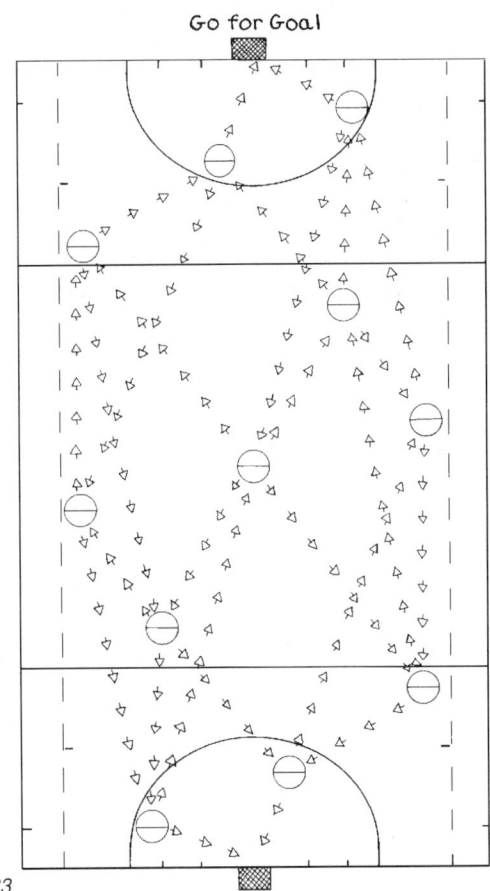

Figure 9.33

turning the card over and placing it alongside the main pack, thus revealing the next card. If a yellow card is displayed, then the player playing Yellow answers first. However, if one of the black cards is displayed, the player who last called correctly has the first opportunity to respond and pass the ball. To pass the ball a player must react correctly to the number sentence on the card. He/she then moves his/her counter down the green pass lines, if Green is playing, or down the yellow pass lines if Yellow is playing. (*Note*: green pass lines take play towards the yellow goal and vice versa.) The game continues until a goal is scored by moving the ball into the opponent's net. Once a goal has been scored, the ball is returned to the centre spot. The game continues until all the cards have been played. You may care to go through the pack again with each player playing a different colour. In this way, each player will have had first 'go' at most of the cards. Shorter games can be played by having a time limit on each half or having the winner as the first player to score, say, three goals. (*Note*: the game board follows the layout of a hockey field to compliment the soccer field used in the Activity Cards for Key Stage 2, Teacher's Guide 1.)

25. Discuss with the children how you can play Go for Goal on a league basis. Arrange the players in four groups and let the children plan the fixtures so that everybody plays the others in their group once. Keep a record on the classroom display area of the results of the games as they are played. Arrange some form of play-off for, say, the top two in each group. Like other games in this series, Go for Goal can be played throughout the year. It is important not to overdo any one activity, but the Go for Goal competition could form a regular feature of the work in class during a particular term, giving regular opportunities for consolidation of multiplication facts. Allow the children to play their 'fixtures' both in and out of lesson time.

26. Play Safari Park (Activity Cards 9.9–9.10). This is a game for up to six players (three is an ideal number). You will need the Safari Park game board (figure 9.34), formed by combining Activity Cards 9.9 and 9.10, one dice marked 1–6, two ten-sided dice marked 1–10, a pack of 60 cards to represent 'photographs' of the animals and a counter for each player.

    The aim of the game is to enter the Safari Park at one of the three entrances, marked 'start', and to go round the park taking 'photographs' of the animals. Once the order of play has been decided, each player puts his/her counter on one of the 'start' positions on the track. The 1–6 dice is then throw, and the player moves forward round the track the number of places shown on the 1–6 dice. If he/she lands on a 'click' zone, then he/she may take a 'photograph' of the animals. To do this the player has to find the product of the two 1–10 dice. If that product falls within the range indicated on the board, then the camera is 'in focus' and a 'photograph' card can be taken. If the product is not within the range, the camera is 'out of focus' and no 'photograph' is taken. Should a player land on a 'double click' zone, then they may throw the 1–10 dice again and have an extra turn. The game ends when all the players have completed a full circuit of the park. The winner is not the first to finish but the player who has collected the most 'photographs'.

    The notation '$19 < P < 101$' is used to mean that the product needs to be greater than 19 and less than 101 for a 'photograph' to be taken. Most players should complete the game in less than 25 throws, find more than 15 products and obtain seven or more pictures.

27. Have the children play World Series Golf (produced by Taskmaster), if available. The game is based on a six-hole golf course and will provide further practice in multiplication. The rules come with the game. The game will be featured in Pupils' Book 3 of Key Stage 2, so it would be advantageous if pupils had

Figure 9.34

experience of this particular activity at this stage in their development.

28. Jump Off is another game (produced by NES/EJ Arnold, ref: SY416/9) which the children may enjoy playing. The game is based on show jumping and uses the full range of multiplication facts.

29. Play Multiplication Dominoes. Activity Cards 9.11–9.14 cover the ranges 5×9 to 9×9, 5×8 to 9×8, 5×7 to 9×7 and 5×6 to 9×6 respectively. As well as competing with each other, get the children to play a form of patience with the dominoes, trying to make complete 'trains'.

30. Play Four in a Line again (see Section 5, Further activity 8), this time to practise multiplication. Figure 9.35 shows a suitable game sheet prepared from Copymaster 5.1. Note that some of the numbers shown involve products outside the range of the 'tables'. Encourage the children to have a go at this type of problem. Also notice that the numbers at the four corners and the centre of the square in the sample shown are all square numbers, and especially worth remembering as far as the children are concerned.

31. Play Calculator Apples. For this game for two players you will need Copymaster 9.9 and a dice marked 6, 7, 8, 9, 8, 9. The object of the game is to be first to colour all the apples on your tree. The players throw the dice to decide who is to go first. The first player then throws the dice and must choose an apple on his/her tree which displays a number which is a multiple of the number shown on the dice. The second player checks that it is correct using a calculator. If the first player is correct, the apple can be coloured in. Play then passes to the second player.
Some of the numbers on the apples are multiples of more than one number on the dice and some are not. Therefore during the game the children will have to make choices as to which apple to colour. (The choice may affect the outcome of the game, because, if no unshaded apple has a multiple of the number shown on the dice, the player misses a turn.)

32. Let the children play the Multiple Flowchart Game on Copymaster 9.10. Up to four players can play. Each player needs a counter. The game also requires two 1–10 dice. Decide on the order of play, for example letting the youngest child go first, etc. Before play starts, complete the decision boxes by filling in the required multiples. The children now follow the instructions on the game sheet.

33. Ask the children to complete an addition matrix for the two dice used in the Multiple Flowchart Game.

```
 + | 1 2 3 4 5 6 7 8 9 10
 1 |
 2 |
 3 |
 4 |
 5 |
 6 |
 7 |
 8 |
 9 |
10 |
```

Have them list how many of the results are multiples of the number in:

(a) the first decision box;
(b) the second decision box;
(c) the third decision box.

Link these results with what they recall from playing the Multiple Flowchart Game. Ask them if they had to wait longer for a move on certain sections than on others. Have the children investigate other multiples with the matrix. Let them consider the likely outcome if other multiples were used in the Multiple Flowchart Game.

34. Play Factor Dominoes (Activity Card 9.15) as shown in figure 9.36. Copymaster 9.11 can also be used, where the children are asked to

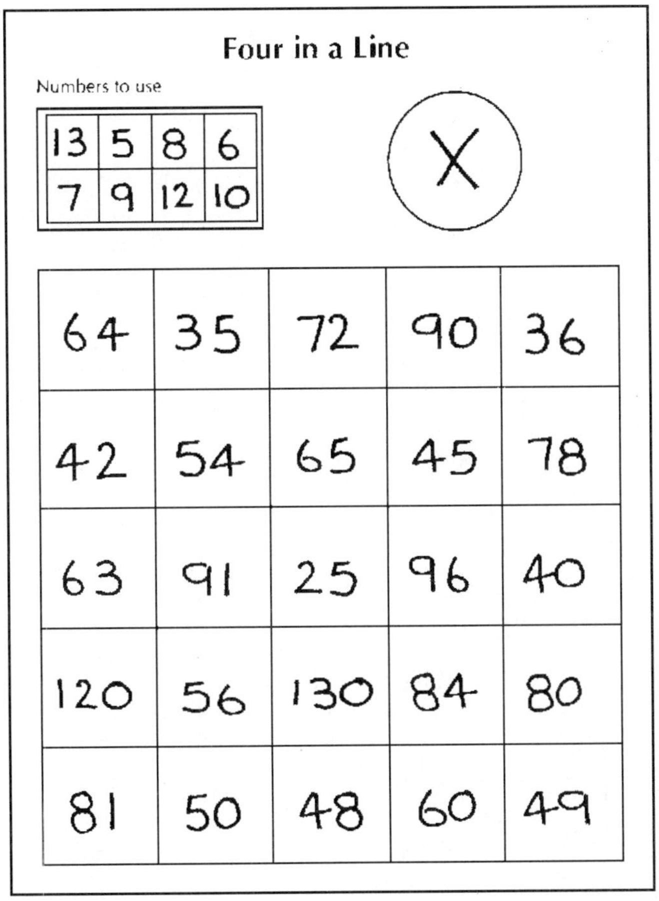

Four in a Line

Numbers to use: 13, 5, 8, 6, 7, 9, 12, 10   ⊗

64	35	72	90	36
42	54	65	45	78
63	91	25	96	40
120	56	130	84	80
81	50	48	60	49

Figure 9.35

New Curriculum Mathematics for Schools Key Stage 2

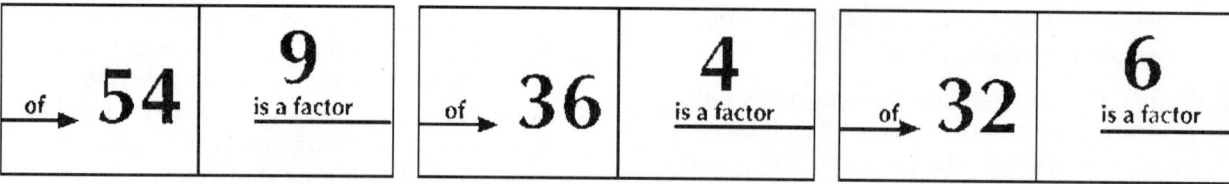

Figure 9.36

complete the dominoes. Make sure the children realise they need to follow the principles of ordinary dominoes; in particular draw their attention to the fact that they must try to avoid repeat dominoes.

35. Let the children play Cross the Board (Activity Cards 9.16–9.21). Two players select one of the game boards and the appropriate cards for the multiplication board being used. Each board is dedicated to one 'table', e.g. '×9' (figure 9.37).

Multiplication Board for x 9

27	9	6	63	45	81	18	72
45	36	27	72	18	54	54	90
0	0	81	72	63	90	45	36
81	18	54	90	9	36	63	27
63	27	6	36	54	90	81	18
45	36	63	90	18	72	0	0
54	90	18	54	27	72	45	36
18	72	45	81	9	63	27	6

Figure 9.37

The aim of the game is to move a given number of counters across the board on the squares of each player's chosen colour. The first to do so wins. It may be helpful in the first instance if only four counters are used. On a player's first move he/she must place a counter on the front row of his/her chosen colour on the board. Subsequent moves are made diagonally to adjacent squares of the player's colour, or a player may decide to enter a new counter on the board.

The multiplication cards are placed in a pile with the unfinished sentences showing face up.

The player whose turn it is looks at the top card and either:

(a) states the number which completes the number sentence if he/she thinks that is a number on a square to which one of his/her counters can be moved legitimately; or
(b) rejects the top card, which is then placed at the bottom of the pile, and tries to state the number for the next card. No more tries are then allowed in that turn.

If a player states a number for the first card, he/she cannot then decide to reject that card. When a number has been stated the card is turned over to see if it is correct. After an attempted statement of a number, correct or not, it is then the opponent's turn. Rejected cards, or cards for which a completed sentence has been attempted, are placed at the bottom of the pack with the number sentence face up.

36. Recall a previous activity in which the children have experimented with solid shapes, making structures to fixed rules (see activity 6 on page

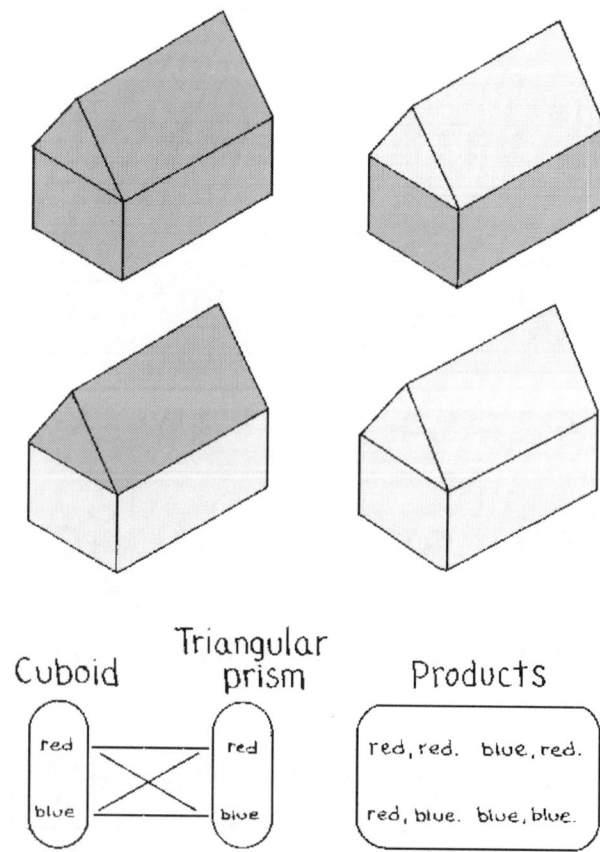

Figure 9.38

88 of Key Stage 2 Teacher's Guide 1). For example, using a cuboid and a triangular prism, in two colours only, how many different structures can they create? Can they link their results to their knowledge of Cartesian products (figure 9.38)? Encourage the children to experiment further, linking their findings to multiplication sentences.

37. Copymasters 9.12 and 9.13 can be used to give further varied practice.

Check-ups

1. Can the children recognise, illustrate and recall the multiplication facts in the 10×10 multiplication matrix?

2. Can the children use the terms factor, product and multiple correctly?

3. Given two sets, A and B, can the children list all the ordered pairs by matching all the elements in Set A with all the elements in Set B in that order?

4. Can the children recall and use the full range of multiplication facts in context?

5. Can the children find products using a calculator?

6. Can the children recall and explain multiplication facts involving zero?

7. Do the children understand the commutative property of multiplication?

8. Knowing the result of a product in a practical situation, can the children produce the commutative equivalent, e.g. knowing that five containers, each holding 8 litres of water, fill a 40-litre tank, can they say how many 5-litre containers of water would be required to fill the same tank?

9. Do the children understand the distributive property of multiplication, e.g. can they partition an array, creating examples and completing a sentence such as: $4 \times 3 = 12$ added to $4 \times 5 = 20$ is the same total as $4 \times 8 = 32$?

New Curriculum Mathematics for Schools Key Stage 2

Section 10

AT 1 3a, 3b, 3c, 3d. AT 2 3b, 3c, 4a. AT 3 2b, 3a, 3b, 4a.

Pages 47–51 Sharing

- **Page 47** The Apple Orchard
- **Page 48** The Bakery
- **Page 49** Make the Shares Equal
- **Page 50** Do It and Undo It
- **Page 51** A Two-stage Function Machine

Purpose

To give children further experience of the relationship between 'equal sharing' and 'equal grouping' operations, and multiplication and repeated 'take away'.

To consolidate children's understanding of 'equal sharing' number sentences, such as 6 ÷ 2 = 3 because 3 x 2 = 6 ('6 shared into 2 sets produces 3 in a set because a set of 3 twice equals 6'), and 'equal grouping' number sentences, such as 6 ÷ 2 = 3 because 2 x 3 = 6 ('6 grouped into sets of 2 produces 3 sets because a set of 2 three times is 6').

To provide further practice in writing 'equal sharing' and 'equal grouping' stories from appropriate number sentences.

To give children practice in recognising 'equal sharing' and 'equal grouping' situations as they arise in context.

To give children experience of situations where 'equal sharing' and 'equal grouping' leaves a remainder, or does not produce a whole number using a calculator.

To introduce the idea of an inverse operation, e.g. 10 x 7 = 70 so 70 ÷ 7 = 10.

To introduce the rules governing equivalent divisions.

Recommended material

1. Small objects such as counters, cubes, etc., for 'equal sharing' and 'equal grouping' activities.
2. Story Pairs (**Activity Card 10.1**).
3. Blank postcards or cards.
4. Calculators.
5. Sharing Touch and Say cards (**Activity Card 10.2**).
6. Metre stick and rods of lengths 1 to 10 cm.
7. Large cardboard boxes for making function machines.
8. **Copymasters 9.1 and 10.1–10.6.**
9. Double Function Pairs (**Activity Card 10.3**).
10. Cards for games (see Pre-page activities 23 and 25, and Further activity 2).
11. 'Any Left Overs'? cards (**Activity Card 10.4**).

Pre-page activities

Note In earlier computation we suggested that in the first instance real objects were used. We then suggested that real objects were replaced by counters, etc., representing the objects. The activities in this section develop previous sharing experiences. As the number involved will be greater than before, small objects such as counters and cubes can be used to represent the items being shared.

1. Play Story Pairs (Activity Card 10.1). Shuffle the cards well and spread them face down on the table as for a memory game. The children take

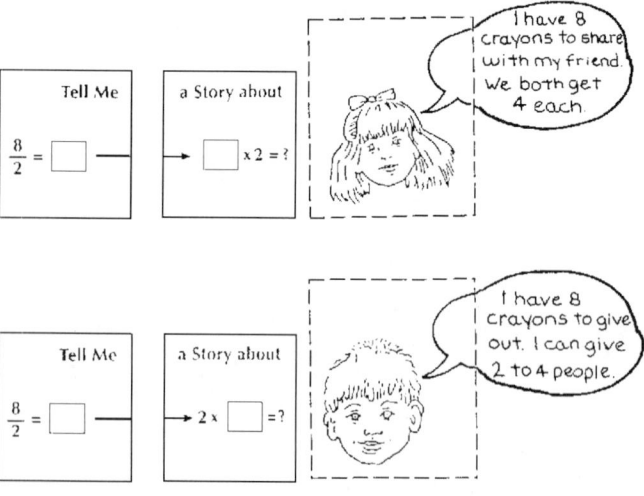

Figure 10.1

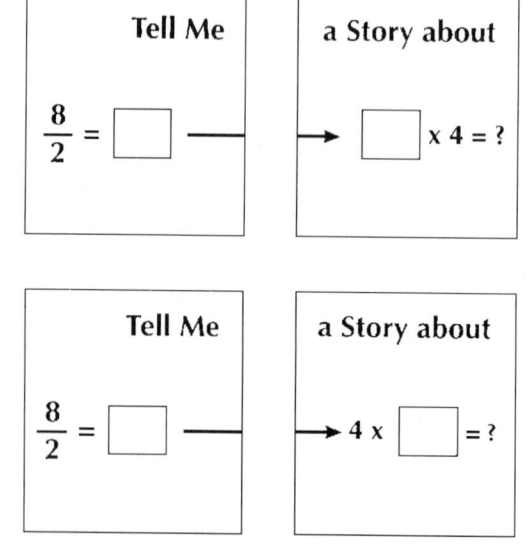

Figure 10.2

it in turns to turn over one red card and one green card. If the cards match, to retain the pair the player must 'tell a story' about the number sentence. Figure 10.1 shows how the number sentence $\frac{8}{2} = \square$ can be paired with either of two cards. The cartoons, though, illustrate two different stories for the paired cards. Figure 10.2 shows a comparable connection which may occur, and which can be linked to the storyline shown in figure 10.1.

2. Give the children some sharing problems to model and solve, involving multiples of 6, 7, 8 and 9. For example, take 27 toy cars (counters) and ask one child to share them equally among nine children. Appoint another child as a commentator and have him/her describe the action, e.g. 'Hannah is now sharing out the cars. She gives one to Sue, one to Ming, one to John, one to Tony, one to Gwen, one to Naseem, one to Kumar, one to Fiona and one to Jamie. They have all got one car and there are 18 left to share out. Now she is giving another to Sue, another one to Ming, another one to John, another one to Tony, another one to Gwen, another one to Naseem, another one to Kumar, another one to Fiona and another one to Jamie. All the cards have been shared out. The children have three cars each.' Record the equal sharing as it takes place. Have the recording show the two stages of the action by encouraging the children to model the problem and record the mathematics 'as it happens' (figure 10.3).
Take the opportunity to stress the relationship between equal sharing and multiplication. Have the children record as:
$\frac{27}{9} = 3$ because $3 \times 9 = 27$;
i.e. a set of three nine times, or nine sets of three. Make sure the children understand where the numbers in the sentence come from. The '27' is the number of cars to share out, the '9' says how many subsets there are (nine children) and the '3' says how many are in each subset (three for each child). As a result of the sharing action, the children should be able to 'see' a set of three nine times, i.e. $3 \times 9 = 27$. Repeat the activity for other situations which produce number sentences involving multiples of 6, 7, 8 and 9, e.g. $24 \div 8$, $36 \div 9$, $40 \div 8$, $56 \div 7$, $42 \div 6$, etc.

3. Give the children a set of 48 objects and ask them to find and record all the possible ways in which the objects can be equally shared among children, for example:

   $48 \div 1 = 48$ because $48 \times 1 = 48$
   $48 \div 2 = 24$ because $24 \times 2 = 48$
   $48 \div 3 = 16$ because $16 \times 3 = 48$
   $48 \div 4 = 12$ because $12 \times 4 = 48$
   $48 \div 6 = 8$ because $8 \times 6 = 48$
   $48 \div 12 = 4$ because $4 \times 12 = 48$
   $48 \div 16 = 3$ because $3 \times 16 = 48$
   $48 \div 24 = 2$ because $2 \times 24 = 48$
   $48 \div 48 = 1$ because $1 \times 48 = 48$

   Have the children make a display of the results. Get them to model some sentences, such as $48 \div 10$, which will not share equally.

4. Develop activity 2 above to consider an 'equal grouping/sharing' problem such as: 28 children are to put in teams of seven. Use counters to represent the children. Have a child put the counters in groups/teams of seven and find how many teams can be formed. Encourage a running commentary, and record the action as it occurs in a picture story and a number story (figure 10.4). Make sure the children appreciate the link with multiplication when they record $35 \div 7 = 5$ because $7 \times 5 = 35$. Check that they understand where each number in the number sentences comes from. Repeat the activity for other 'equal grouping' situations which produce number sentences involving multiples of 6, 7, 8 and 9, e.g. $24 \div 8$, $36 \div 9$, $40 \div 8$, $56 \div 7$, $42 \div 6$, etc.

5. Give the children some number sentences such as $63 \div 7 = \square$. Ask them to write both an 'equal sharing' and an 'equal grouping' story for the sentence, as well as providing the result. Take care that the children link the sentence with multiplication and in doing so put the numbers in the correct place. For example, for

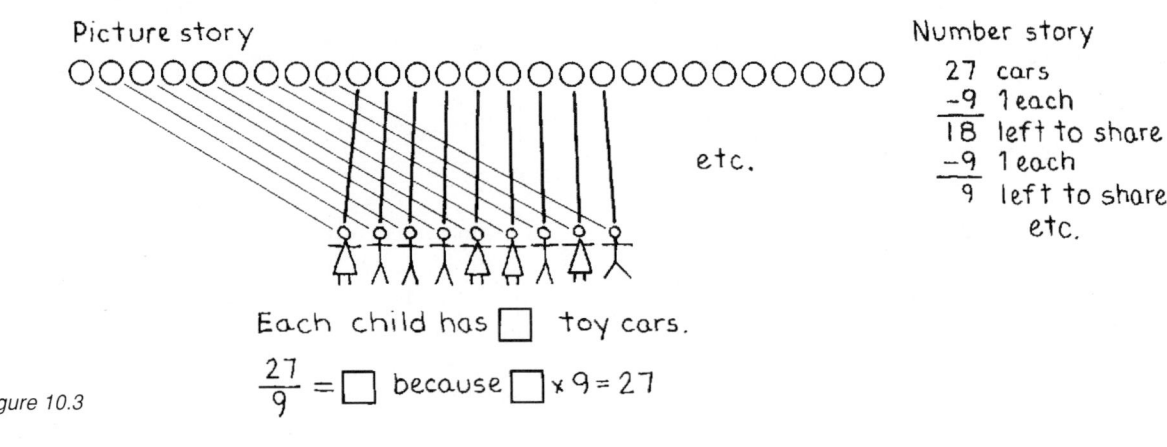

Figure 10.3

Picture story   Number story

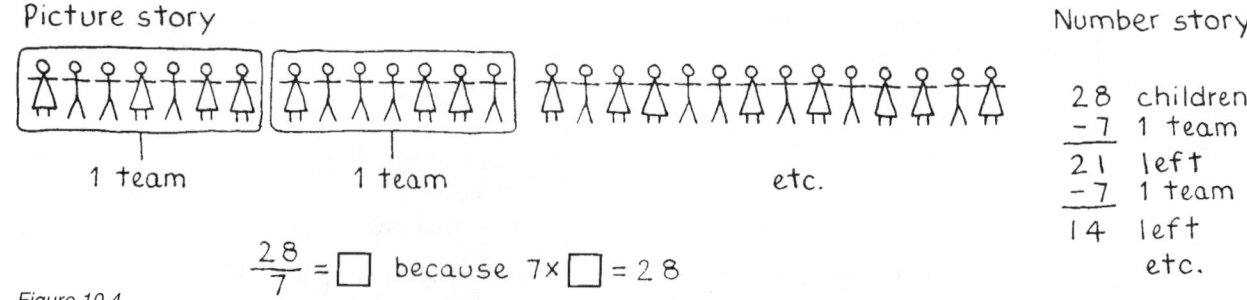

Figure 10.4

'equal sharing', 63 ÷ 7 means 'put 63 into seven equal subsets and find how many are in each subset'. The final sentence will be 63 ÷ 7 = 9 because 9 × 7 = 63. When 63 ÷ 7 becomes an 'equal grouping' situation it will mean 'find how many subsets with seven members can be made from 63 objects'. This time the final sentence will be 63 ÷ 7 = 9 because 7 × 9 = 63. Get the children to display their two different images side by side to illustrate the contrast.

6. Ask the children to find answers to problems where equal grouping is not possible, for example:

   (a) At a sale of work there are 50 cakes and they are sold six in a box. How many boxes are filled?
   (b) Mr Price buys pencils in packs of eight. He requires one pencil for each of 30 children. How many packs must he buy?

   Have the children make up similar stories.

7. Let the children make and play Sharing Trivia. The players should form teams of two. Provide each team with a series of 12 blank postcards, on each of which they must write a sharing story. Get them to include the answer number sentence in red at the bottom of the card. Once the cards are completed, let the teams decide who is playing by allowing teams to challenge each other. Appoint a question master/mistress and a scorer from another team. The question master/mistress reads the question devised by one team to the opposing team, taking it in turns to ask one team and then the other. (Questions are asked from the opponents' pack.) For a correct result a score of two points is awarded. However, if the actual question is wrong, the answering team gets three points. Calculators can be used by the scorer to settle arguments. The teams can work together to solve the questions. If a team is not actually playing, they are free to amend their question cards.

8. Put a pile of 12 counters on the table. Share the counters into four equal piles. Discuss the sharing with the children. Have them record the operation and note the resulting number of counters in each pile. Now place 24 counters on the table and repeat the operation, sharing them

into eight piles. Have the children relate the experience to the one before, to emphasise the equivalence of the result. Repeat the activity for $\frac{12}{4}$ followed by $\frac{6}{2}$. (*Note*: the fraction notation is suggested as a link with other activities related to equivalent fractions.) Repeat the activity using other quantities. Discuss what has been done to the dividend (total quantity), and to the divisor, to produce the same result in each case.

9. Ask the children to draw picture stories and write number stories for the following number sentences: 3 ÷ 3 = ☐, 4 ÷ 4 = ☐, 5 ÷ 5 = ☐, 6 ÷ 6 = ☐, 7 ÷ 7 = ☐, ... etc. See activity 10 below.

10. Have the children use sharing number sentences to find other ways of writing 1 (figure 10.5).

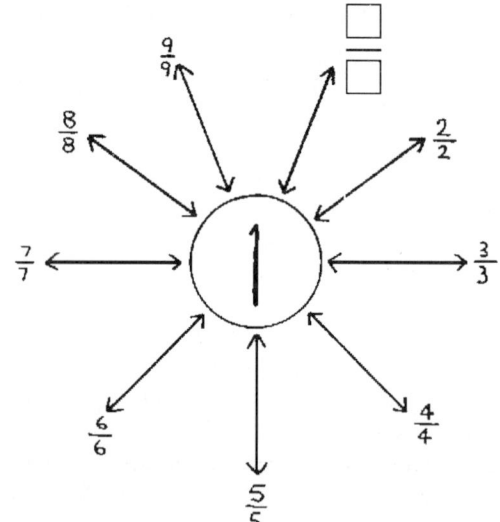

Figure 10.5

11. Let the children use their calculators to investigate sharing sentences. Have them put, say, 21 ÷ 7 into their calculators and find the result. Get them now to multiply both the numbers by, say, 5, and use their calculators to find the result. Have the children record their activity as: $\frac{21 \times 5}{7 \times 5} = \frac{105}{35} = \square$.

Remind the children that 5 ÷ 5 = 1 and that multiplying by 1 produces 'no change' (figure 10.6). Let the children use numbers outside their normal experience and demonstrate that, provided they are really multiplying by 1, the answer will stay the same. You might also like

to let the children see that:
$$\frac{21}{7} \neq \frac{(21+5)}{(7+5)} \text{ since } \frac{26}{12} \neq 3.$$

Figure 10.6

12. Let the children play Sharing Touch and Say (Activity Card 10.2). As a variation, get each child to 'tell a story' about the number sentence before retaining the card.

13. Choose a length of, say, 20 cm on a ruler. Ask the children to find five rods, all of the same length, which will fit end to end against the ruler, reaching the chosen length. Record the operation as before:
$20 \div 5 = 4$ because $4 \times 5 = 20$.
Double the chosen length and now get the children to find ten equal rods to match against it. Record the number sentence in the usual way and get the children to notice the relationship between the two sentences.
$20 \div 5 = 4$ because $4 \times 5 = 20$
$40 \div 10 = 4$ because $4 \times 10 = 40$
Repeat for $15 \div 5$ and $30 \div 10$; $15 \div 3$ and $30 \div 6$; $12 \div 4$ and $24 \div 8$; etc.

14. Place eight counters on a table in one pile, then form two more similar piles. Discuss what you are doing with the children and ask them to make a number sentence to match. From their suggestions choose the multiplication sentence. Represent the total by bringing all the counters into one pile. Ask the children how many counters there will be in each pile if you now share the total equally into three piles. Have the children record the related multiplication and division statements. Repeat using other quantities and different numbers of piles. Reverse the activity and start with a total number of counters. Share them into equal piles, then bring them together again. Discuss the actions as before. Get the children to record their number sentences.

15. Get the children a number sentence such as $28 \div 4 = \square$ which relates to a problem such as 'How many 4 cm strips of ribbon can be cut from a 28 cm length?' Have the children model the situation with a ruler and 4 cm strips or rods. As the children place each strip/rod alongside the ruler, get them to say the multiplication situation they are building, i.e. $4 \times 1 = 4$, $4 \times 2 = 8$, etc., until the strips/rods extend to 28 cm. Discuss the two related sentences ($28 \div 4 = 7$ and $4 \times 7 = 28$) in terms of the model. Repeat with other similar problems.

16. Make and use a 'function machine'. Take a large cardboard box (from a new cooker or fridge, etc.) and let the children decorate it as a robot or computer. Make sure it has one slot for the input and another one for the output. Also arrange for it to display a label, which will indicate the function. Allow a child to sit inside the 'function machine' and explain that every time a number is fed into the machine through the input, they must carry out the function, e.g. $\div 6$, and write the result down on another card which they must then feed out through the output. The children should be allowed to have suitable materials to help them with their calculations. Two machines can be used side by side (figure 10.7), where the first machine feeds into the second and the second outputs the result. For example, if the functions are $\div 2$ then $\div 3$ and a 12 is fed in, the first child will pass a 6 into the next stage and the child operating the second machine will output a 2. Change the functions around and see which functions produce the same output and which do not. Get the children to say which 'machines' can be replaced by a single function.

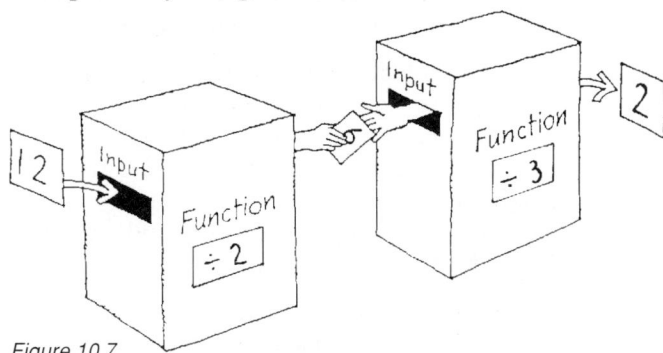

Figure 10.7

17. Set up individual calculators as function machines with functions such as $\div 6$, $\div 7$, $\div 8$ and $\div 9$. Let the children put in various inputs so that they can discover what the function is. Encourage the children to try the function, then predict, then generalise, e.g. 'The input was 30, the output 5. The input was 60, the output 10. I think if I input 24, the output will be 4. I think the function is $\div 6$.'

18. Have the children complete Copymaster 10.1. You may wish to have them set up their calculators as function machines to help them. Because the children are looking for the inputs,

the calculators can be used to give instant feedback as to whether their predictions for input are correct. The mappings at the bottom of the sheet are deliberately open and the children are asked to find more than one solution for each.

19. Have the children play Double Function Pairs (Activity Card 10.3). This is a game for 2–4 players. The cards are shuffled and spread face down on the table. The players take it in turns to pick up a blue card and a yellow card. If the two functions on the yellow card can be replaced by the one function on the blue card (figure 10.8), the player keeps the pair. If not, the cards are shown to the other players before being replaced face down on the table. The player with the most pairs at the end of the game is the winner.

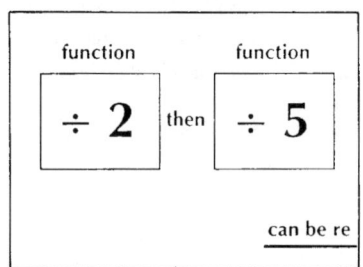 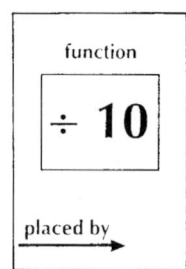

Figure 10.8

20. Using one function machine, have the children say what function would reverse the process. Allow the children to use materials if they wish.

21. Use two function machines in which the second function is the 'inverse' of the first, e.g. $+3, -3$; $\times 5, \div 5$; etc. Discuss with the children the effect of using the two machines in this way.

22. Have the children carry out investigations with their calculators to find pairs of inverse functions. Each time get them to check with more than one input that they have a correct pair. Discuss with the children what they notice about the pairs. Copymasters 10.2 and 10.3 can be used for further practice.

23. Make and play Inverse Pairs. On a set of nine red cards write the functions $\times 2, \times 3, \times 4, \times 5, \times 6, \times 7, \times 8, \times 9, \times 10$, and on a set of nine blue cards write the functions $\div 2, \div 3, \div 4, \div 5, \div 6, \div 7, \div 8, \div 9, \div 10$. Shuffle the cards and spread them face down on the table. The children take it in turns to select one red card and one blue card to try and make a pair (figure 10.9). The player who collects the most pairs wins.

24. Use the two-stage function machine with a mixture of + and −, and a mixture of × and ÷ (e.g. × 10, ÷ 2). Again ask the children to predict the intermediate and final outputs, and see if they can replace the two-stage machines with a one-stage.

25. Play Calculator Challenge – a game for two players and one referee. Make up 30 cards with sharing sentences written on them from the 6, 7, 8 and 9 multiplication tables. The referee draws a card from the pack. One child gives the answer from memory while the other uses the calculator (figure 10.10). The first player to give the correct answer retains the card. The player with most cards wins.

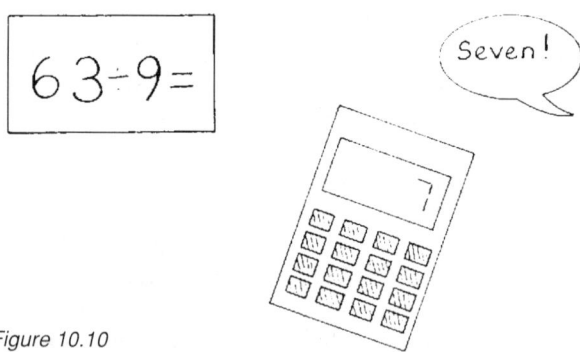

Figure 10.10

26. Write a number sentence such as $63 \div 9 = 7$ on the chalkboard and then discuss with the children how the multiplication sentence will help with sentences like: $63 \div 7 = \square$, $7 \times 9 = \square$, $63 \div \square = 7$ and $63 \div \square = 9$. Make a workcard which requires the children to use other sentences in a similar way.

 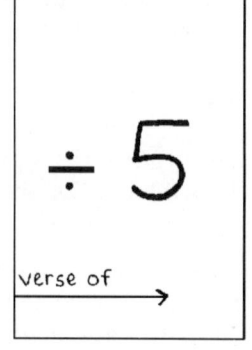

Figure 10.9

Key Page points

Page 47 Remind the children that the picture stories in these situations are similar to those shown in the 'think bubbles' of the sharing out procedure, and the number story is the recording of the repeated 'subtraction' (take away) aspect of the sharing out. Make sure the children can state what each part of the number sentences represents, i.e. $18 \div 6 = 3$ because $3 \times 6 = 18$, the '18' represents the number of apples to share, the '6' represents the six children and the '3' represents the number of apples each child should get. In a different situation these numbers could mean something different (see next page).

Page 48 Although this page doesn't specifically require the children to complete a picture story, you may feel it advisable if some children do so. (The page essentially highlights the number story.) As before, make sure the children can state what each part of the number sentences represents, i.e. in 24 ÷ 8 = 3 because 8 × 3 = 24, the '24' represents the number of rolls to place in bags, the '8' represents the number of buns in each bag, and the '3' represents the number of bags used.

Page 49 Discuss the picture at the top of the page and relate the set of cubes to the associated number sentences. Explain that the number sentences are in pairs and that the children should look for a connection between each pair.

Page 50 Let the children describe what is happening in the two pictures at the top of the page. Check that they can represent the scenes as 'sharing' and 'multiplication'. Relate the pictures to the paired number sentences below them. Make sure that the children understand that they are to complete the unfinished statements as in the example.

Page 51 On completion of this page, you might like to ask the children to create their own two-stage mappings and say which can be replaced by a single function.

Further activities

1. The children might like to take examples of simple whole number divisions and expand them, using their calculators, to equivalent divisions involving large numbers, e.g.
$$\frac{6}{2} = \frac{119 \times 6}{119 \times 2} = \frac{714}{238} = 3.$$
Their results can form the basis for a wall display.

2. Make and play Fours, a game for four children. Prepare a set of 36 cards with number sentences as shown below.

6 × 2 = 12	2 × 6 = 12	12 ÷ 2 = 6	12 ÷ 6 = 2
6 × 3 = 18	3 × 6 = 18	18 ÷ 3 = 6	18 ÷ 6 = 3
6 × 4 = 24	4 × 6 = 24	24 ÷ 4 = 6	24 ÷ 4 = 6
6 × 5 = 30	5 × 6 = 30	30 ÷ 5 = 6	30 ÷ 6 = 5
6 × 6 = 36	6 × 6 = 36	36 ÷ 6 = 6	36 ÷ 6 = 6
6 × 7 = 42	7 × 6 = 42	42 ÷ 7 = 6	42 ÷ 6 = 7
6 × 8 = 48	8 × 6 = 48	48 ÷ 8 = 6	48 ÷ 6 = 8
6 × 9 = 54	9 × 6 = 54	54 ÷ 9 = 6	54 ÷ 6 = 9
6 × 10 = 60	10 × 6 = 60	60 ÷ 10 = 6	60 ÷ 6 = 10

   Each card in a set of 'Four' shows a different form of each multiplication/division relationship. The cards are shuffled and each player is dealt four cards. The remaining cards are placed face down in a pile on the table. The children play in turns, trying to collect sets of four. When a set of four is made, it is shown to the others and placed on the table (figure 10.11). The next top four cards on the pile may be taken to replace them. If a player cannot put down a set, he or she can discard one of his/her cards by placing it on a discard pile and taking the discard card on view or the next top card. The winner is the first to form a chosen number of sets of four. Other cards can be designed based on different multiplication 'tables' or a mixture used as appropriate.

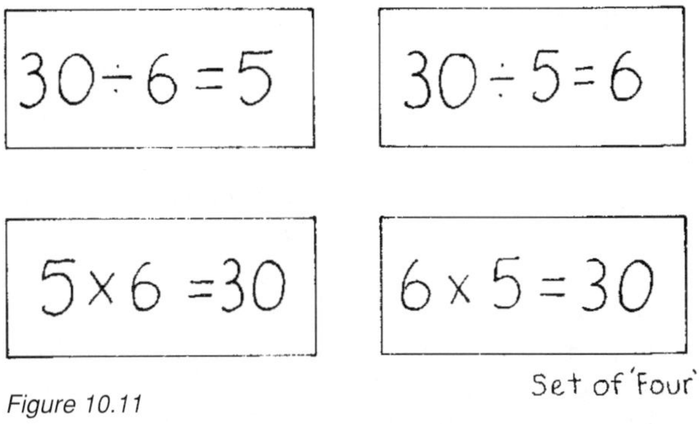

   $$\boxed{30 \div 6 = 5} \quad \boxed{30 \div 5 = 6}$$
   $$\boxed{5 \times 6 = 30} \quad \boxed{6 \times 5 = 30}$$

   Figure 10.11   Set of 'Four'

3. Have the children consider a problem such as 'I have 25 marbles to share between two people. How many does each person get?' Get the children to model the situation and consider what to do with the spare marble. Change the situation to one of, say, apples, where 25 apples need to be shared between two people. What can happen to the spare apple? Challenge the children by considering both sharing situations practically. Get the children to see how their calculators will respond. Repeat with other sentences, introducing fractional parts where appropriate.

4. Have the children use their calculators to investigate the sharing number sentences in the range 3 ÷ 3, 4 ÷ 3, 5 ÷ 3, 6 ÷ 3 … 29 ÷ 3, 30 ÷ 3. The children should record on part of a 1–100 square which numbers give a 'simple' answer. Explain to the children that these 'simple' answers are whole numbers and that the others are whole numbers and part (a bit!) of a whole number. Can the children recognise which numbers give simple answers? Let the children repeat the investigations for other divisors from within the range of multiplication tables they are comfortable with. Ask them to generalise about how they can decide if a number can be 'divided' exactly by another number. Copymasters 10.4 and 10.5 can be used for further practice.

5. Play 'Find the Hidden Number'. Tell the children that you have hidden a number in their calculator and that it is 6, 7, 8 or 9. To do this press ⑥ (or ⑦ or ⑧ or ⑨) ÷ ÷ = ⓪ =. This will show a 0 in the display. (Some calculators may vary in the way a number can be 'hidden'. You will need to consult the

maker's instructions.) Tell the children they have to try to find the number by putting a number in the calculator and pressing =. The calculator will then 'divide' by the hidden number and they are to try and estimate as quickly as possible what the hidden number is. You may wish to restrict the numbers which they can try initially. However, once the children are able to tell from the display whether a number has been 'divided' exactly or not, they will be able to try any number. You will need to discuss with the children what they need to record to help them remember the numbers they have tried and what the output tells them.

6. Let the children play 'Any Left Overs?' (Activity Card 10.4). The two sets of cards are shuffled separately and placed face down in two piles on the table. The children then take it in turns to pick up two cards, one from each set (figure 10.12). When they pick up the cards they have to say if they think there will be a remainder when the sentence is completed. The other player checks using a calculator. If the first player is correct, he/she keeps the pair of cards. If not, the cards are returned to the bottom of the piles on the table. The cards can also be spread on the table as in a memory game.

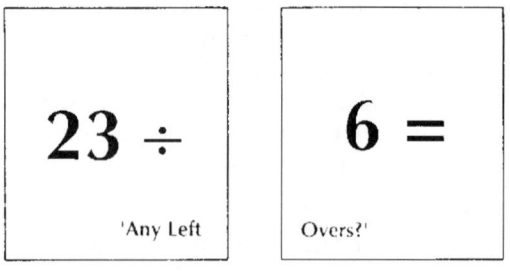

Figure 10.12

7. Copymaster 10.6 is available for further practice.

8. Encourage the children to use a full range of operations to find 'other ways of writing' a number (figure 10.13).

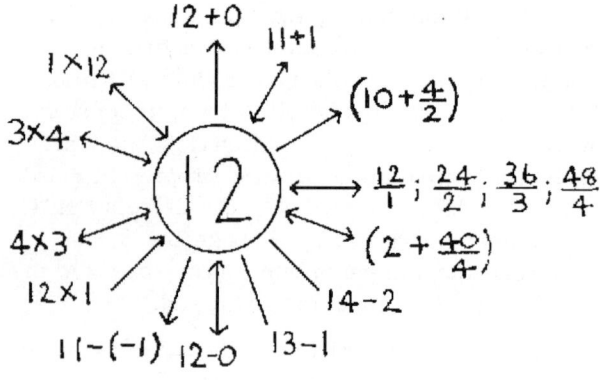

Figure 10.13

Check-ups

1. Can the children illustrate an 'equal sharing' and an 'equal grouping' activity with materials?

2. Can the children record an 'equal sharing' or an 'equal grouping' activity such as 6 ÷ 2 = 3 in terms of multiplication and repeated 'take away'?

3. Can the children recall and use the 'equal sharing' and 'equal grouping' facts they have experienced in the multiplication tables?

4. Can the children write 'equal sharing' and 'equal grouping' stories from appropriate number sentences?

5. Can the children recognise situations where 'equal sharing' and 'equal grouping' do not produce a whole number result?

6. Can the children find 'equal sharing' and 'equal grouping' facts using a calculator?

7. Given a 'sharing' number sentence, can the children rearrange it to form a sentence for multiplication?

8. Can the children replace two functions with a single function?

9. Do the children understand the inverse relationship between '÷' and '×'?

Section 11

AT 1 3a, 3b, 3c, 3d. AT 2 3c, 3e, 4e. AT 3 2b. AT 4 4d, 5d.

Pages 52–53 Measurement: Area

Pages 52 and 53 The Classroom Floor

Purpose

To introduce the square metre as a unit of area.
To give the children experience of measuring area using square metres.
To give the children practice in making simple scale drawings.

Recommended material

1. A number of square metres made from newspapers, etc.
2. Metre sticks.
3. Squared paper.
4. **Copymaster 11.1**.
5. A collection of clothes (e.g. skirts and trousers) in different sizes and styles.

Pre-page activities

Note The square metre is quite a large unit. Nevertheless it is important that displays involving this unit are mounted in the classroom, and other areas around the school. In the Pupil's Book it is suggested that a plan of a classroom floor is made on squared paper, letting one square represent one square metre. Teachers should encourage the children to make similar scale plans where appropriate, again using one square to represent a square metre.

1. Remind the children how they used square centimetres to find the surface area of different surfaces. Mention some surfaces with larger areas and discuss the need to have a larger unit than the square centimetre. Introduce the square metre. Make one out of some newspaper. Let the children see how each side of the square is 1 metre in length. Take great care in making this first unit, so that it can become the class standard unit and can be displayed alongside a square centimetre. Draw the children's attention to the fact that the sides must all be a metre in length, and that the angles are right angles. Have the children use metre sticks, cellotape and newspapers to make their own square metres. Have them compare their units with the class standard. Discuss with them just how accurate they have made them. Are the sides equal and a metre in length, and are the angles right angles? Remember that measurement is approximate, but set a certain acceptability level when checking against the class standard. Let the children use their square metres to find surfaces which are less than a square metre, about the same as a square metre, and greater than a square metre.

2. Ask the children to take a square metre and cut it up into different shapes, and then reform it into another shape. Let them see that, by using all the square metre, the new shape will still cover 1 square metre.

3. Let the children make a tangram out of a square metre (figure 11.1). Encourage them to use their tangrams to make shapes which are all 1 square metre in area.

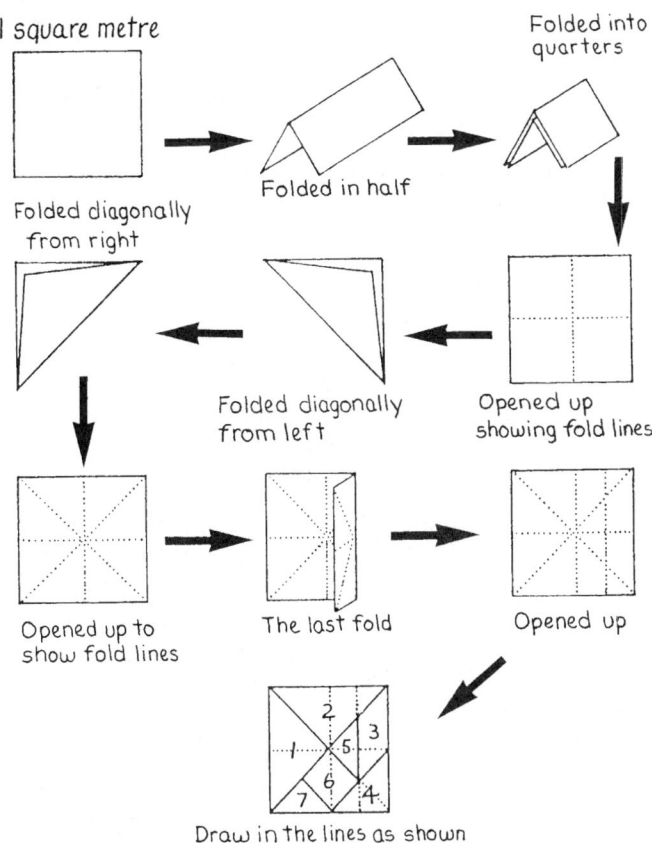

Figure 11.1

4. Provide the children with a square metre and get them to fold it into fractions as shown in figure 11.2. Discuss the link with earlier experiences of the fraction $\frac{1}{2}$, recalling that this involves 'one set partitioned into two parts', e.g. 'a square metre can be cut into two equal parts and each part covers half a square metre'. Discuss the other fractions in a similar way, even the very small ones!

New Curriculum Mathematics for Schools Key Stage 2

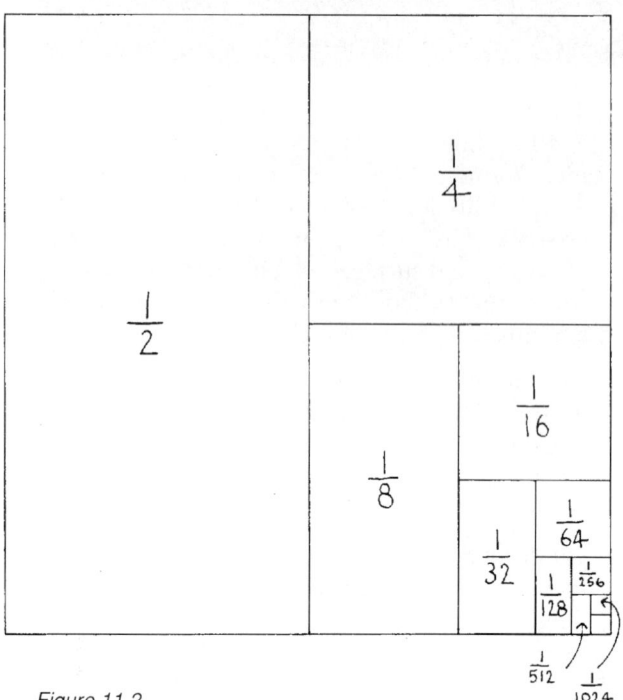

Figure 11.2

floor area on squared paper and can then find the area by:

(a) counting the squares;
(b) 'having a go' at finding the product using previous knowledge (see also page 41 of the Pupils' Book);
(c) recognising that the problem is a multiplication situation and using a calculator to find the product.

Discuss with the children how to make a plan of the room on squared paper. Make sure they realise that one of the squares on the paper represents one square metre on the classroom floor. Emphasise that the number of squares down one side of the room gives the length of the room in metres, and that a metre stick could also be used to indicate how many squares they could fit into the row and, indeed, how many rows there are. When measuring rooms in your school, be prepared to deal with 'bits' of area, and hence fractions. Make sure the children are aware of simple fractions of a square metre (see Pre-page activity 4). Copymaster 11.1 is available for further practice.

5. Have the children find different ways of cutting a square metre into four equal parts.

6. Encourage the children to devise a way of cutting a square metre into ten equal parts. Allow them to practise on smaller squares. Get them to explain to you why they think the parts are equal.

7. A number of the above activities have asked the children to make parts of a square metre. Now let the children use these parts to make a display of, for example, areas which are about half a square metre, etc.

8. Let the children find out how many copies of their mathematics book will cover about a square metre. Encourage them to use other similar objects to fit into their square metre. Have the children record their findings as '15 of the mathematics books cover about one square metre', etc.

9. Devise an experiment to find how many children can stand in a square metre. Have the children cut out a pair of 'footprints' for each child and stick them inside a square metre model.

Further activities

1. Make a collection of some different sizes and styles of skirts and trousers (figure 11.3). Ask the children to find the area in square metres of the material required to make the garments. Have them compare the area of the material as the size increases. Does the cost increase in proportion as the amount of material increases?

Figure 11.3

2. Get the children to make a copy of the shape of their own outline and find its area. They could find the area of their shadow at different times on a sunny day (figure 11.4).

Figure 11.4

Key page points

Pages 52 and 53   These pages show Sue and Gwen discussing how to measure the area of the classroom floor without moving the furniture. Discuss the pictures with the children and make sure they understand why Sue and Gwen have worked out the number of squares in a row and how many rows there are. Sue makes a plan of the

Section 11

Newspaper Survey

Sport Advertisements News

Figure 11.5

3. Have the children compare the amount of surface area of paper in a number of daily newspapers. Get them to join together all the sheets of a newspaper and then mark it off in square metre units. Display the findings. Newspapers from other countries would make an interesting comparison.

4. Extend the newspaper survey in activity 3 above to find what area of a paper is devoted to news, sport, advertising, etc. Have the children cut up a two identical newspapers (two because they will need to consider both sides of each page), and paste them on separate square metre sheets (figure 11.5). Ask the children to estimate the area devoted to each selected topic in terms of square metres and fractions of a square metre (see figure 11.2).

5. On a visit to the park or woods, get the children to estimate and then measure the areas covered by the fallen leaves of different trees such as fir, oak, beech, chestnut and pine (figure 11.6). From the measurements the children may be able to order the trees according to ground coverage.

6. Discuss with the children how they might find the area of surfaces such as games courts, which are perhaps marked on their playground, using a metre stick. Have them carry out the activity and then write about it, saying what the area of the surface is.

7. Make careful arrangements for the children to find out how much space a car occupies in the school car park. Have the children find a number of areas for different cars, and see if they can say what a typical area would be for a particular car, or for cars in general. Encourage the children to design a simple car park for their school, using squared paper for a scale drawing.

8. Ask the children to make a list, for display, of all the occasions they can find where square metres are used in everyday life.

9. Have the children find the dimensions of the goals in hockey, ice hockey, soccer, five-a-side soccer and shinty, and draw a scale drawing of them on squared paper. Get them to work out the area the goalkeepers have to defend.

10. Find a map of your locality which is covered by a one kilometre grid. Have the children study the map to see what part of their town covers a square kilometre.

Check-ups

1. Can the children estimate the size of a surface with an area of about 1 square metre?

2. Can the children use square metres to find the area of a reasonably sized room?

3. Can the children make a scale drawing of a rectangular room using squared paper?

4. Can the children find the area of a rectangle?

Figure 11.6

New Curriculum Mathematics for Schools Key Stage 2

Section 12

AT 1 3a, 3c, 3d. AT 3 2b, 3a, 4a.

Pages 54–55 Pattern

Page 54 Puzzle Patterns

Page 55 More Puzzle Patterns

Purpose

To enable children to describe, develop further and then use patterns.
To explain how patterns result when operations are applied in accordance with fixed rules that can be applied to predict members in the pattern.
To give the children practice in finding patterns from numbers arranged in order in rows and columns, e.g. patterns of multiples.
To introduce the conditions which maintain a constant difference between two numbers:
(a) the same number may be subtracted from each;
(b) the same number may be added to each.
To encourage children to look for relationships and express the relationships in words.
To provide experiences in first and second order number sequence patterns.
To encourage children to create number patterns with a calculator.

Recommended material

1. A good supply of interlocking cubes.
2. Counters.
3. Rulers marked in centimetres, and rods in lengths from 1 to 10 cm.
4. **Copymasters 12.1–12.6.**
5. Calculators.
6. Matchsticks.
7. Small balls of spheres.
8. Squared paper.
9. Calendars.

Pre-page activities

'At all ages, pupils should be encouraged to look for 'pattern' in the results they obtain and to explain this in words even though they may not be able to express in algebraic terms what they have observed.'
(*Mathematics Count*: paragraph 227)
Note In the following activities it is suggested that sequences are made with materials such as interlocking cubes and counters, etc. Teachers may feel it would help if these materials were pre- prepared and kept in 'pattern boxes', so that the children can open the box, order the sequence and perform the activity. It is important that children can make a model of a pattern from a picture and from words. The activities should therefore be varied in their presentation. Teachers should be aware that sequencing can be heavy on resources.

1. Have the children create a model for the counting numbers as shown in figure 12.1. Get them to sort the odd numbers from the even, and display the two sets as sequences. Ask them to rearrange each sequence as a staircase.

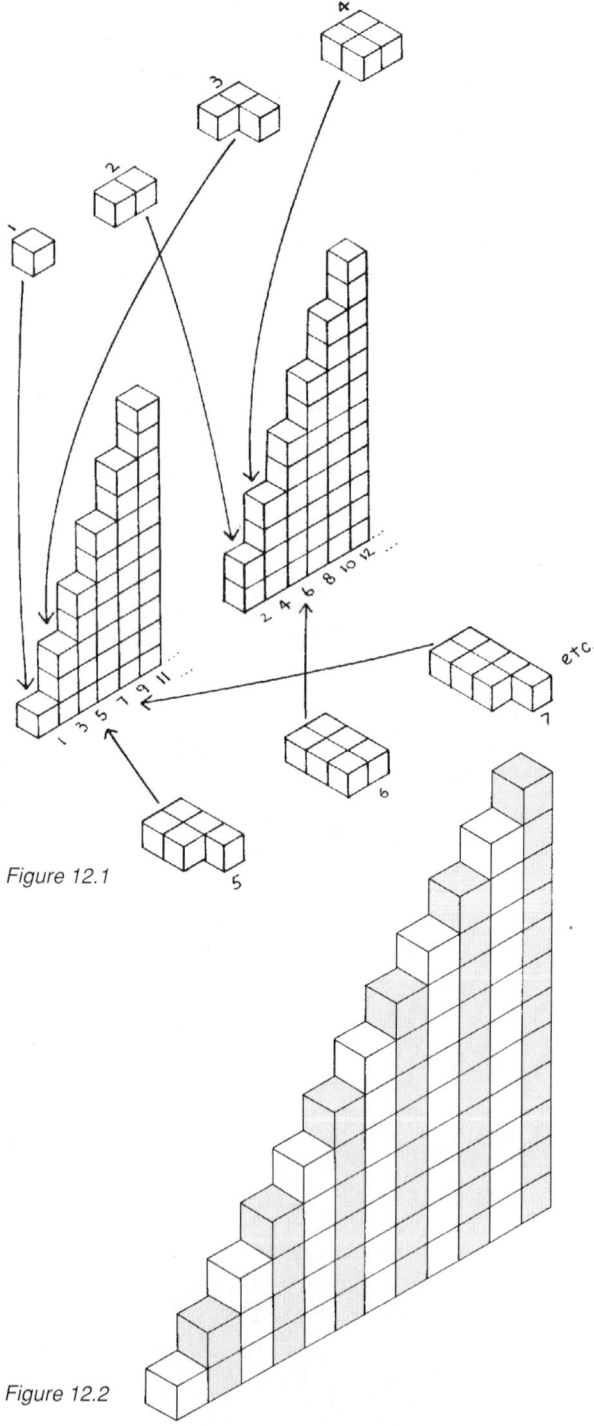

Figure 12.1

Figure 12.2

Discuss with them the slope of each staircase and show that the two can be formed into one (figure 12.2) since the slope is the same for each one. Get them to make a copy of their model on isometric paper. (Copymaster 12.1 can be used.) Have them describe the two patterns in words. Ask the children to define, then make, say, the twenty-fifth and twenty-sixth numbers in each sequence.

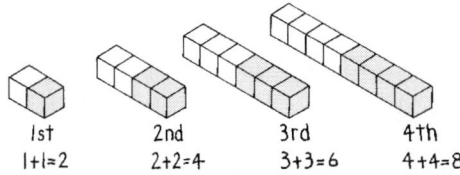

Figure 12.3

2. Use interlocking cubes in two colours, say red and blue, to create the pattern shown in figure 12.3. Ask the children to make the next two members in the sequence using their interlocking cubes, and to record the associated addition sentences. The children should be asked to write down, for example, the tenth and fifteenth number sentences in the pattern, and then make the sequence to verify their prediction. Have the children investigate other sequences, such as those shown in figures 12.4 and 12.5, in a similar way.

3. Remind the children that sequences which involve repeated addition of the 'quantity' will produce first 'multiplication tables' patterns (figure 12.6). Have the children make models of such sequences with interlocking cubes, and display them side by side (see figure 12.7).

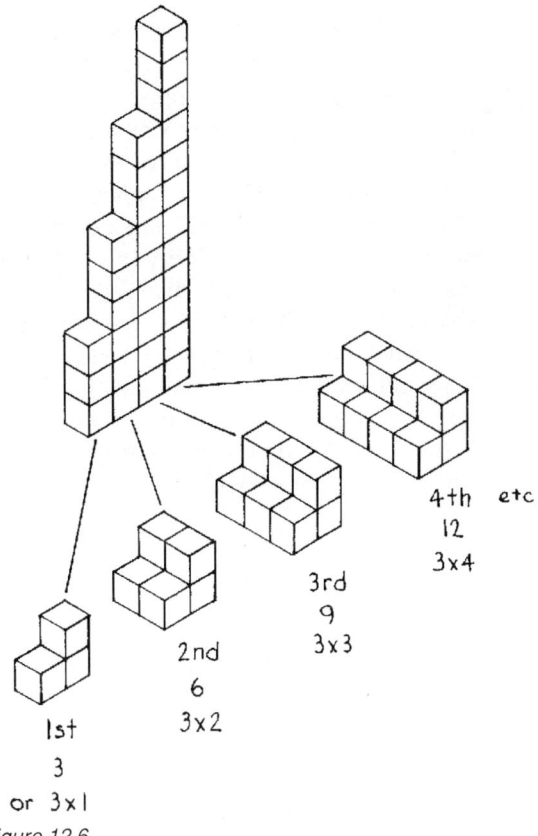

Figure 12.6

4. Lay out some counters (or draw small circles on the chalkboard) arranged as for the first pattern on Copymaster 12.2. Discuss the number of circles in each row and assess the children's facility with their table facts. Relate the separated counters or circles to the array on the copymaster. Have the children complete the copymaster.

5. Write some number sentence patterns on the chalkboard and ask the children to complete the number sentences and continue the patterns, for example:

1 + 5 =	3 + 5 =
2 + 8 =	6 + 10 =
3 + 11 =	9 + 15 =

2 + 6 =	14 − 8 =
4 + 12 =	13 − 7 =
6 + 18 =	12 − 6 =

15 − 9 =	30 − 10 =
16 − 10 =	40 − 20 =
17 − 11 =	50 − 30 =

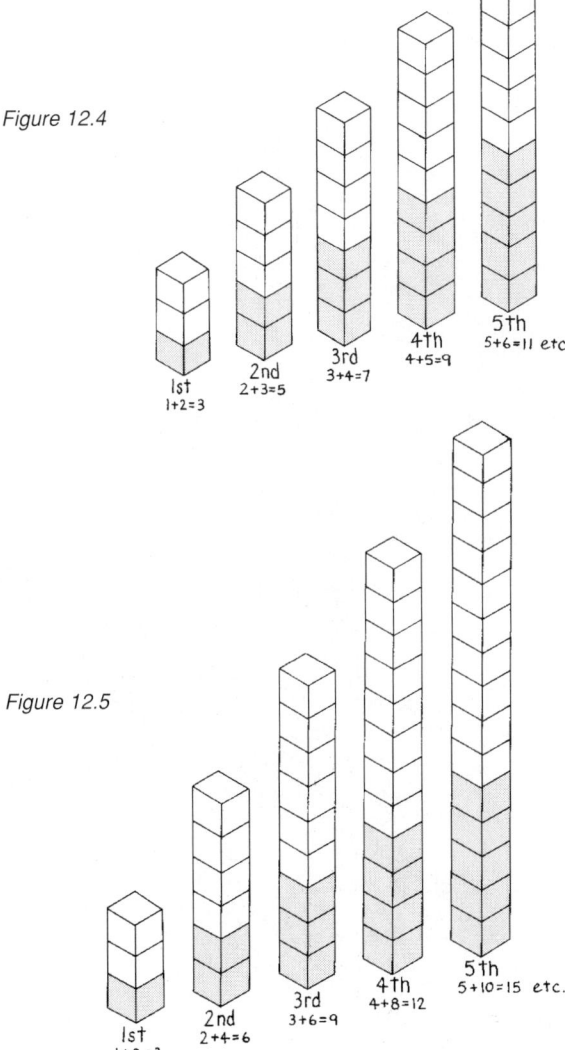

Figure 12.4

Figure 12.5

New Curriculum Mathematics for Schools Key Stage 2

27 + 18 =   91 − 67 =

37 + 28 =   81 − 57 =
47 + 38 =   71 − 47 =

The children should describe each pattern in their own words. Have them make up their own number sentence sequences and ask a friend to continue them. Encourage the children to extend their sequences to involve negative numbers.

6. Have the children investigate some of their patterns for 'first differences'. For example, in the pattern in figure 12.8, the cubes form a repeated '5' pattern. The difference between the numbers in the sequence is 5. Have the children continue the 'square number' sequence shown in figure 12.9 and make the 3-D block graph. Get the children to notice not only the 1, 4, 9, 16, 25 pattern of the 'squares', but also the 3, 5, 7, 9 pattern of the difference between each square number. Have the children also find the difference between the differences, which is a constant 2. Encourage them to find some sequences where the first difference is constant, and others where the second difference is

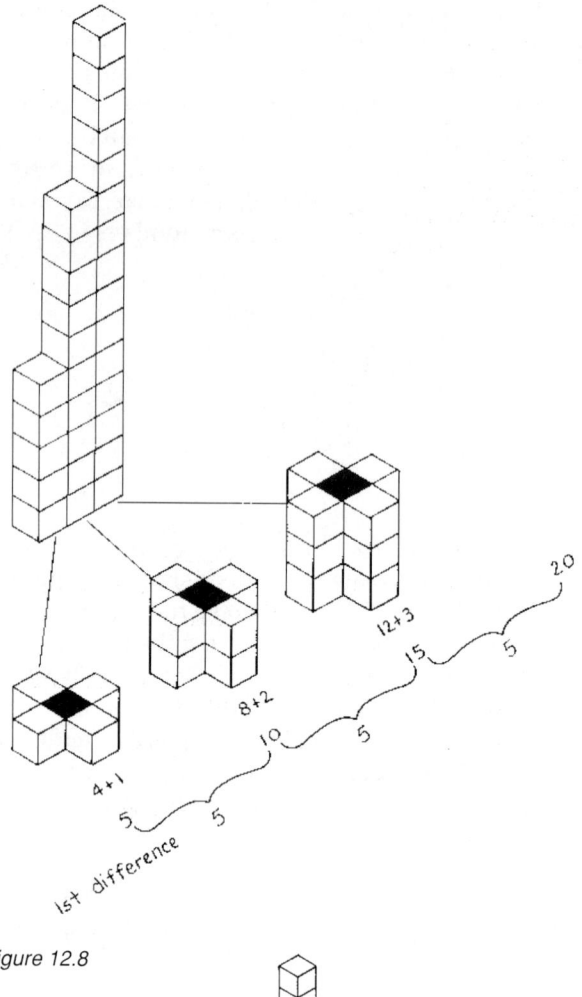

Figure 12.8

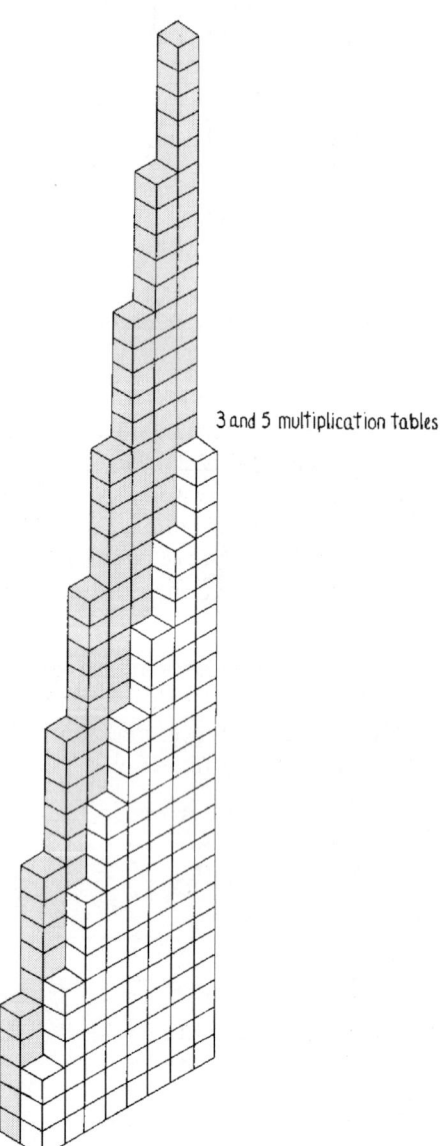

Figure 12.7

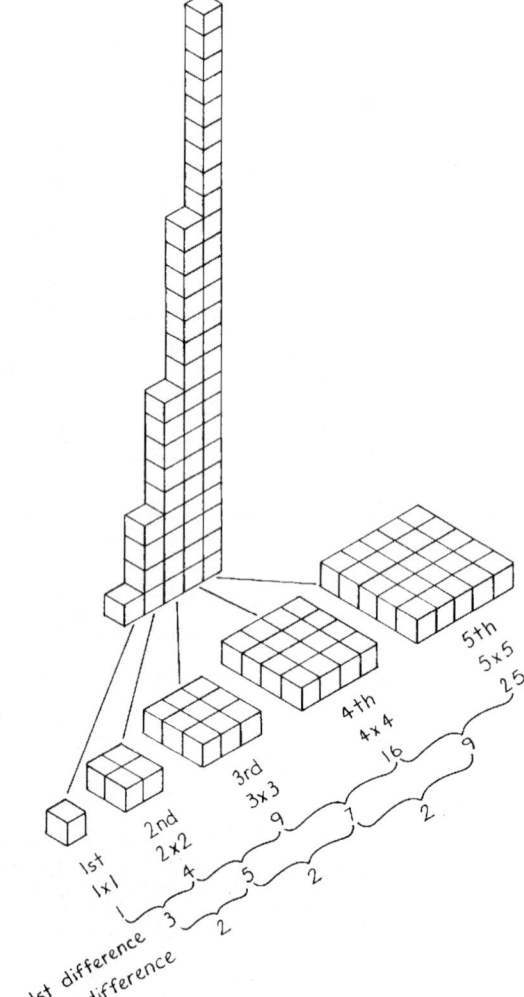

Figure 12.9

constant.

7. Give the children some counters and have them investigate ways of arranging them to form 'hexagons' (figure 12.10). Encourage the children to look for hexagonal arrays in the

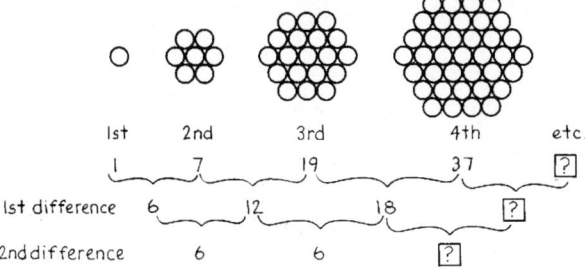

environment.

8. Present the children with some matchstick sequences, as shown in figure 12.11, to be continued. Emphasise the idea of predicting the member of the sequence and then checking by drawing, or making, that member. These patterns are first order, i.e. the differences between successive terms are constant. Counting the sticks in the second pattern produces the sequence 5, 9, 13, 17, 21, with a constant difference of 4. Other sequences can be found by counting the regions, or the vertices, in each shape. Have the children create their own matchstick sequences to investigate. Copymasters 12.3 and 12.4 are available for further practice. It is suggested that the copied sheet is attached to a blank sheet for the children to work on.

9. Let the children make some fraction patterns. Give them a sheet of squared paper and have them 'define' a fraction, say a half, and then make a sequence as shown in figure 12.12. They should record the numbers as they go. Have them repeat the experiment with other 'fractional parts'.

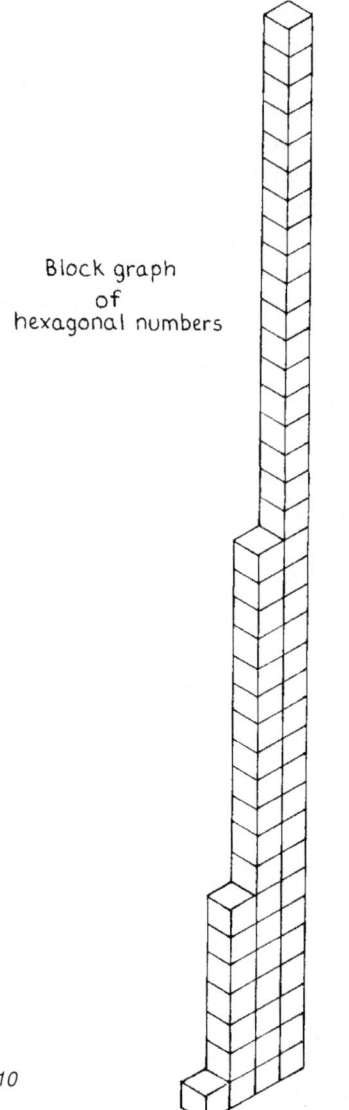

Figure 12.10

Figure 12.12

Key page points

Page 54 Let the children have coloured counters to create the patterns. Discuss with the children how the patterns could be described.

Page 55 Make sure the children understand what

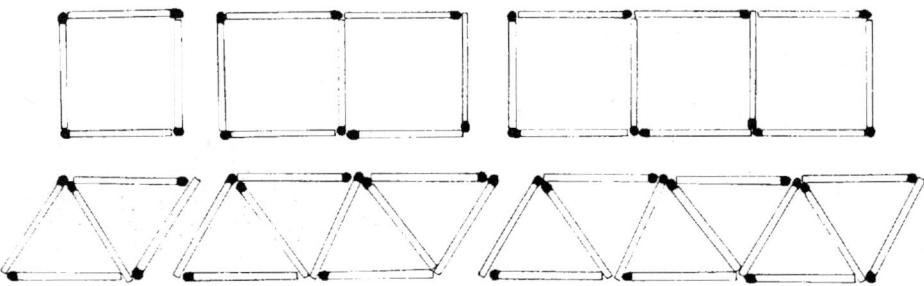

Figure 12.11

Further activities

1. Ask the children to record the first eight members of any multiplication table and study the pattern formed by the units. Let them use the discovered pattern to continue the sequence for a further eight members. For example, for multiples of 6:

   6   12   18   24   30   36   42   48
   Units digit: 6   2   8   4   0   6   2   8

   Ask the children to find out if there are any multiplication tables where the units digits do not have a similar repetitive pattern.

2. Give the children 125 unit cubes and have them try to make a single larger cube. Repeat with 64, 27 and 8 cubes. Have them arrange their cubes in order of size, using a single cube as the smallest. Ask the children to investigate the pattern, examining the first difference, etc. For example:

   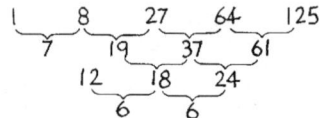

   Have the children say how many unit cubes are needed for the seventh and eighth cubes in the pattern.

3. Give the children a month from a calendar and ask them to look for patterns. For example, given August 1993 they might find:

   (a) +7 patterns going from Sunday Week 1 to Sunday Week 2, to Sunday Week 3, etc.
   (b) +8 patterns going from Monday Week 1 to Tuesday Week 2, to Wednesday Week 3, to Thursday Week 4.
   (c) other addition patterns such as +9, +10, +14.

   Have the children examine relationships within the dates in figure 12.13. They should test whether the relationship is true for other dates, then try to find a reason for the relationship.

4. Draw a large four-column numbered array on the chalkboard (or project one from an overhead projector). Draw a 2 by 2 square, as shown in figure 12.14a, and explain that you are going to make a rule for choosing numbers to add. Choose the numbers diagonally and ask the children what they notice. Try several examples, then extend the idea to rectangles, gradually increasing the complexity (figure 12.14b). In all cases add the numbers in pairs about the centre of symmetry. Introduce the latter phrase informally as the idea of the rule becomes established. Have the children investigate other rectangular arrays. Copymaster 12.5 can also be used.

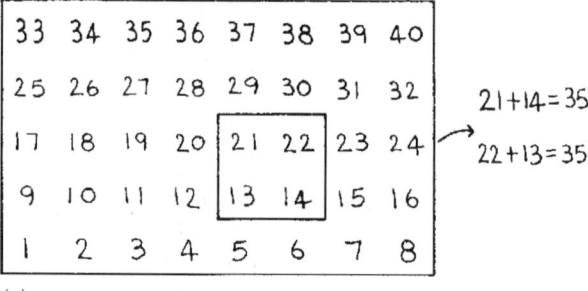

(a)

(b)

A progression of complexity for the rectangles. Pairs with the same letter add to the same sum. In the larger rectangles, other equal sums may be made from other lettered pairs. More than two numbers may also be combined to give equal sums, e.g. a, b, g and f in the last rectangle.

Figure 12.14

5. Show the children how a rule may be made for difference/take away patterns. Note that the operation must always be performed in the same parallel direction when 'taking' a smaller number from a larger one (figure 12.15).

Figure 12.13

Section 12

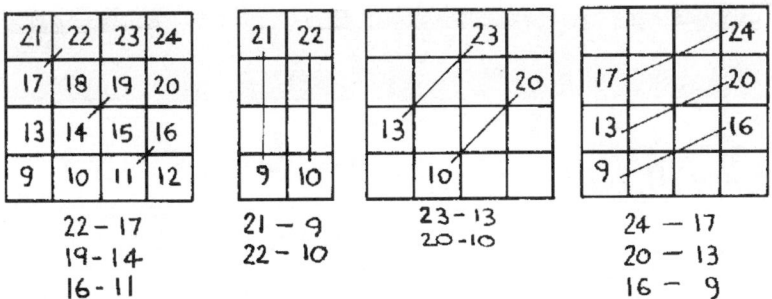

Figure 12.15

6. Introduce the pattern of constant differences between products from numbers chosen according to a rule. The rule is: multiply the numbers in the diagonal corners of identical rectangles taken from the same numbered array (figure 12.16). Copymaster 12.6 provides further practice.

7. Have the children look at sets of ordered pairs such as (2, 6) (3, 9) (4, 12) (5, 15) (6, ☐) and (1, 5) (2, 9) (3, 13) (4, 17) (5, ☐) to see if they can spot a pattern which can be expressed in 'code' form. The children who spot the relationship between each of the first and second numbers of every ordered pair will express their discovery in words such as 'the second number is the first number multiplied by three' (for the first sequence). In the second sequence, the children might say 'the second number is the first number multiplied by 4 and 1 is then added'. Have the children plot the ordered pairs on a graph and compare their findings to the work done in Section 6 for pages 28 and 29 of the Pupils' Book.

8. The Code Game can be played by two children. One child is asked to think of a code. His/her partner suggests the first number of each ordered pair, and the codemaker completes the second number in accordance with his/her code. For example, Sara suggests the first number (2) and Ann, with a code in mind, records the second number (6). Others in the sequence could be (3, 8), (4, 10), (5, 12), etc.

When the code is discovered, in this case 'multiply by 2 and then add 2', the children change roles.

9. Let the children use their calculators to produce number sequences. Give them the first three members of a pattern and ask them to continue it, using the calculator as a function machine. For example, to continue the pattern 3, 8, 13, …, which is an 'add 5' pattern, enter [0] [+] [+] [5] [=] into the calculator. Key in [3] [=] [=], etc., and the numbers in the sequence will appear on the display. Have the children explore sequences such as: 92, 79, 66, …. The children should also be allowed to set up their calculators as function machines to produce their own patterns, and get their friends to predict the next three numbers. Let the children verify the predictions.

10. Have the children investigate some 'cannonball' clusters. Some are piled in triangular-based pyramids, while others are in square-based pyramids. Have the children use spheres to model these sequences. They will have to devise a method to stop them rolling! Encourage them to explore the sequences and to make a block graph with their interlocking cubes. Get them to compare the steepness of the slope of these models with some of the others they have made.

Check-ups

1. Can the children describe how a pattern is created and then continue the pattern?

2. Can the children continue a number sequence where the first differences between members are constant?

3. Can the children continue a number sequence where the second differences are constant?

4. Can the children continue patterns using a calculator?

5. Can the children model a sequence with materials, and describe how the model illustrates the pattern?

6. Can the children draw a graph of a sequence and make a mathematical comment about the relationship illustrated?

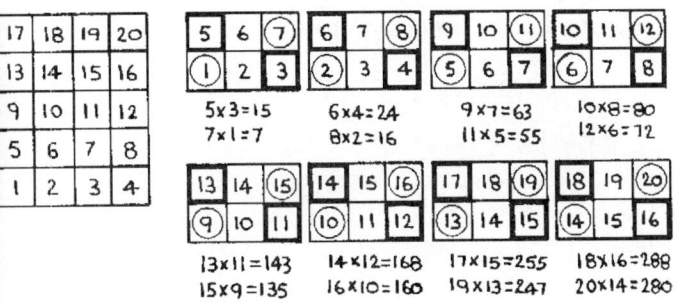

Equal differences between products of numbers in opposite corners of identically shaped rectangles. In this example the difference is 8.

Figure 12.16

New Curriculum Mathematics for Schools Key Stage 2

Section 13

AT 1 3a, 3b, 3c, 3d. AT 2 3a, 3d, 4a, 4b. AT 3 2b, 3a, 4a. AT 5 3b.

Pages 56–63 Difference (H.T.U.)

Pages 56–59 A Petrol Survey
Page 60 What's the Difference?
Page 61 Card Games
Page 62 Weighing in the Kitchen
Page 63 Fly Away

Purpose

To promote understanding and proficiency in 'finding the difference' between two three-digit numbers.
To introduce situations involving the comparison of numbers made up of hundreds, tens and units.
To give children practice in modelling the process of comparison of numbers involving hundreds, tens and units.
To put the addition and comparison of three-digit numbers in the physical context of mass/weight.
To give children the opportunity to develop an algorithm for the addition of three-digit numbers.

Recommended material

1. Structural apparatus: Multibase materials (base 10) and interlocking cubes.
2. Hundreds, tens and units counting boards and counters.
3. Difference Algorithm Cards (**Activity Cards 13.1–13.4**).
4. Cards for games (see Pre-page activity 8 and Further activities 2, 11 and 14).
5. Calculators.
6. Balance scales with standard masses, measuring down to 1 gram if possible.
7. Sand, pebbles, etc., for weighing.
8. Various containers and bags.
9. Commercial products on which the weights are marked in grams.
10. Compression balances capable of showing as near to 1 gram as possible.
11. Cubes for making dice.
12. 'Nearly' Difference Triples (**Activity Card 13.5**).
13. **Copymaster 13.1**.
14. A stopwatch.
15. Spinners and overlays.
16. Blank golf scorecards.

Pre-page activities

See the note at the start of the activities in Section 5 for details about the approach to computation work used in this series. In this section, our models of 'subtraction' are built by comparing sets and using the base 10 structure of the number system in exchange experiences. The notes and figures which follow here are presented in the traditional format, moving from no exchange to exchange involving both tens and units. Teachers are strongly recommended to read the section as a whole before planning their programme. Whatever order of presentation is chosen, a variety of materials should be used. In the following illustrations base 10 materials are used, along with counting boards and coins. Teachers will wish to 'mix and match', and consider the use of other materials as necessary.

1. Present the children with a situation where you have to use materials to represent the items being considered, selecting numbers which do not involve exchange in the process, for example: 'On the school open day 286 people visited in the morning and 143 visited in the afternoon. How many more visited in the

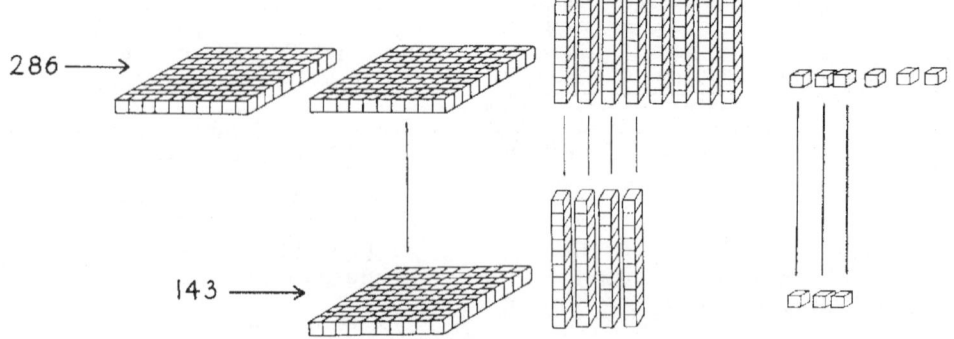

Figure 13.1

'The difference is 143'.

morning than in the afternoon?' The number of people in the morning can be modelled as two '100' pieces, eight '10' strips and six cubes, and the number in the afternoon as a '100' piece, four '10' pieces and three cubes. Once the model has been established, the children can use a problem solving approach to find the difference. They can match the cubes, the '10' strips and the '100' pieces because they all represent people (figure 13.1). Get the children to record the mathematics as they go:

$$\begin{array}{r}286\\-143\end{array} \xrightarrow{\text{can be written as}} \begin{array}{r}(200+80+6)\\-(100+40+3)\\\hline 100+40+3\end{array} \longrightarrow 143$$

Make sure the children see that 143 is a reasonable result since 286 is nearly 300, and 143 is nearly 150, so the result should be nearly 150 as well!

2. Suggest a situation where children will have to exchange a 'ten' in solving the problem, for example: 'If a shop sold 127 cans of Fizz and 352 cans of Pop on one day, how many more cans of Pop than Fizz were sold?' Have the children model the situation, comparing the regrouping as necessary (figure 13.2). Again, get the children to record the mathematics:

$$\begin{array}{r}352\\-127\end{array} \xrightarrow{\text{can be written as}} \begin{array}{r}(300+50+2)\\-(100+20+7)\end{array} \longrightarrow \begin{array}{r}(300+40+12)\\-(100+20+7)\\\hline 200+20+5\end{array}$$
$$\longrightarrow 225$$

Have the children say whether the result looks 'about right', and why it could not be greater than 300 or, indeed, less than 100.

4. Invent a situation where finding the difference involves exchanging a '100' piece for ten '10' strips, for example: 'In a one-day international cricket match, India scored 428 and the West Indies scored 163. Who won and by how many?' Again, have the children model the situation, comparing the sets and regrouping as necessary (figure 13.3). Make sure the children record the mathematics as before:

$$\begin{array}{r}428\\-163\end{array} \xrightarrow{\text{can be written as}} \begin{array}{r}(400+20+8)\\-(100+60+3)\end{array} \longrightarrow \begin{array}{r}(300+120+8)\\-(100+60+3)\\\hline 200+60+5\end{array}$$
$$\longrightarrow 265$$

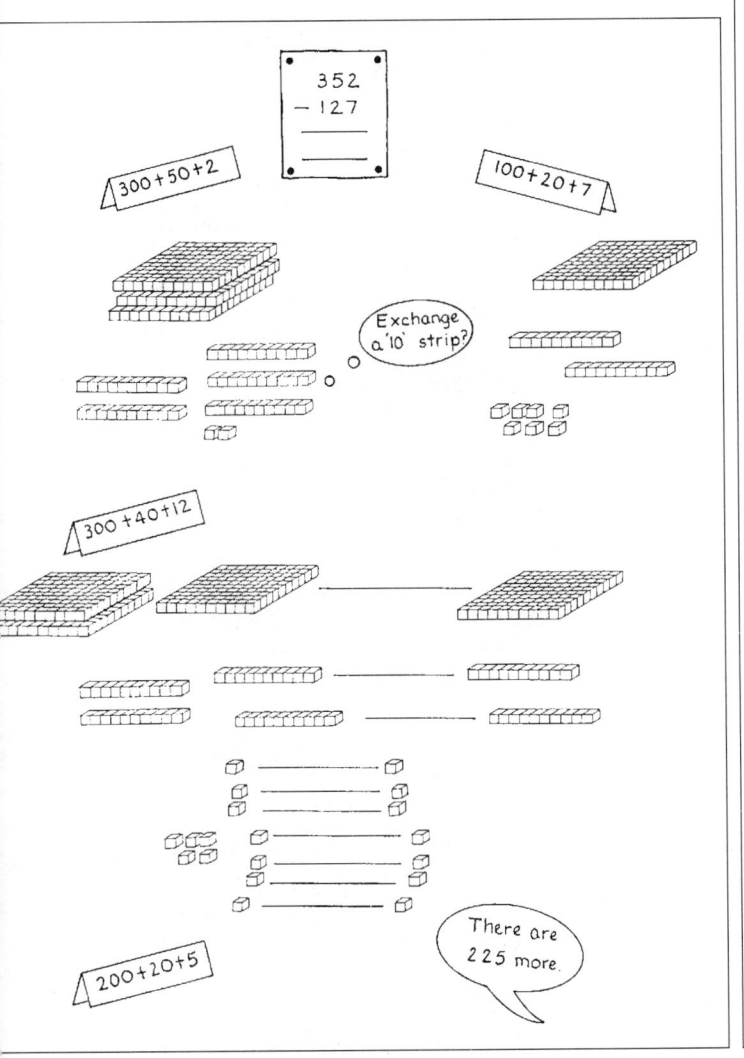

Figure 13.2

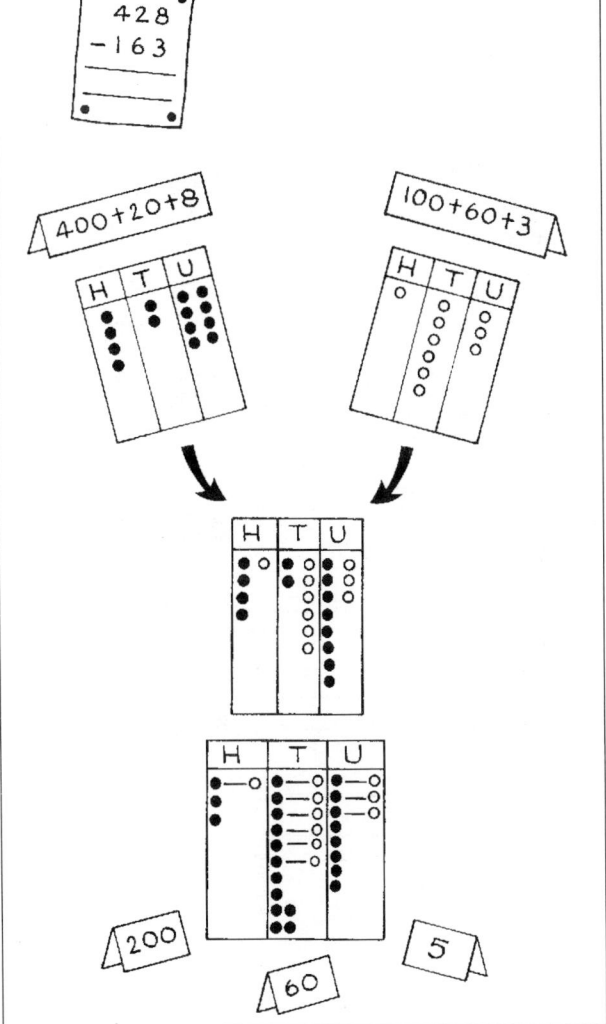

Figure 13.3

Have the children say if this is a reasonable result, and why.

5. Repeat the above activities with situations which involve exchanging a '10' strip for ten cubes, and a '100' piece for ten '10' strips, for example: 'In her Saturday job at the supermarket, Hannah's sister stacked 327 packets of Flakes and 158 packets of Bran. How many more packets of Flakes than Bran did she stack?' (figure 13.4). This time the children can record their actions as:

$$\begin{array}{r} 327 \\ -158 \\ \hline \end{array} \xrightarrow{\text{can be written as}} \begin{array}{r} (300 + 20 + 7) \\ -(100 + 50 + 8) \\ \hline \end{array} \longrightarrow \begin{array}{r} (300 + 10 + 17) \\ -(100 + 50 + 8) \\ \hline \end{array}$$

$$\longrightarrow \begin{array}{r} (200 + 110 + 17) \\ -(100 + 50 + 8) \\ \hline 100 + 60 + 9 \end{array} \longrightarrow 169$$

or if tens are exchanged first:

$$\begin{array}{r} 327 \\ -158 \\ \hline \end{array} \xrightarrow{\text{can be written as}} \begin{array}{r} (300 + 20 + 7) \\ -(100 + 50 + 8) \\ \hline \end{array} \longrightarrow \begin{array}{r} (200 + 120 + 7) \\ -(100 + 50 + 8) \\ \hline \end{array}$$

$$\longrightarrow \begin{array}{r} (200 + 110 + 17) \\ -(100 + 50 + 8) \\ \hline 100 + 60 + 9 \end{array} \longrightarrow 169$$

Have the children say why they think the result is reasonable.

6. Activity Cards 13.1–13.4 can be used by the children to make flowcharts showing the solutions to given problems. There are three sets of cards. Each set depicts a problem and a possible solution modelled with both base 10 materials and counters and a counting board. Have the children discuss the situations on these cards, put them in order (figure 13.5) and complete the recording as suggested. Have the children say if they can find another way to perform the operations required to solve the problems on the cards. These cards should not be used until the children have actually modelled similar situations with cubes or counters.

Figure 13.4

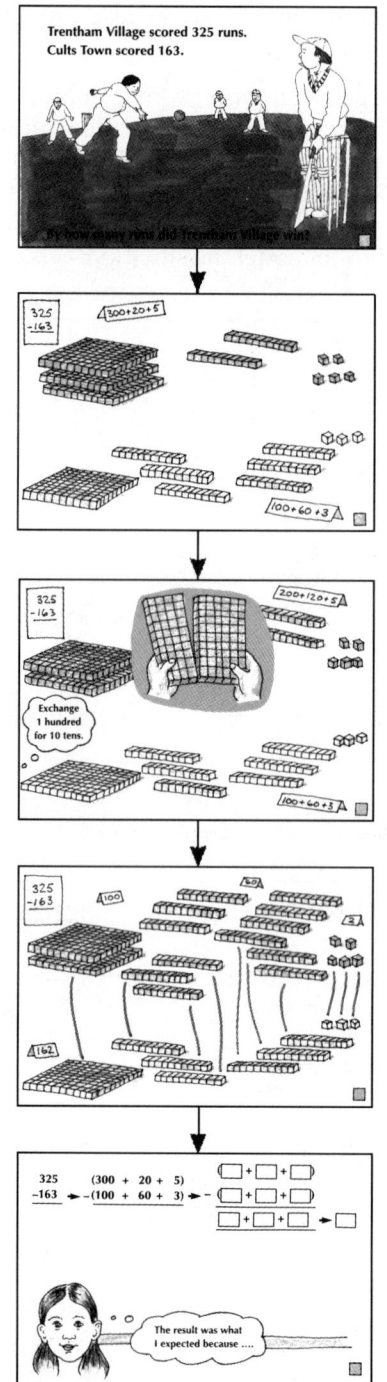

Figure 13.5

7. Write sentences such as 427 − 135 = ☐ on the chalkboard. Ask the children to write both difference and comparison stories for the sentences.

8. Make and play Difference Pairs. Write incomplete difference/comparison sentences involving multiples of one hundred (400 − 100 = ☐, 900 − 200 = ☐, 800 − 300 = ☐, etc.) on a set of, say, red cards, and on a set of blue cards write the differences (300, 700, 500, etc.). Have the children play a game of trying to collect matching pairs. The game can be repeated but with difference sentences involving multiples of ten (460 − 130 = ☐, 890 − 270 = ☐, 320 − 180 = ☐, etc.). As a variation, have the children describe a situation for their pair before retaining it.

9. Let the children use their calculators to find differences between three-digit numbers. Have them try various ways of finding the differences, e.g.

   | 3 | 4 | 6 | − | 1 | 5 | 8 | = |

   | 3 | 4 | 6 | − | 1 | 0 | 0 | − | 5 | 0 | − | 8 | = |

   | 3 | 4 | 6 | − | 1 | 6 | 0 | + | 2 | = |

   | 3 | 4 | 6 | M+ | 1 | 5 | 8 | M− | MR |

10. Suggest to the children that they find the difference of two numbers such as 479 and 734 by counting on, e.g.

    $479 \xrightarrow{+1} 480 \xrightarrow{+20} 500 \xrightarrow{+34} 534 \xrightarrow{+200} 734.$

    The difference is 1 + 20 + 34 + 200 = 255. Give the children other differences to find in this way.

11. Write some difference sentences such as 821 − 319 = ☐ on the chalkboard and ask the children to estimate the result by saying which multiple of 100 the difference is nearest to, i.e. 821 − 319 is nearly 500.

12. Prepare two bags of sand, one weighing 50 grams, the other weighing 150 grams. Ask children from the group to weigh both bags separately and record the weights on the chalkboard. Ask the children what weight they will need to balance the scales if both bags are placed on one pan. Encourage them to consider which arithmetic operation can be used to find the total. Have them find the weight practically to check the calculation. Repeat using other bags of sand, made to balance with exact multiples of ten at first. Suggest some activities where the bags of sand are placed on different pans. Ask the children to work out what extra weight will be needed to balance the bags. Have them relate this to finding the difference between the two bags. Encourage the children to record the calculation in a way which matches the action. Repeat the activity with pebbles, or commercial products, etc. An important aspect of this activity is the modelling of the operation using place value apparatus, leading on to calculations on paper. You may wish to combine the mathematics with an activity based on the decoration of pebbles found by the children (see Section 5, Further activity 9).

13. Weigh an empty container, then weigh the container filled with sand. Discuss the calculation which will find the weight of the sand only. You may wish to connect the calculation with the idea of taking away a part of a quantity. Show the children how to obtain feedback on their calculations by weighing the sand on its own. Repeat using other granular material, and with water if the scales are suitable. In later work in science, this method can be used for finding the weight, and hence the volume, of water in a container.

14. Have the children weigh a number of groceries and find the difference, if any, between the total weight and the weight listed on the container. For example, they may be able to find a selection similar to the following:

Item	Total weight	Weight of contents
Mincemeat	575 g	411 g
Jam (large)	575 g	340 g
Jam (small)	280 g	100 g
Coffee	400 g	100 g
Soup	525 g	435 g
Chilli beans	525 g	425 g
Tinned vegetables	325 g	283 g
Muesli	375 g	375 g
Shredded wheat	535 g	500 g
Washing powder	850 g	690 g

Have the children model their weighings, partitioning the total so that they 'see' the contents within the package. For example, having weighed a large jar of jam as above, they can display the total weight as 575 g and partition the base 10 materials to show how the contents represent part of the whole (figure 13.6).

In the above situation no exchanging is required. Other situations may well require exchanging, as outlined in previous activities. In all the weighing activities, ensure that the children appreciate the approximate nature of the weighings and the effect of this when the calculated result is compared with that found practically.

New Curriculum Mathematics for Schools Key Stage 2

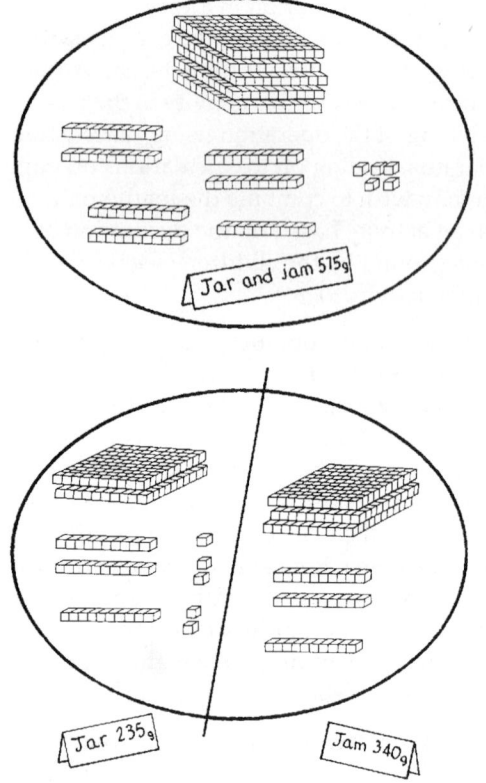

'The difference between the weight of the jar with the jam and the jam on its own is 235 grams. 575 − 340 = 235 because 340 + 235 = 575'

Figure 13.6

Key page points

Pages 56–59 Before starting these pages you might like to discuss with the children the environmental issues arising from the use of leaded and unleaded petrol. Make sure the children have structural apparatus available to recreate the models. The children may use their calculators to check the answers. Give the children a selection from the following for further practice, either after you have discussed a particular page or after you have discussed the group of pages.

After page 56 Exchange in tens only

737	806	617	512	644	708
−486	−651	−237	−351	−463	−263

516	587	604	547	643	814
−256	−394	−481	−366	−142	−352

After page 57 Exchange in both tens and units

731	410	860	643	701	441
−585	−191	−195	−297	−194	−257

835	861	320	573	611	385
−168	−577	−199	−288	−355	−196

After page 58 Exchange in units only

750	752	885	852	781	761
−511	−346	−547	−329	−139	−248

761	850	864	862	855	634
−336	−235	−226	−224	−337	−229

After page 59 No exchange

755	874	666	842	674	588
−422	−642	−211	−531	−231	−148

337	765	558	858	823	685
−123	−414	−336	−346	−611	−330

Pay particular attention to the bottom half of page 59 in any discussion: if the children fully understand the reasons for the exchange, one of the main causes of mistakes can be eliminated.

Page 60 This page should consolidate the children's experiences of finding the difference. Make sure the children have materials to set up the models in question 1. When questions 2 and 4 have been completed, record and display the children's responses. In question 4, the children should find some sentences which will help them with ways of writing 200 in question 5. When the page is finished, the children could use their calculators to check their answers.

Page 61 This page further consolidates the children's work on difference. Note that in the last 'game' in question 1, Sue would have won if she had expressed her score as 874 and not 748. (Did anyone notice?) In question 2 have the children link their answers in each row.

Page 62 To solve the problem in question 1 on this page, Kumar and Fiona need to compare the actual weight of the jar and the honey (363 g) with the weight of the honey alone (227 g). In her model Fiona thinks of the 363 g as 227 + ☐. Encourage the children to 'see' the contents within the whole quantity and record their number sentence in the form 363 − 227 = ☐ because 227 + ☐ = 363. Try not to let the children regard this as a 'take away', as it is not intended that the honey will be removed from the jar. Make sure the children have access to structural apparatus or counting boards.

Page 63 On this page the seating capacities of different aircraft are compared. Make sure the children realise they have to compare the number of seats in the aircraft with the number of passengers travelling.

Further activities

1. Make and play Difference Throw. Take three

cubes and on the faces of the first cube write the numbers 9, 8, 7, 6, 5, 4; on the second write 90, 80, 70, 60, 50, 40; and on the third write 100, 200, 300, 100, 200, 300. Each player throws all three cubes twice, recording the score each time and then finding the difference between the two scores. The child with the greatest difference is awarded points equal to the difference. The first child to reach 900 wins. The players may use counting boards to keep their scores.

2. Make and play 'Close to' Pairs. On a set of, say, blue cards write the following differences:

   412 920 798 612 801 911 693 897
   −231 −197 −192 −497 −521 −489 −211 −121

   On another set of, say, red cards write:

   is close to 100   is close to 200   is close to 300
   is close to 400   is close to 500   is close to 600
   is close to 700   is close to 800

   Shuffle the cards and spread them face down on the table. The children take it in turns to turn over a red card and a blue card. If the cards match (figure 13.7), the player keeps the pair. The winner is the player who collects the most pairs. The cards can also be used by an individual as a sorting activity.

   [412 − 231 is]   [200 close to]

   Figure 13.7

3. Play 'Nearly' Difference Triples (Activity Card 13.5).

4. Write some difference sentences such as 637 − 412 = 225 on the chalkboard. Ask the children to say how the sentence helps with other sentences such as:

   637   637   637   421
   −225   −325   −425   +225

5. Have the children make up difference/comparison stories, involving three-digit numbers, from everyday situations.

6. Write number sentences such as those shown below on the chalkboard. Ask the children to complete them and continue the pattern.

   321 − 3 =   484 − 36 =
   421 − 3 =   584 − 36 =
   521 − 3 =   684 − 36 =
   etc.   etc.

   986 − 235 =   871 − 147 =
   986 − 335 =   871 − 157 =
   986 − 435 =   871 − 167 =
   etc.   etc.

   You may find that the children extend their patterns to include negatives. If so, have them explain their sequences to you and/or their friends.

7. Ask the children to make up a three-digit number, and then make up a second one with the digits reversed, for example 862 and 268. They should then set out to find (a) the two such numbers with the greatest difference, (b) the two such numbers with the least difference.

8. Get the children to explore other methods of finding differences and have them record and discuss their methods.

9. Have the children complete 'other ways of writing' three-digit numbers, using difference sentences in the first instance (figure 13.8).

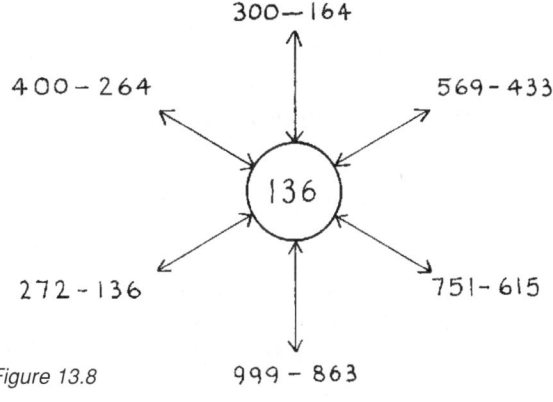

Figure 13.8

10. Play Calculator Trail, a game for two players. Prepare some calculator trails using Copymaster 13.1. Make a number of blank copies of the master and prepare a variety of trails. For example, one trail could be marked 100 → 232 → 386 → 404 → 291 → 474 → 658 → 331 → 196 → 587 → 741 → 999, and the other trail marked 100 → 265 → 497 → 264 → 425 → 694 → 858 → 401 → 574 → 714 → 581 → 856. One of the players, e.g. the younger of the two, chooses a trail, leaving the other trail for the other players. Each player places a counter on his/her start position, and a calculator is switched on and 100 entered on its display. The players take it in turns to enter a three-digit number, press a function key and then the equals key. If the display shows the next number on the trail, the player's counter can be moved up the trail. If not, a player has to wait until his/her next turn to try to get the next number on the trail. If a player accidentally presses 'clear' he/she must move his/her counter back one place and enter the

number shown on the trail. The first player to reach the end of the trail wins.

11. Make and play Match. On a set of, say, blue cards write the following difference sentences:

    648 852 704 594 824 983 611 738
    −217 −518 −196 −238 −581 −875 −234 −254

    On another set of, say, red cards write the differences:

    431 334 508 356 243 108 377 484

    Shuffle the cards and spread them face up on the table. Each child is timed trying to match the blue cards with the correct differences on the red cards. The winner is the child who completes the matching in the shortest time. Draw up a chart showing the time each child takes. The children may be given second chances to improve their times.

12. Let the children weigh objects from the nature table, or items which they have brought to school. Suggest the possibility of finding the combined weights of two or more objects. Some science experiments investigate the weights which will cause paper to tear, twigs to bens, etc. Make sure the children take the opportunity to add weights in such experiments.

13. Weighing a container full, and then empty, can be used to investigate the relative densities of powders or granular materials. The same container is used for all the weighings but it is filled with different materials for each weighing. A graph of the results can be a useful basis for discussion.

14. Make and play the Largest Difference Card Game. Prepare 30 cards with the numbers 0 to 9 on them, so that there are three of each number in the pack. You will also require a tens and units scoreboard. The game is for four players. Spread the cards face down on the table and mix them up well. Allow the children to take one card at a time until they have six cards each. The players then sort their cards into two three-digit numbers with the largest possible difference. They then take it in turns to declare their difference, and the player with the largest difference scores five points, the second player three, the third player two and the last player one. The first to reach a set total, or with the highest score after an agreed number of rounds, wins.

15. Make and play Mini Golf, a game for two. The players require a spinner marked off in equal parts and numbered 1 to 8, a scorecard from any golf course, a dice with the faces numbered 1, 1, 2, 2, 3, 3, and two counters. The Mini Golf Course as shown in figure 13.9 should also be provided on a card. To play a hole, players must first find out from the real score card if it is par 3, 4 or 5. They then put their counter on the appropriate tee. Each player spins the spinner and moves his/her counter to the number thrown which gives the distance of the tee shot. (This counts as one stroke.) If the distance is within 10 metres more or less than the length of the hole as shown on the real scorecard, the ball is deemed to be on the putting green. No calculation is required. The player rolls the dice to see how many 'putts' he/she takes. If the distance to the hole is more

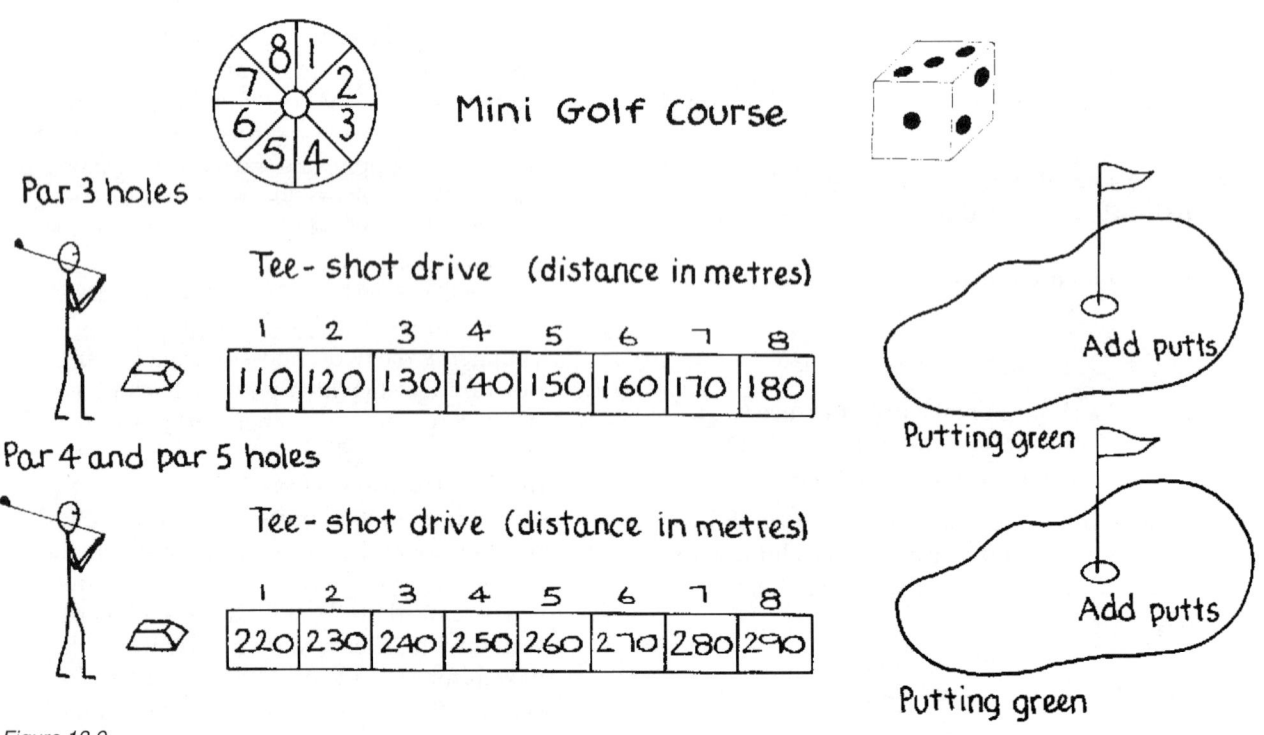

Figure 13.9

than 10 metres, a calculation is required. (The player calculates the difference between the length of the hole and the length of the drive as in figure 13.10.)

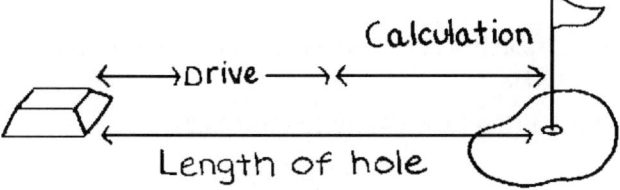

Figure 13.10

For the par 3 and par 4 holes:
if the calculation is correct, count one stroke;
if the calculation is wrong, count two strokes.

For the par 5 hole:
if the calculation is correct, count two strokes;
if the calculation is wrong, count three strokes.

Each player needs to check his/her opponent's calculation. The players now place their counters on the putting green, and each player then rolls the dice. The number thrown gives the number of putts taken. The players add the number of strokes taken to the green to the number of putts taken to obtain the score for the hole. Have them record the score on their scorecard. The players play holes 1 to 18 and find the total strokes for the 18 holes.

Sample scores:

Par 4 hole		Par 5 hole	
Drive	1 stroke	Drive	1 stroke
Calculation correct	1 stroke	Calculation correct	2 strokes
Number of putts	2 strokes	Number of putts	4 strokes
Total score	4 strokes	Total score	7 strokes

16. When the children are confident with the extended form of recording you may wish to introduce them to more streamlined ways.

Check-ups

1. Can the children recognise a difference situation involving three-digit numbers?

2. Can the children model a difference situation involving three-digit numbers and develop an algorithm?

3. Can the children understand various algorithms used to find the answers to difference problems?

4. Can the children follow a difference algorithm created by another person and make a model using materials?

New Curriculum Mathematics for Schools Key Stage 2

Section 14

AT 1 3a, 3b, 3c. AT 2 3e, 4c. AT 3 2b. AT 4 4d. AT 5 3b.

Pages 64–65 Measurement: Capacity

Page 64 Full Measure

Page 65 The Lemonade Stall

Purpose

To give children experience of finding the relationship between the size of containers.
To provide practice in working with measures less than 1 litre, and in finding halves, thirds and quarters of containers.
To give children experience of using small measures such as cupfuls, capfuls and spoonfuls.
To introduce the millilitre and cubic centimetre.
To encourage children to work out prices based on the capacity of a container and unit costs.

Recommended material

1. A selection of scientific measuring containers with litre, half litre and quarter litre as well as millilitre and cubic centimetre markings.

2. Kitchen measuring containers with graduations clearly marked showing litres, half litres, quarter litres, millilitres, cubic centimetres, fluid ounces, etc.

3. An assortment of clean safe bottles and containers, including 1 litre and 2 litre clear plastic lemonade bottles, sauce bottles, 5 ml, 10 ml, 25 ml, 50 ml and 100 ml medicine or shampoo bottles, garden fertilizer bottles, etc. Some labels may be marked in cubic centimetres.

4. Bottle caps which are used for measuring purposes.

5. Cups, eggcups and mugs (plastic or paper or otherwise).

6. Teaspoons and tablespoons.

7. Kitchen measuring spoons.

8. Set(s) of metric spoons.

9. An eyedropper.

10. A set of ten graded metric measures.

11. **Copymasters 2.1 and 14.1–14.2.**

12. A commercially produced clear plastic 10 cm cube container, complete with centimetre cubes to fit into it.

13. A plentiful supply of Centicubes.

14. A graduated litre cube.

15. Capacity Touch and Say cards (**Activity Card 14.1**).

16. Pouring Pairs (**Activity Card 14.2**).

17. Plastic container with juice extractor.

Pre-page activities

Note It is important that all containers used in this section are both safe and clean.

1. Take the labels off a set of four or five differently shaped bottles. Have the children compare them and order them by capacity. Use a scientific metric measuring container to check the predictions.

2. Design a variety of logic mats (figure 14.1) and provide the children with a range of different sized containers, asking them to place them on the mats so all the conditions hold. Include some similarly-sized containers where it is not so obvious which holds more. Consider 'holds less than' relationships as well as 'holds more than'.

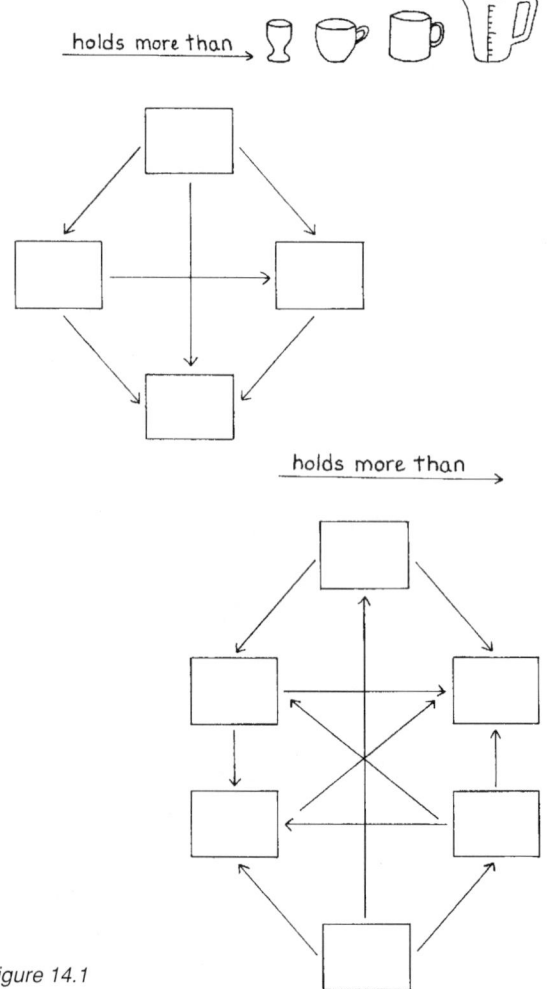

Figure 14.1

3. Provide the children with a range of containers and have them estimate and then mark the water level on the side when they are half full. Make sure the children have some straight-sided containers as well as some with sloping sides. If possible, have them seal the end and invert a container (figure 14.2). Does the water still reach the same mark? Make sure the children realise that two halves produce the whole.

Figure 14.2

4. Have the children try to find a third of a container and mark the water level on the side. Let them test their prediction. Make sure they realise that there are three thirds in the whole container (figure 14.3). Have the children experiment with a variety of shaped containers. Let them repeat the activity and try to find a quarter of a container, making sure they realise there are four quarters in the whole. Repeat again with a variety of containers.

Figure 14.3

5. Give the children some containers which hold a litre and have them find a half, a third and a quarter of each one. Ask them to use their new measures to find other containers, such as mugs and beakers, etc., which will 'just' hold a half, third or quarter of a litre. Have them demonstrate that the 'cup' they say holds a quarter of a litre needs to be filled four times to fill the litre container.

6. Provide the children with a range of containers and have them find relationships between them (figure 14.4). For example, can the children predict and verify that four half-litre containers will fill a 2 litre bottle? If a 1 litre bottle will fill four cups, how many of the same sized cup will the 2 litre bottle fill?

7. Develop some 'holds more than'/'costs more than' logic activities, as in 2 above. Provide the children with some containers of the same item but of different sizes, with clearly displayed

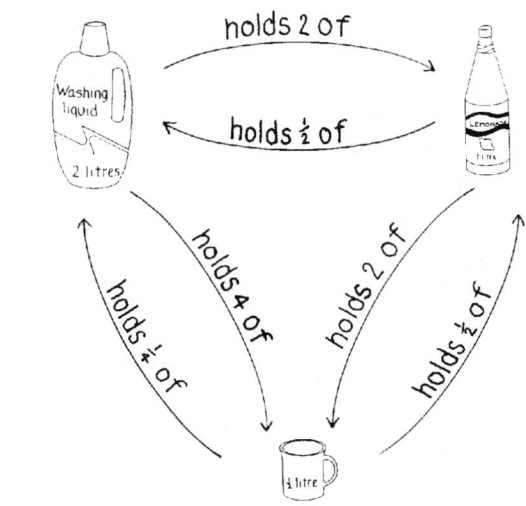

Figure 14.4

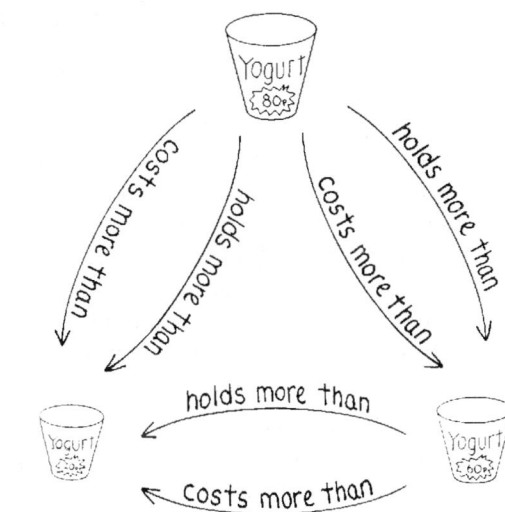

Figure 14.5

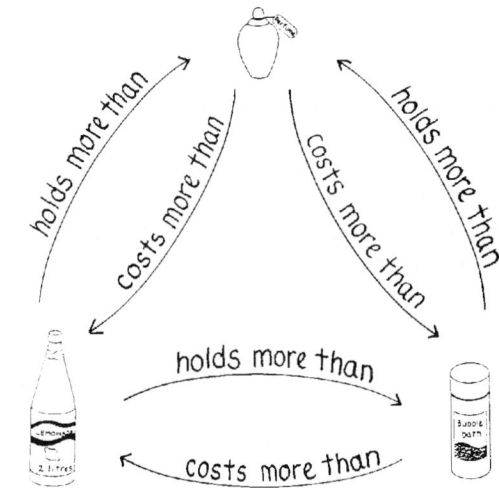

Figure 14.6

prices on them. Ask the children to place them on a logic mat as before. Have them replace the 'holds more than' relationship arrows with 'costs more than' arrows (figure 14.5). Will the two 'results' be the same? Repeat the activity but this time compare different commodities, which may well result in a change in the direction of the arrows. For example, a small bottle of perfume will no doubt hold less than a bottle of bubble bath but it will probably cost more (figure 14.6)! Have the children say when they think a price relationship is directly proportional to quantity and when it does not appear to be so.

8. Introduce the children to a scientific measuring jar which has both litre, millilitre and cubic centimetre graduations. Explain the standard units used to measure capacity and let them experiment and find out that a half litre is 500 ml, a quarter is 250 ml and three quarters of a litre is 750 ml. Have the children act as Weights and Measures Inspectors, testing a variety of containers to see if they hold what the labels claim. Explain that the Weights and Measures Inspectors are there to see that short measures are not given. Hopefully the children will find the containers will hold what is claimed.

9. Have the children collect, say, five different teaspoons and see if they can find how much a teaspoon will hold. (The British Standard teaspoon holds 5 ml.) Encourage them to tip, say, ten teaspoons of water into a scientific measuring jar and carefully read the level. Have the children use their number skills to compute the value of one teaspoonful.

10. Collect the prices of some everyday commodities which come in large and small sizes marked in millilitres. Have the children represent these amounts on a graph (figure 14.7). Ask the children to say how much a third container in the series would hold, and to find out from the graph what the likely cost would be.

11. Have the children work through Copymasters 14.1 and 14.2. You will need to first take a few copies of Copymaster 14.2 and write in some costs for the cups for each child, as shown in figure 14.8. You can use a variety of prices as indicated in the table, so that you have a selection of masters which can be copied and filed.

Naseem	Ming	Hannah	(Extra)
5p	10p	15p	(20p)
10p	20p	30p	(40p)
15p	30p	45p	(60p)
20p	40p	60p	(80p)
25p	50p	75p	(100p)
30p	60p	90p	(120p)
40p	80p	120p	(160p)
50p	100p	150p	(200p)
60p	120p	180p	(240p)

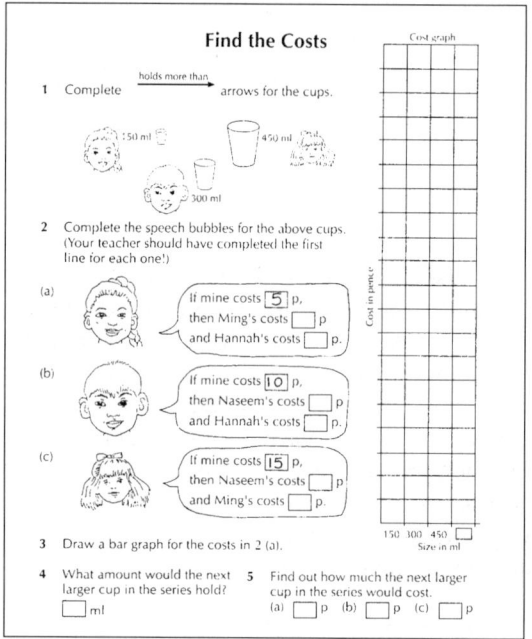

Figure 14.8

12. Fill a clear measuring jar to a certain level, say 400 millilitres. Have the children make up a $5 \times 5 \times 5$ cube with their centimetre cubes and immerse it in the measuring jar water. It should sink and the level of the water will rise. Get the children to record the results, e.g.
initial water level = 400 ml
size of cube = 125 cubic cm
second water level reading = 525 ml (?)
difference in water level readings = 125 ml (?)

Cost graph: soft drinks

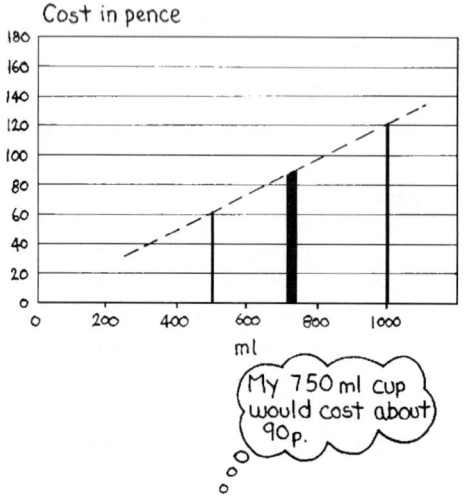

Figure 14.7

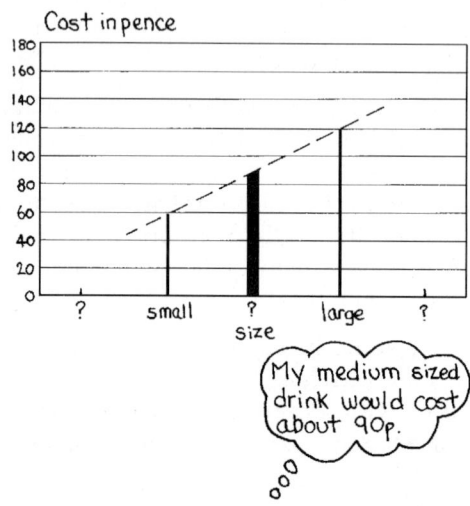

Repeat the activity several times using the same number of cubes to make up shapes other than cubes. What results do the children get? What do they find out about the volume of the shape and its relationship to the difference in water levels?

Key page points

Page 64 The cartoons on the page lead children to see that ¼ of a litre is the same as 250 ml, etc. Have the children look at the markings on the containers and see the implications. They can use Copymaster 2.1 to complete the bubbles. In question 2 provide the children with a variety of eggcups and get them to discuss their results. Have them try to decide how much water an eggcup holds!

Page 65 Identify the characters on the page. (Kumar in green, John in blue, Tony in red, Fiona in yellow and Sue in blue.) Discuss the thought and speech bubbles with the children and have them complete what Hannah is thinking (i.e. '... that's a quarter of a litre'). Have the children say what each of the coloured bottles is worth if a full litre costs 40p.

Further activities

1. Have the children discuss the question 'how big is a drop of water?' (10 drops are approximately equal to 1 ml).

2. Repeat Pre-page activity 12 by giving the children 64, 27 and 8 cubes and have them make a variety of shapes to immerse in the water. Can the children find a relationship between the size of the cube/shape and the difference in the water levels? Have the children draw graphs of their results, showing both the number of cubes in their shape and the rise in water level. In this activity and Pre-page activity 12, the children will have made cubes of sides 2 cm, 3 cm, 4 cm and 5 cm. They should make a graph of their results for these cubes as shown in figure 14.9.

3. Pour a litre of water into a 10 × 10 × 10 cm clear plastic cube. What do the children find? How many millilitres does the cube hold? Now empty the water out of the cube and find out how many cubic centimetres can be stacked inside the 10 cm cube, either by counting or some other method. Can the children find any relationship between the number of cubes and the millilitres?

4. Have the children play Capacity Touch and Say (Activity Card 14.1). These cards require the children to read scales marked in millilitres.

5. Let the children play Pouring Pairs (Activity Card 14.2). The cards are spread out face down on a table. The children take it in turns to turn over two cards, one of each colour. If the card showing two containers matches with the single container card, then the player keeps both cards. If the cards do not match, they are turned face down again and play moves to the next player. The player with the most pairs wins.

6. Ask the children to devise an investigation to find out how much juice is in an orange (or a grapefruit or lemon). Have the children squeeze an orange or similar fruit, collecting the juice as they do so and measuring the amount collected. If possible, squeeze three oranges of the same size and take the middle value of the juice collected as the 'norm'.

Check-ups

1. Can the children compare the capacity of a variety of containers?
2. Can the children recognise containers which hold a litre?
3. Can the children find a half, third and a quarter of a container?
4. Are the children able to recognise containers which hold half a litre?
5. Can the children classify containers which hold small quantities?
6. Do the children understand the millilitre as a unit of capacity and know that a teaspoon holds about 5 ml?
7. Can the children measure quantities in millilitres, e.g. 125 ml, 250 ml, etc?
8. Do the children know that there are 1000 ml in a litre and that 500 ml is half a litre, 250 ml a quarter and 750 ml three quarters?
9. Do the children understand what is meant by a measuring scale and can they use a variety of different scales?
10. Can the children see the relationship between the cubic centimetre and the millilitre?

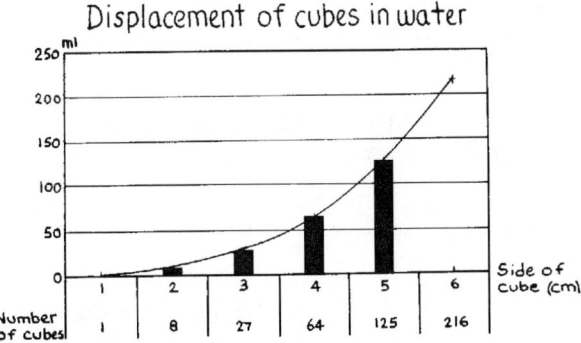

Figure 14.9

New Curriculum Mathematics for Schools Key Stage 2

Section 15   AT 1 3b, 3c, 4a. AT 2 3c, 3d, 4a. AT 3 4b. AT 5 3a, 3b, 3c, 3d, 4c.

Pages 66–69   Data Handling

Page 66   Holiday Pocket Money

Page 67   The Charity Stall

Pages 68 and 69   Clearing the Playground

Purpose

To consolidate the children's knowledge of 'sharing', especially with regard to situations where there are 'left overs'!

To consolidate the children's experience of using a calculator to solve sharing problems and to review how the calculator displays amounts 'in between' whole number results.

To introduce the children to the idea of the arithmetic mean.

To give the children practice in calculating the mean.

To give the children experiences where the mean is useful for making predictions.

To introduce the children to the bar line graph as a means of pictorial representation.

Recommended material

1. 'Any Left Overs?' cards (**Activity Card 10.4.** **Activity Card 17.2** from the previous pack relating to Book 1 would also be useful.)

2. Calculators.

3. **Copymasters 15.1–15.6.**

4. Cards for Between Pairs game (see Pre-page activity 3).

5. Sweets, stamps, toys, coins, counters, cubes, etc., for sharing activities.

6. Blank dice.

Pre-page activities

1. Review the 'Any Left Overs?' game (Activity Cards 17.2 from Book 1 and 10.4 from Book 2), and take the opportunity to use the cards to model some sharing situations. For example, for 23 ÷ 6 = ☐, have the children recount a sharing situation, such as 'Teacher asks Hannah to share out 23 pencils among six tables. How many pencils should go on each table?', and use materials to model it. Modelling on a 'one for you, one for you, etc.' principle, there will be three per table with five left over. Make sure the children realise that as there are five left over, there are 'nearly' enough for another one on each table. If the situation had been 'Teacher asked Hannah to share out 23 pencils by putting six on each table. How many tables would get six pencils?', then modelling would again show that three tables would get six pencils and that the five left over would be nearly enough for another table. Each time have the children check the model with their calculator and have them realise that 3.833333 is more than 3 and nearly 4. Repeat with other random cards from the set. Get the children to record their findings on paper (figure 15.1), each time writing the number sentence, the picture story, the number story and the result, verified with the calculator. If the situation and number sentence make it appropriate, have the children consider the effect of sharing out the 'left overs'. For example, for 15 ÷ 6 it may be possible for the children to model on a 'one for you, one for you, etc.' basis and then consider fractional parts.

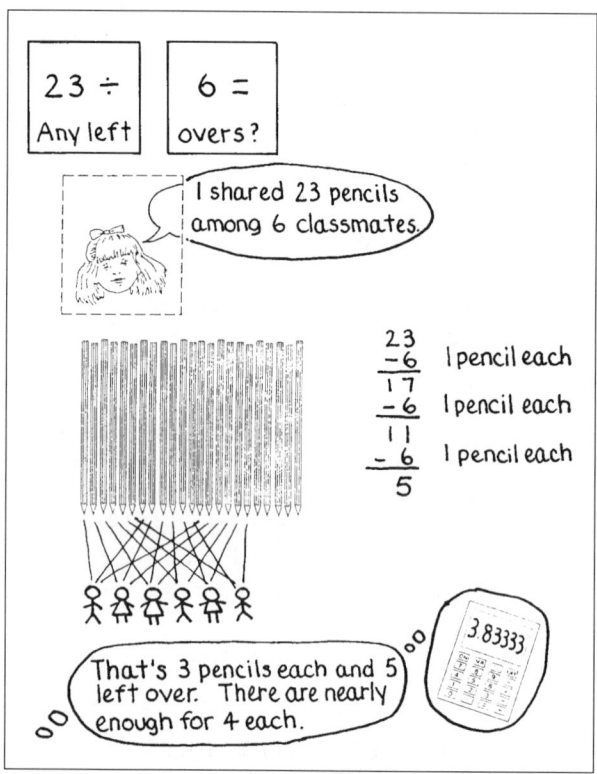

Figure 15.1

2. Give the children a series of sharing number sentences involving the number 10, e.g.

10 ÷ 1 = ☐, 10 ÷ 2 = ☐, 10 ÷ 3 = ☐,
10 ÷ 4 = ☐, 10 ÷ 5 = ☐, 10 ÷ 6 = ☐,
10 ÷ 7 = ☐, 10 ÷ 8 = ☐, 10 ÷ 9 = ☐,
10 ÷ 10 = ☐. Have the children mark the results on a number line (figure 15.2a).
Consider the 'in-between' results (figure 15.2b).

108

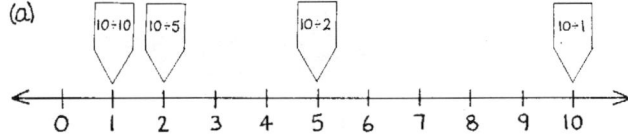

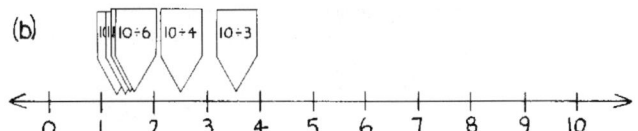

Figure 15.2

Have the children notice that, for a constant numerator, the smaller the denominator the larger the number, and the larger the denominator the smaller the number. Copymasters 15.1 and 15.2 are available for further practice.

3. Make and play Between Pairs using sharing number sentences. You will need a set of, say, 18 number sentence cards in one colour, and a set of 18 'between' cards in a different colour, as follows.

Number sentence cards:

$3 \div 2 = \square$ $8 \div 5 = \square$ $5 \div 2 = \square$ $29 \div 10 = \square$
$15 \div 4 = \square$ $30 \div 9 = \square$ $17 \div 4 = \square$ $25 \div 6 = \square$
$35 \div 6 = \square$ $42 \div 8 = \square$ $37 \div 6 = \square$ $65 \div 10 = \square$
$63 \div 8 = \square$ $30 \div 4 = \square$ $65 \div 8 = \square$ $25 \div 3 = \square$
$99 \div 10 = \square$ $19 \div 2 = \square$

'Between' cards (two of each):

is between 1 and 2
is between 2 and 3
is between 3 and 4
is between 4 and 5
is between 5 and 6
is between 6 and 7
is between 7 and 8
is between 8 and 9
is between 9 and 10

Shuffle the cards and spread them face down on the table. The children take it in turns to turn over a number sentence card and say what they think the result is. They then turn over a 'between' card. If the result is 'between' the values displayed on the card then a pair is formed (figure 15.3) and that player keeps the cards. The player who collects most pairs wins the game.

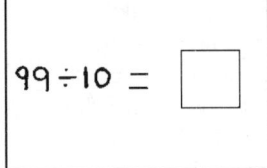 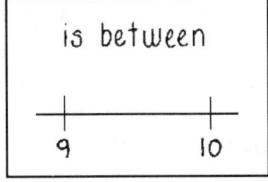

Figure 15.3

4. Discuss a situation with the children where a 'survey' of the cost of, say, chews at five shops in the district has revealed prices of 9p, 8p, 10p, 7p and 11p for the same packet. The information can be displayed on a chart as shown in figure 15.4a. Discuss with the children how they could express what the price of chews is, saying perhaps that it is 'between 7p and 11p'. If the prices are arranged in order, i.e. 7p, 8p, 9p, 10p and 11p, the middle value of 9p could be selected as 'the price'. Have the children say how many packets were actually above this selected price, and how many were below. Levelling out the prices amongst the shops would also give an indication of 'the price', and this is known as the (arithmetic) mean/average of the prices. The levelling/averaging/sharing out can be done by collecting all the prices together, adding them and then sharing them out among the five shops (see figure 15.4b). In this case the mean is 9p, and could represent 'the price'. The mathematics of this action can be recorded as: $(9 + 8 + 10 + 7 + 11) \div 5 = 9$ because $9 \times 5 = 45$. Select some other values to model in a similar way. *Note*: take the opportunity to refer to the arithmetic mean where appropriate.

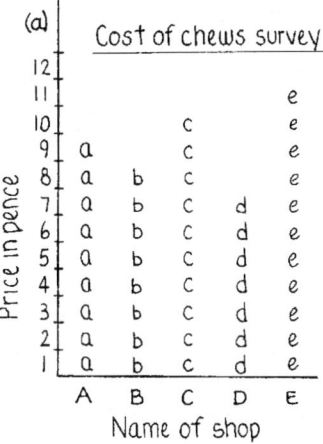

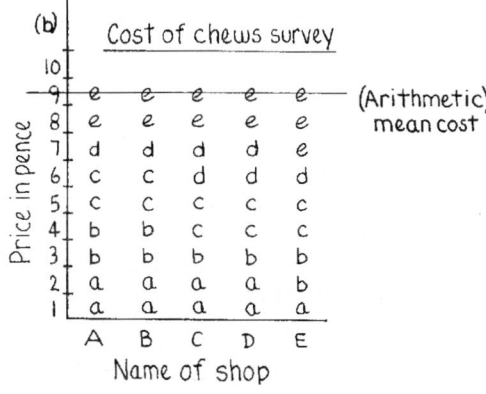

Figure 15.4

5. Have the children cut out three strips of paper 5 cm, 7 cm and 9 cm long. Tell them these are to represent the number of, say, sweets which

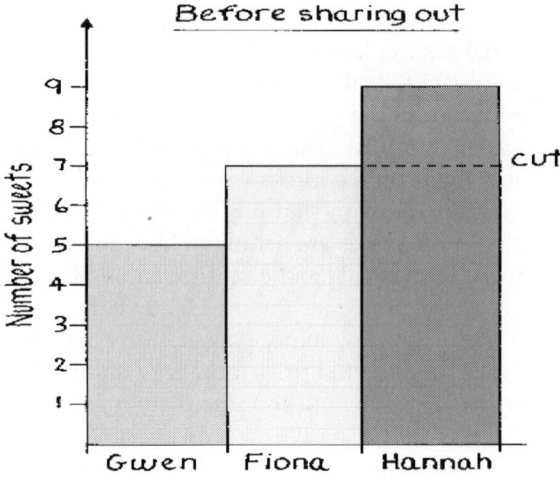
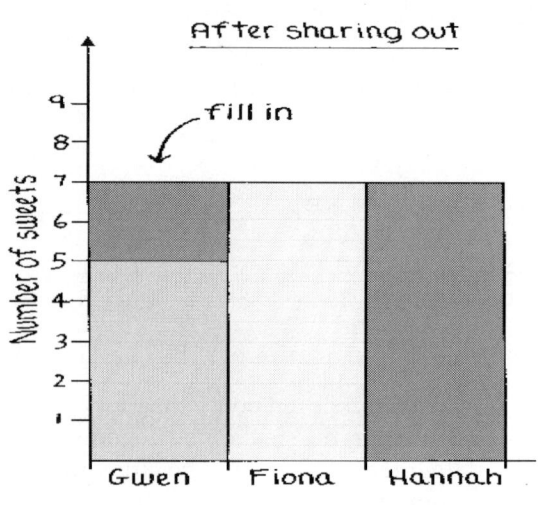

Figure 15.5

three girls have. Get the children to arrange the strips in bar chart form. Discuss with them how the height of the strips may be made uniform 'by cutting down the hills and filling the valleys' until the bar chart has been levelled (figure 15.5). Discuss what the level is. Relate this to sharing out the sweets equally as in activity 4. Discuss the recording of the calculation and encourage the children to notice that the three girls will have seven sweets each, that $7 \times 3 = 21$, and that 21 is the total number of sweets. Repeat the activity with strips of 6 cm, 9 cm, 7 cm and 10 cm, representing items which four children are going to share.

6. Give one child three sweets, another four sweets and a third five sweets. Tell the children that these three are good friends and that they want to put the sweets together and share them out equally. Get the children to do that. Discuss with them how to record the practical activity. Explain that, as all three of them now have the mean number of sweets each, one has lost out while one has gained. Repeat the activity, adjusting the number of children and sweets. You might also wish to set up some situations using coins, stamps, toys, etc.

7. Have the children complete Copymaster 15.3. Make sure that they have coins, sweets, toys, etc., (or counters to represent them) and that they actually do the 'putting together and sharing out'. Get the children to colour the names of those who gained by sharing out their sweets, etc., in red, and those who lost out, in blue.

8. Tell the children that John, Jamie and Kumar have put their sweets together and that they now have three each. Ask the children to investigate how many sweets each of the boys might have had originally, perhaps recording their results in a table like the one shown.

| How many sweets did each boy have? ||||
John	Jamie	Kumar	Total
3	3	3	9
1	4	4	9
2	4	3	9

Repeat with other quantities.

9. Let three children each throw a dice marked 3, 3, 6, 6, 9 and 9, recording the scores and finding the total. Have them say what score they would have had to throw to get that total if all three scores were the same. Could they have got that score with this dice? Have them repeat this activity several times, recording their investigations in a table like the one shown below.

Scores thrown	Total	Scores if all the same	Possible with this dice?
3, 6, 9	18	6, 6, 6	✓
3, 3, 3	9	3, 3, 3	✓
9, 6, 6	21	7, 7, 7	✗
9, 9, 6	24	8, 8, 8	✗

Key page points

Page 66 The calculations on this page are all concerned with the number of 10p coins. Explain to the children that although the Williams children need different amounts of pocket money when they are at home, they think it would be fairer if they had the same amount to spend whilst on holiday, even though someone may lose out! Encourage the children to reproduce the pocket money chart using 10p coins. They should then move the coins so that the four children have the same amounts. When doing the calculations for the three families in question 3, encourage the children to predict first, check using the coins and then record their calculations, e.g. 5 + 6 + 7 = 18 and 18 ÷ 6 = 6 because 6 × 3 = 18. Provide the children with copies of Copymaster 15.4. Discuss with them how the pocket money was shared out and have them consider the fact that in averaging out there will be some who gain and some who lose … and perhaps some who stay the same! Get the children to draw portraits of the Williams and Roberts families, showing how the individuals might feel after the share-out, e.g. winners could look happy and losers sad or grumpy. The questions to the right of the portraits are to encourage the children to realise that the total gains should equal the total losses, though not necessarily by the same number of people.

Page 67 The children should use the graph to help them answer the questions. Although they calculate the mean amount, they will find that in this case it is not very helpful in making a prediction about what might happen in the future. The important factor in this case is the total amount spent because that is unchanging. When writing the report, the children should aim to give enough information to enable another child to plan and run a stall.

Pages 68 and 69 The children need to calculate how many tubs were collected per child. On page 68 they are actually calculating the (arithmetic) mean/average number of tubs collected for each group. When writing about the graphs the children should note, in particular, that they are not the same shape. Discuss with the children the fact that the groups have different numbers of children in them. The children can use Copymaster 15.5 to help with the completion of the tables. Point out to the children that when the total of the group totals and the total of the daily totals have been found they should be equal, and that this 'grand total' is a good check on calculations. Discuss the statements at the bottom of page 68 with the children. Ask them if they agree with Naseem's suggestion about how the competition could be made fairer. Page 69 should provide a fairer way of judging.

Further activities

1. Have the children complete Copymaster 15.6. Explain that we know what pocket money the Partons are to have on holiday, but that we don't know what the usual weekly amounts are. Can the children chart five different possibilities?

2. Give the children a copy of Copymaster 15.5 with the names of the children removed. Allow them to fill in the number of children in each group and the number of tubs collected each day. Have them explain the situation they have created, and then let them complete the totals as before.

3. Remind the children of Pre-page activity 9 and ask them to investigate how they might get a mean/average score of 3, then 4, 5, … 9. How many ways can they find to get each score? Point out to the children that in this case it does not matter in which order the numbers are thrown, since scores of 3, 3 and 6 are the same as 3, 6 and 3, and 6, 3 and 3. Repeat using a dice marked 10, 20, 30, 10, 20, 30. In this case you could let the children use 10p coins to help with their calculations. Encourage them to predict and then use a calculator to check their predictions.

4. Let the children play Mean Grab. Place some coloured cubes, all of the same size, in a bag. Ask a child to take a handful and then count the number of cubes taken. Repeat the experiment a number of times and then ask the children to find the mean value of their handfuls. If the result is not a whole number, have the children say that the mean is, for example, 'between 7 and 8'.

5. Have the children consider the following problem. In the time allowed for an aeroplane flying competition, Peter had four tries. His plane flew 8 m, 6 m, 4 m and 6 m. Dawn had more tries. Her plane flew 8 m, 4 m, 6 m, 7 m, 5 m, 6 m and 6 m. Robert's plane flew 8 m, 7 m, 6 m, 6 m and 8 m. Who should be declared the winner? Ask the children to work out the mean for each competitor. You could organise an actual competition, if wished.

6. Ask the children to count the number of words on, say, five lines of their reading book and work out the mean number per line. Explain to them that if this mean/average value was really the actual number on each line in the book, you could work out the total number of words on each page. Compare the results obtained by calculating in this way and by counting. If the mean is not a whole number, talk about the total being 'between' the limits of the mean value.

Check-ups

1. Using numbers within their experience, can the children calculate the arithmetic mean?

2. Given the mean and the number of items, can the children suggest possible distributions?

3. Do the children realise that the mean × the number of items = the total?

New Curriculum Mathematics for Schools Key Stage 2

Section 16

AT 1 3a, 3b, 3c, 3d. AT 2 3a, 3d, 4a, 4b, 4d. AT 3 2b, 4a.

Pages 70–74 Take Away (H.T.U.)

Page 70 Desktop Publishing: The School Newspaper
Page 71 Ways of Writing
Page 72 Sentences to Read
Page 73 Other Ways of Doing
Page 74 At School: The Maths Class

Purpose

To give the children practice in 'taking away' one three-digit number from another.
To introduce situations involving the 'taking way' of numbers made up of hundreds, tens and units, and to encourage the children to model the process using apparatus.
To give children the opportunity of developing an algorithm for the 'taking away' of three-digit numbers.
To contrast 'difference' and 'take away' situations.
To relate 'take away' and 'addition' with reference to three-digit numbers.

Recommended material

1. Structural apparatus: Multibase materials (base 10) and interlocking cubes.
2. Hundreds, tens and units counting boards and counters.
3. Calculators.
4. Cards for games (see Further activities 1 and 4).
5. **Copymasters 5.1 and 16.1–16.4.**

Pre-page activities

Note As in Section 13, our models of 'subtraction' are built by comparing sets and using the base 10 structure of the number system in exchange experiences. The notes and figures which follow here are presented in the traditional format, moving from no exchange to exchanging both tens and units. Teachers are strongly recommended to read the section as a whole before planning their programme. Whatever order of presentation is chosen, a variety of materials should be used. In the following illustrations base 10 materials are used along with counting boards and counters. Teachers will wish to 'mix and match', and consider the use of other materials as necessary.

1. Suggest a situation where you have to let materials represent the items being considered, selecting numbers which do not involve exchange in the process. For example: 'A publisher has 478 books in stock. They send out an order for 125, how many have they left in stock?' The number of books in stock can be modelled as four '100' pieces, seven '10' strips and eight single cubes. Once the model has been established, the children can actually 'take away' 125 'books' (figure 16.1).

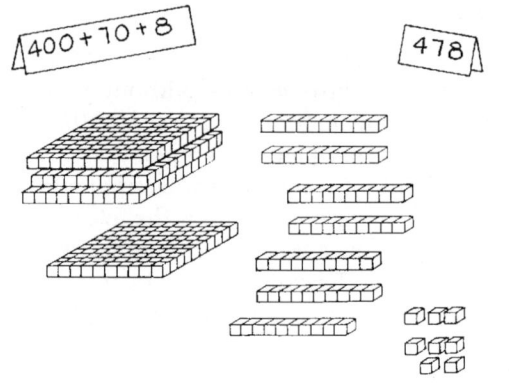

Figure 16.1

Get the children to record the mathematics as they model.

$$\begin{array}{r} 478 \\ -125 \\ \hline \end{array} \text{ can be written as } \begin{array}{r} (400 + 70 + 8) \\ -(100 + 20 + 5) \\ \hline 300 + 50 + 3 \end{array} \longrightarrow 353$$

Check that the children can see that 353 is a reasonable result since 478 is nearly 500, and 125 is close to 100, so the result should be about 400. As appropriate, discuss with the children that the books left, together with the books 'taken away', constitute the total, i.e.
478 − 125 = $\boxed{353}$ because 125 + 353 = $\boxed{478}$.

2. Make up a situation where children will have to exchange a '10' in solving the problem. For example: 'A shopkeeper has to cut 125 cm from a roll of ribbon which is 362 cm long. How

much will she have left on the roll?' Have the children model the situation, regrouping as necessary (figure 16.2).

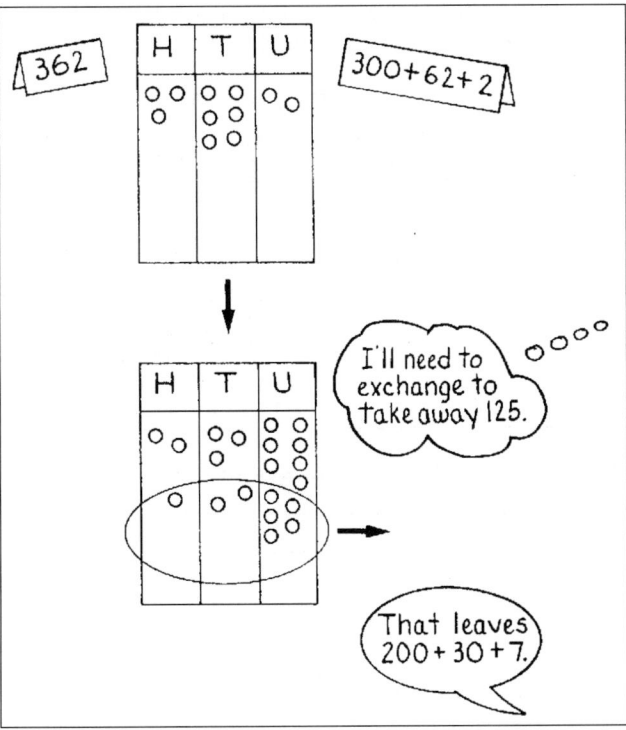

Figure 16.2

Again get the children to record the mathematics.

$$\begin{array}{r} 362 \\ -125 \end{array} \xrightarrow{\text{can be written as}} \begin{array}{r} (300 + 60 + 2) \\ -(100 + 20 + 5) \end{array} \rightarrow \begin{array}{r} (300 + 50 + 12) \\ -(100 + 20 + 5) \\ \hline 200 + 30 + 7 \end{array} \rightarrow 237$$

Encourage the children to say whether this result is 'about right'. In all 'take away' models, make sure the children see the link with addition where, in this case, the ribbon which is left and the ribbon cut off represents the total started with. Have the children record this situation as:
362 − 125 = 237 because 125 + 237 = 362.

3. Suggest a situation with numbers which involve exchanging a '100' piece for ten '10' strips. For example: 'A lorry fills up with petrol at a garage. If the owner knows his pump is nearly empty with only 725 litres left in it and the driver takes out 175 litres, how much will be left in the pump?' Again have the children model the situation, exchanging where necessary and recording the mathematics at the same time (figure 16.3).

$$\begin{array}{r} 725 \\ -175 \end{array} \xrightarrow{\text{can be written as}} \begin{array}{r} (700 + 20 + 5) \\ -(100 + 70 + 5) \end{array} \rightarrow \begin{array}{r} (600 + 120 + 5) \\ -(100 + 70 + 5) \\ \hline 500 + 50 + 0 \end{array} \rightarrow 550$$

Have the children say whether the result is reasonable, and why.

Figure 16.3

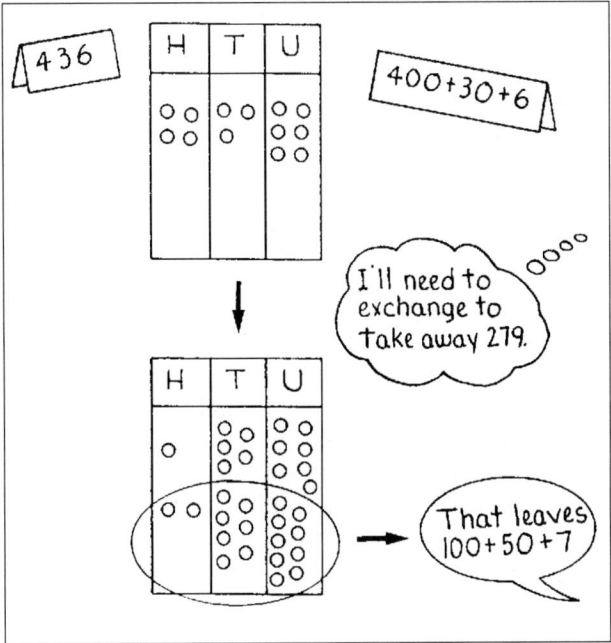

Figure 16.4

4. Ask the children to consider a problem such as: 'On a full jumbo jet equipped to carry 430 passengers, the flight attendants gave out 279 headsets. How many headsets did the crew have left if they had one headset for each possible passenger and six extra?' Have the children model the situation (figure 16.4).

This time the children can record their actions as:

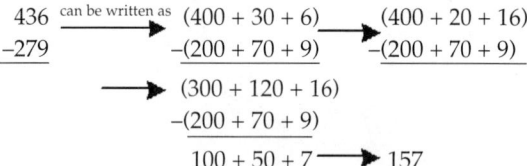

or if tens are exchanged first:

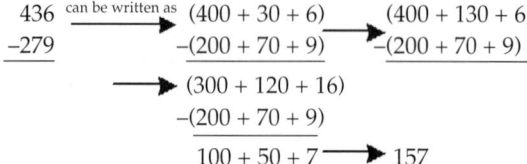

Have the children say why they have confidence in the result. As recommended in earlier activities, make sure the children notice the link with addition where:
436 − 279 = 157 because 279 + 157 = 436.

5. Make up a 'take away' situation such as 523 − 398 = ☐ for the children to solve. Have them find the result in as many ways as possible:
523 take away 300 → 223 take away 90 → 133 take away 8 → 125;
523 take away 8 → 515 take away 90 → 425 take away 300 → 125;
523 take away 23 → 500 take away 300 → 200 take away 75 → 125.

6. Have the children use their calculators to solve some 'take away' number sentences involving three digits in different ways. Make sure they write down what they do as they proceed, e.g. for 846 − 287 = 559:

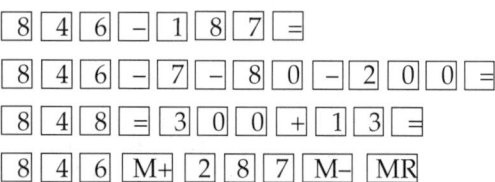

7. Write a number of 'take away' number sentences on the chalkboard and have the children make up 'take away' stories. Encourage a variety of responses. Discuss some of the stories with the children and have them say which are allowed and which are not, e.g. 'If I take away this car number from that one I get …'!

8. Let the children make up some of their own 'take away' patterns:

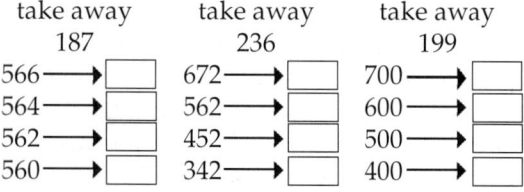

Encourage the children to consider negative numbers in their sequences.

9. Have the children study some different algorithms as shown in figure 16.5. Ask them to explain the algorithm and write a situation for the number sentence solved by that algorithm.

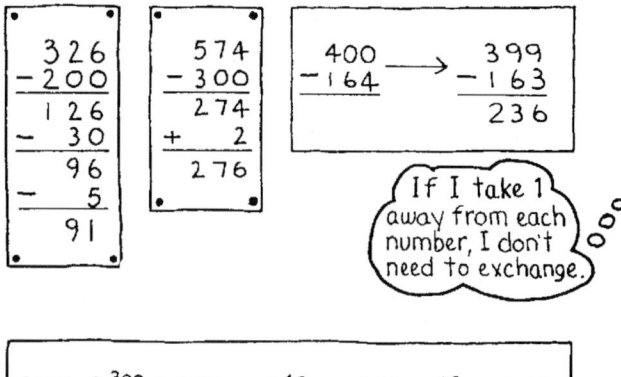

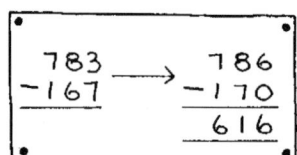

Figure 16.5

Key page points

Page 70 Discuss the cartoon on the page where Hannah and John are doing some stock control. Have your children say how they think John knows that he will need to exchange a ten (question 2). Get the children to make a model of the situation with familiar materials. Questions 3 and 4 develop from the first question, and question 5 asks the children to find the total cost of the papers if each costs 10p.

Page 71 The ways of writing the number in question 1 should lead to question 2. All the 'answers' on the page are 186. The models should be a little different and the children should be able to explain why the results are the same. It is important therefore that the children can model these situations.

Page 72 This page should consolidate the children's experiences of 'take away' in different ways. Let the children have familiar materials to set up the models in question 1. When questions 2 and 4 have been completed, display the children's responses. In question 3 the children should find some of the sentences help them with ways of writing 155 in question 5.

Page 73 The questions on this page will require a lot of exchanging if the traditional approach is adopted. However, the children in the cartoon at the bottom of the page seem to have come up with another solution! Discuss alternative ways of solving the questions in number 7.

Page 74 Discuss the illustrations on the page with your children. You will note that Fiona uses the memory keys on her calculator. Make sure your children are familiar with theirs.

Further activities

1. Make and play Below 400, a game for two players. Prepare 20 cards each carrying one of the following numbers on them: 103, 107, 112, 118, 122, 129, 134, 137, 140, 149, 155, 156, 166, 169, 174, 178, 182, 188, 193 and 194. Shuffle the cards well. Each player starts with 900 points, and takes it in turn to pick a card from the set and 'take away' that number from his/her total. The results are checked with a calculator, and a point is awarded for each correct answer. If an answer is wrong, no points are scored and the players reverts to the total he/she had before the error. On each round a bonus point is given to the player with the lower score. Play continues in this way until one player is left with less than 400. The winner is the player with the highest number of points.

2. Write on some cards a number of incomplete 'take away' number sentences and have the children complete them, e.g.

   ```
     8 6 7        6 7 8        7 8 1         ☐ ☐ ☐
   -3 ☐ ☐      - ☐ ☐ 2      - ☐ ☐ ☐       -2 8 7
   ─────        ─────        ─────         ─────
     4 9 5        4 6 6        4 1 7         5 3 7
   ```

3. Let the children use a calculator as a function machine with a 'take away' function such as −198 as the constant. Have the children input numbers such as 346, 457, 893, etc., each time encouraging them to say what they think the output will be before pressing the = key. Repeat with other functions and have the children see if they can generate some negative numbers.

4. Play Calculator *v* Paper and Pencil, a game for two players. On twenty cards write 'take away' three-digit number sentences. Make sure you have an evenly balanced number of those without exchange, those with exchange in one place only, and those with exchange in two places. Shuffle the cards well and place them face down on the table. Decide who is to use the calculator first and who will use pencil and paper first. One card is turned over. The two players now have to complete the sentence and the first with the correct answer wins, and keeps the card. After ten cards have been played the players change roles. After all the cards have been played, the winner is the player retaining most cards. Have the children say which types of sentence they were able to do quickest and by which method.

5. Have the children play Four in a Line using Copymaster 5.1. Figure 16.6 shows a suitable game sheet prepared for use with three-digit numbers. See Section 5, Further activity 8 for details of how to play the game.

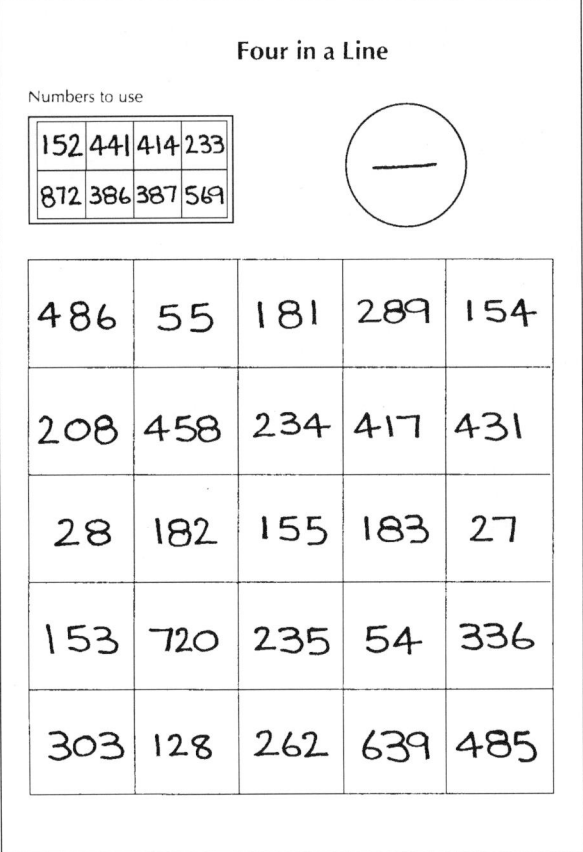

Figure 16.6

6. Use Copymaster 16.1 for further practice in 'taking away' three-digit numbers.

7. Write some number sentences on the chalkboard and have the children write a 'take away' and a 'difference' story for each one.

8. Have the children explain how knowing that 864 −375 = 489 helps them with sentences such as 864 − 377 = ☐, 864 − 365 = ☐ and 864 − 475 = ☐. Repeat with other starting sentences. Copymaster 16.2 provides more work on related sentences.

9. Give the children an addition sentence such as 387 + 258 = 645 and have them use it to make up some 'take away' sentences.

10. Have the children complete Copymaster 16.3. They should colour the two half slabs, and the space to be filled in, the same colour. Encourage the children to use their calculators to check their predictions.

11. Copymaster 16.4 can be used to provide practice in estimating by rounding off to the nearest 100.

12. Let the children use their experience to find other ways of writing three-digit numbers (figure 16.7).

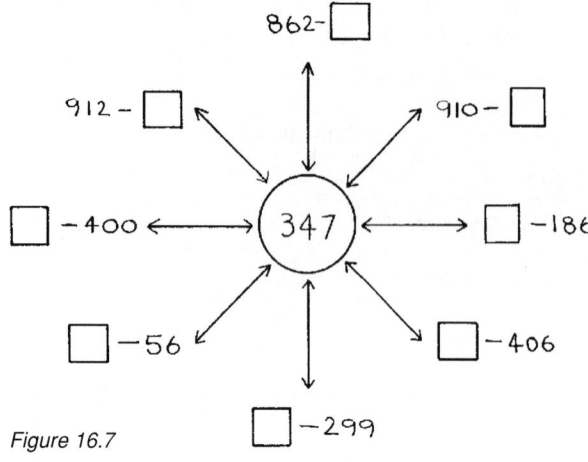

Figure 16.7

Check-ups

1. Can the children recognise a 'take away' situation involving three-digit numbers and solve it?

2. Can the children model a 'take away' situation involving three-digit numbers and develop an algorithm?

3. Do the children understand various algorithms used to find the answers to 'take away' problems?

4. Can the children follow a 'take away' algorithm created by another person and make a model using familiar materials?

5. Can the children use their calculators with confidence to perform 'take away' operations?

Section 17

AT 1 3a, 3b, 3c. **AT 2** 3b, 3c, 3d, 3e, 4a, 4c, 4d.

Pages 75–78 Money

Page 75   Shopping for a Present
Page 76   At the Supermarket
Page 77   Mother's Day
Page 78   At the Station

Purpose

To introduce children to the decimal form for recording pounds and pence.
To give the children further practice in shopping situations involving paying bills.

Recommended material

1. A collection of coins of all values.
2. Items for a class shop.
3. Cards for recording prices.
4. Calculators.
5. Decimal Money Position Value cards (**Activity Cards 17.1–17.3**).
6. **Copymasters 17.1–17.4**.
7. Gummed paper coins.
8. Cards for games (see Pre-page activity 9 and Further activity 5).
9. The Money 'Nearly' Game (**Activity Cards 17.4–17.5**).
10. Supermarket Checkout cards (**Activity Card 17.6**).
11. Supermarket Triples (**Activity Cards 17.7–17.8**).
12. Catalogues for cutting up.

Pre-page activities

Note The computational models in this section follow on from those in the addition, difference and 'take away' sections. Children should be presented with a situation and model the processes, developing and recording an algorithm as they go. Later the recording can be streamlined and alternative ways of finding the answers can be discussed and used. It may help to read again the introductory note to the pre-page activities for Section 5 before starting this section.

1. Price some articles in the class shop at over £1. Give the children a collection of coins and ask them to pay for the articles. Discuss the notation with them, for example that £5.36 represents £5 and 36 pence. They should also appreciate that £5.36 can be written as 536p because 100p is worth £1, and there are £5. (At this stage the decimal point will merely be a point separating the pounds and pence. Later when the decimals are discussed you will be able to refer to the experiences the children have gained using money and these will help them to understand decimal notation.) Have the children use the Decimal Money Position Value cards (Activity Cards 17.1–17.3) to show the decimal recording of prices in the class shop (figure 17.1). The cards show the amounts as pictures of coins with the decimal equivalents written below on the number strips. A card which shows an amount less than 10p is placed under a card which shows a multiple of 10p so that the number strips overlap; similarly a card which shows a multiple of 10p is placed under a card showing a multiple of £1. Also take the opportunity to display the prices on a calculator, and encourage the children to use their calculators throughout these activities. Copymaster 17.1 consists of eight calculator pictures with blank displays which the children can write in. Copies of the master can also be made on card and cut up for display purposes.

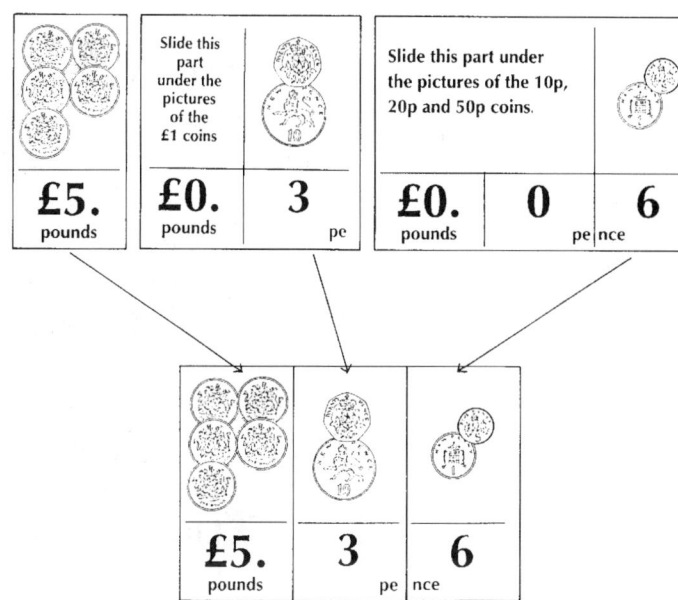

Using the cards to show the decimal recording of 5 complete pounds, 30 pence in complete tens, and 6 extra pence.

Figure 17.1

2. Repeat activity 1 but this time price the items at less than £1. Emphasise the difference in recording amounts such as 7p and 70p, i.e. £0.07 and £0.70, etc.

3. Ask the children to select, say, two position value cards such as £0.07 and £0.08, and count that number of individual 1p coins onto a 100 pence sheet (Copymaster 17.2), i.e. 15 1p coins. Have them count in the decimal notation, i.e. £0.01 ('zero point zero one pound'), £0.02 ... £0.10 ('zero point one zero pound'), £0.11 ('zero point one one pound'), £0.12 ('zero point one two pound'), etc. This is to associate the counting with the representation on the card. Stress to the children that after the decimal point we count by saying the figures separately, i.e. 'zero point one two' and *not* 'zero point twelve', even though the figures represent 12p. Also point out that although we write the pound sign first, we say 'pounds' last. Give the children practice with other small amounts which 'cross the ten boundary'.

4. Contrast the counting sequence of activity 3 by using a calculator as a function machine and keying 1p as 0.01 into the constant memory. Have the children count on with the calculator. Draw their attention to the fact that when they move on from 0.09, the next in the sequence is 0.1, leading to 0.11, 0.12, ... 0.19, 0.2, 0.21, etc. Have the children say how many times they will have to add 0.01 (1p) into the calculator to get 1.00 (i.e. £1), shown as 1 in the display. Repeat the activity with other amounts such as 0.02, 0.05, etc.

5. Prepare a series of money boxes using plastic coins with amounts over £1. Ask the children to count the money in each box and record the total, e.g. £1 + £1 + 50p + 10p + 5p + 2p = £2.67.

6. Give the children some coins and a scoop. Have them dip into the pile of coins with their scoop and take out a scoopful of coins. Get the children to sort the coins and say how much money they have collected. As a variation, you could make the game competitive, e.g. by letting the children take it in turns to take two scoopfuls each, with the one scooping the most money winning the round.

7. Use gummed paper coins to make a set of Touch and Say cards to encourage coin recognition.

8. Give the children some prices below £5 and have them find as many ways as they can of using coins to make the total. Ask the children to consider the minimum number of coins needed to make the total, e.g.

    £1.36 → £1+ 10p + 10p + 10p + 1p + 1p + 1p + 1p + 1p + 1p   10 coins
    → £1 + 20p + 10p + 2p + 2p + 2p   6 coins
    → £1 + 20p + 10p + 5p + 1p   5 coins
    → 50p + 50p + 10p + 20p + 5p + 1p   6 coins

9. Make and play Memory Money Bingo, a game for four players. You will need four game mats and 32 memory cards as shown in figure 17.2. Give each player a game mat. Shuffle the cards

Game mats

	£1.01	£2.25	
£0.10			£3.15
	£1.50		
£0.05		£2.59	£5.32

£0.50	£1.05		
		£2.49	£5.30
	£0.09	£2.95	
	£1.90		£2.53

£0.20		£2.51	
	£1.10		£3.51
		£2.94	£2.35
£0.01	£1.02		

		£2.52	£3.50
£0.02	£1.09		
		£1.20	£3.25
£0.90		£2.15	

Memory cards

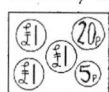 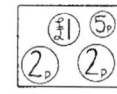 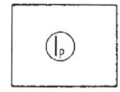 etc.

Figure 17.2

well and spread them face down on the table. The children take it in turns to turn over a card. If the card belongs on their mat they place it in the correct position. If it does not, the card is turned face down again and the play moves to the next player. The first to complete his/her game mat wins.

10. Write some prices on separate cards and ask the children to order them from cheapest to dearest, e.g. £0.04, £0.08, £0.18, £0.24, £0.40, £0.63, £0.80, £1.00, £1.29, £1.92, £2.11, £2.87.

11. Price all the goods in the class shop in decimal notation. Have the children buy single items, giving the correct coins each time.

12. Ask the children to 'buy' two items priced at over £1 from the class shop. Get them to use their calculators to find the total price after estimating it first. Ensure you include in the discussion the rounding down, rounding up and rounding off ways of estimating, for example:

```
£1.35                                                £1
+£2.89   rounded down to the nearest pound becomes  +£2
                                                     £3

£1.35                                                £2
+£2.89   rounded up to the nearest pound becomes    +£3
                                                     £5

£1.35                                                £1
+£2.89   rounded off to the nearest pound becomes   +£3
                                                     £4
```

Discuss with the children the merits of each method, identifying which is the most accurate, which is the quickest and which is safest when you are shopping with a fixed sum of money.

13. Play the Money 'Nearly' Game, a game for four players (Activity Cards 17.4–17.5). Shuffle both sets of cards separately. Place the target cards face down on the table. Deal out five of the other cards to the four players. A target card is then turned face up. Players take a card from their hand and place it face down on the table. When all have made a selection, the cards are turned face up in order of play. The player closest to the target wins four points. The player coming second gets two points. If two players tie, then each gets three points. If three players tie, then they score two points each. If all four players tie, then they all score one point. There is no score for ties in second place. At the end of each round the used cards are put to one side and not used again until the next game. The game is over when all five cards have been played, with a new target card each time, and the winner is the player with most points.

14. Present the children with a situation such as 'Hannah has £2.23 and she is given £1.35. How much has she altogether?' Have the children model the addition situation with their coins (figure 17.3).

Figure 17.3

In this situation have the children record the process as:

£2.23 ⟶   £2 + 20p + 3p
+ £1.35   + £1 + 30p + 5p
           ─────────────────
           £3 + 50p + 8p ⟶ £3.58

Make sure the children see that £3.58 is a reasonable result. You may care to compare this action with the modelling of 223 + 135 (i.e. as in Section 5). Explain to the children that £2.23 can be regarded as 223p and £1.35 as 135p. Have the children model other situations where no exchanging is required, e.g.

£5.41	£3.72	£1.67	£6.12
+£1.13	+£4.15	+£3.32	+£1.24

15. Have the children consider a situation such as 'Gwen earned £1.49 collecting bottles on Saturday and £2.15 on Sunday. How much did she earn over the weekend?' Get the children to model the addition situation with their coins (figure 17.4).
Have them record the process as:

£1.49   ⟶   £1 + 40p + 9p
+ £2.15   + £2 + 10p + 5p
            ─────────────────
            £3 + 50p + 14p
        ⟶   £3 + 50p + 10p + 4p
        ⟶   £3 + 60p + 4p
        ⟶   £3.64

New Curriculum Mathematics for Schools Key Stage 2

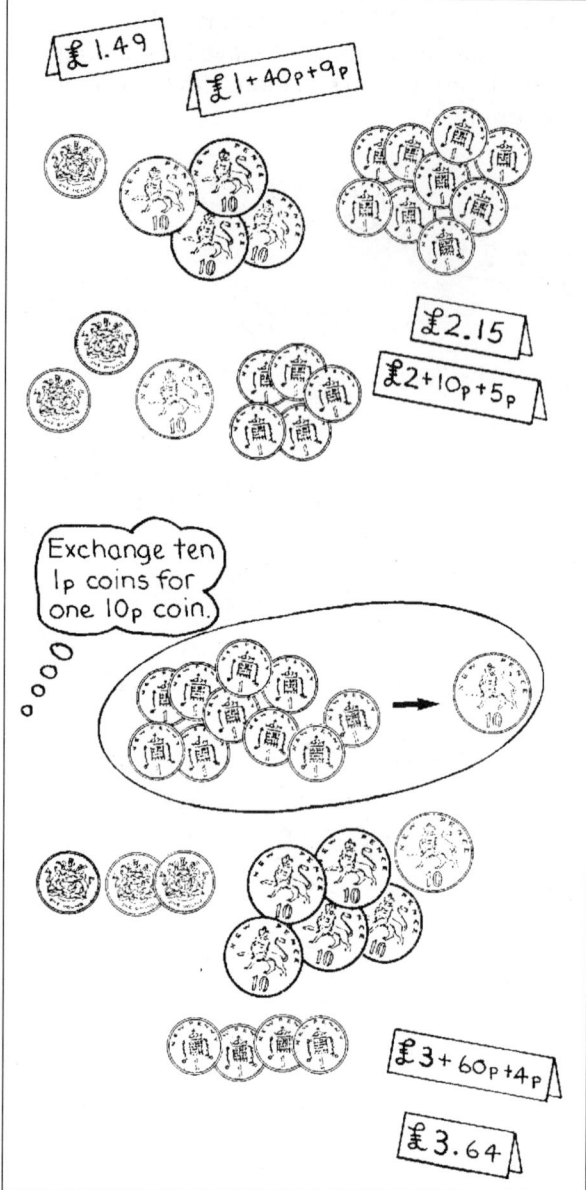

Figure 17.4

Figure 17.5

Have the children explain why the result could not be less than £3 or more than £4. Give the children some other situations involving a single exchange to model, e.g.

£1.29	£1.12	£3.15	£5.29
+£1.64	+£6.58	+£3.39	+£3.39

16. Discuss a situation such as 'John buys two cricket books in a sale. On the first he 'saves' £1.46 and on the second £2.72. How much does he 'save' at the sale?' Get the children to model the situation with coins as before (figure 17.5). They should record the process as:

$$\begin{array}{l} £1.46 \\ + £2.72 \end{array} \longrightarrow \begin{array}{l} £1 + 40p + 6p \\ + £2 + 70p + 2p \end{array}$$

$$£3 + 110p + 8p$$

$$\longrightarrow £3 + £1 + 10p + 8p$$
$$\longrightarrow £4 + 10p + 8p$$
$$\longrightarrow £4.18$$

Again, make sure the children say why they think £4.18 must be the correct total. Give them some further similar situations to solve, e.g.

£1.33	£2.93	£1.93	£1.74
+£3.93	+£2.63	+£2.75	+£3.33

17. Have the children model situations such as 'Naseem finds £2.45 in her money bank and £1.76 in her purse. How much has she altogether?' (figure 17.6). Record the process as:

$$\begin{array}{l} £2.45 \\ + £1.76 \end{array} \longrightarrow \begin{array}{l} £2 + 40p + 5p \\ + £1 + 70p + 6p \end{array}$$

$$£3 + 110p + 11p$$

$$\longrightarrow £3 + (£1 + 10p) + (10p + 1p)$$
$$\longrightarrow (£3 + £1) + (10p + 10p) + 1p$$
$$\longrightarrow £4 + 20p + 1p$$
$$\longrightarrow £4.21$$

120

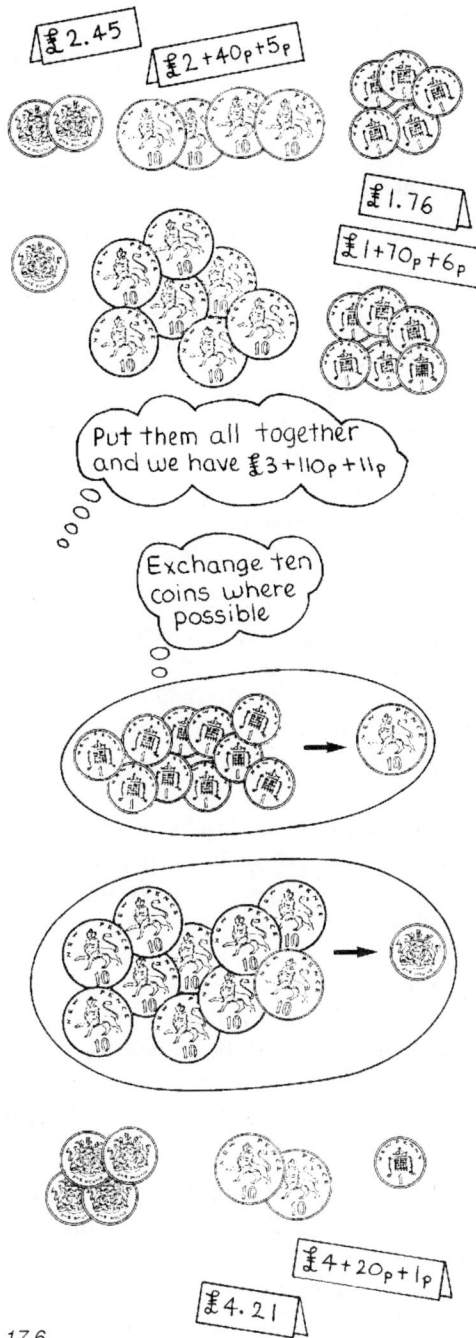

Figure 17.6

Provide the children with some similar sentences to model, e.g.

£1.85	£3.37	£1.86	£2.75
+£2.25	+£1.95	+£2.88	+£1.56

Note: if modelling with a full range of coins, the children may have to exchange a number of times (figure 17.7). For example, modelling £1.46 + £2.72 with 20p and 50p coins:

£1.46 → £1 + 20p + 20p + 5p + 1p
+ £2.72   + £2 + 50p + 20p + 2p

  £3 + 50p + 20p + 20p + 20p + 5p + 2p + 1p
→ £3 + 50p + 20p + 20p + 10p + 10p + 8p
→ £3 + £1 + 10p + 8p
→ £4 + 10p + 8p
→ £4.18

Figure 17.7

18. Have the children estimate the difference in two prices using the rounding down, rounding up and rounding off of prices, for example:

£6.12		£6
−£4.78	rounded down to the nearest pound becomes	−£4
		£2

£6.12		£7
−£4.78	rounded up to the nearest pound becomes	−£5
		£2

£6.12		£6
−£4.78	rounded off to the nearest pound becomes	−£5
		£1

Have the children confirm with their calculators that £6.12 − £4.78 = £1.34, which is close to £1.

19. Give the children two prices, say for an item such as ice-cream in 2 litre and 4 litre sizes. Have the children find the difference between these prices by counting on. For example, if the prices are £1.95 and £3.30:

$$195 \xrightarrow{+5} 200 \xrightarrow{+100} 300 \xrightarrow{+30} 330.$$

The difference is 135 which is £1.35. Explain that these were the prices for a certain brand in 1988 and that in 1990 the prices were £2.10 and £3.50. Have the children find the difference again, i.e. £1.40. Help the children to represent these quantities on a graph (figure 17.8). Can

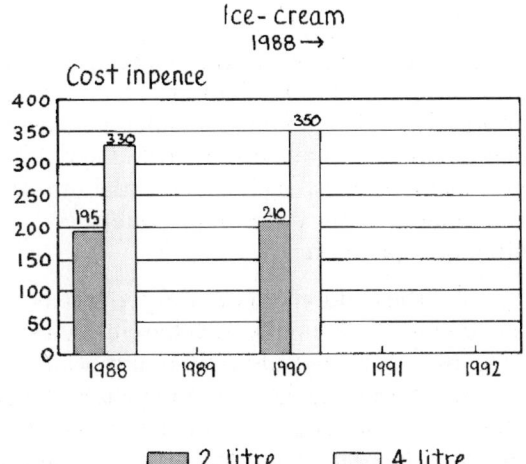

Figure 17.8

they suggest from the graph a price for an 'in-between' size for the ice-cream? Have the children collect prices of other series of commodities and draw graphs of the results.

20. Have the children act out and model some money problems where change has to be found. For example: 'Sue spends £2.36 at the fruit shop. She gives the shopkeeper a £5 note. How much change should she expect?' Have the children act out the counting on procedure, making sure they realise that the value of the goods is part of the equation! Provide the children with other 'bills' where change is required. At this stage make sure the amount offered in payment is realistic, e.g. in the above example £7.89 would be unlikely to be offered! (See also Further activity 1.)

21. Take an article priced at over £1 from the class shop and ask the children how much four of the articles would cost. Have the children estimate first and then find the cost in different ways.

Key page points

Page 75 Finding the sum of a collection of coins and comparing amounts of money are the two concepts developed on this page.

Page 76 Calculators should be available for this page as the children have to estimate the total price for two and three articles, and then find the total using their calculators. Before starting question 6, the children should have decided on the best estimating method to use. Some children might obtain two estimates; one by rounding off the prices to the nearest pound and the other by rounding up to the next pound. When the page is complete discuss with them the three methods of estimating: rounding off, rounding up and rounding down; noting any advantages of each. Coins should be available for children to model the addition operation. Ensure that the children have confidence in their calculators and that they give the correct results.

Page 77 This page gives the children experience in using estimating for the difference process. For questions 5, 6 and 7, the children should estimate the answers before finding the differences using their calculators. Again discuss with them the three methods of estimating, and make sure coins are available for the children to model the difference operation.

Page 78 The children's money experience is extended into situations which the children should recognise as repeated addition/multiplication. They are to estimate the costs and then find them using calculators. Again ensure that the children have confidence in their calculators and that the correct results are given. Discuss once more the three methods of estimating, and again make sure that coins are available for the children to model the multiplication operation.

Further activities

1. Develop Pre-page activity 20 above. Again have the children act out and model some money problems where change has to be found. For example: 'Sue spends £2.36 at the fruit shop. This time she offers £5.36 so that she gets the fewest coins in her change. How much change should she expect and how could it be provided using the minimum number of coins?' Have the children consider the change required if £3.86 was offered (e.g. by someone needing three 50p coins for a machine).

2. Have the children play Supermarket Checkout, a game for 2–4 players (Activity Card 17.6). Decide on a total to have as the 'target', e.g. £5.50, £6.00, £6.50 or £7.00. Deal out three cards to each player and place the rest in a pile face down on the table, with the top card placed face up alongside the pile. Players take it in turns to draw a 'shopping card'. They decide which three of the four cards to keep, attempting to keep the sum as close to the predetermined 'target' as possible without going over. When a player chooses to stop shopping, he/she announces the fact and each remaining player takes one last turn. Each player then uses his/her calculator to find the sum of the items on their cards. The winner is the person who comes closest to the spending 'target' without going over.

3. Let the children play Supermarket Triples (Activity Cards 17.7–17.8). Shuffle all the cards well and spread them out face down on the table. The children take it in turns to turn over a red 'Today's price' card and a blue 'Special offer' card. They then have to turn over a green 'Total to pay' card. If this green card has the sum of the two item cards they have revealed (figure 17.9), then they keep the green card and turn the other cards over again for another player to use. Play continues in this fashion until all the green cards have been claimed. The winner is the player with most green cards at the end of the game.

Figure 17.9

4. Give the children collections of coins and ask them to sort them into sets of each coin and then complete a matrix like the one below.

	1p	2p	5p	10p	20p	50p	£1	
No. of coins								Total value
Value								

5. Have the children play Price Pairs. On one set of cards write prices in decimal notation and on another set, in a different colour, write the same prices in pence, e.g. £0.08, 8p; £0.80, 80p; £8.00, 800p; £1.30, 130p; £2.56, 256p; £0.35, 35p; etc.

6. Ask the children to make displays using cut-outs from catalogues with the prices in decimal notation. Have the children investigate how many prices involve 45p, 49p, 95p and 99p, and discuss with them the implications these popular amounts have when working out change!

7. Have the children price (using decimal notation) an outing to the seaside, cinema, theatre or any local attraction which includes travel, snack and entry money.

8. Get the children to construct ready reckoners for use in the class shop or at a railway or bus station, e.g.

Number \ Cost	£1	£2	£4	£8
1	1	2	4	8
2	2	4	8	16
4	4	8	16	?
8	?	?	?	?

Have the children use their tables to find out how much four items at £5 would cost, e.g. by adding the figures for £1 × 4 and £4 × 4, then ten items at £5, etc. Remind the children of the link with multiplication where they will have seen that 5 × 4 = (1 × 4) + (4 × 4), etc.

Other amounts can also be used, e.g.

Number \ Cost	£1.34	£2.16	£3.42
1 ticket	£1.34	£2.16	£3.42
2 tickets	?	?	?
4 tickets	?	?	?
8 tickets	?	?	?

9. Provide the children with simple shopping problems where they need to find the total cost of their purchases and check the change they get.

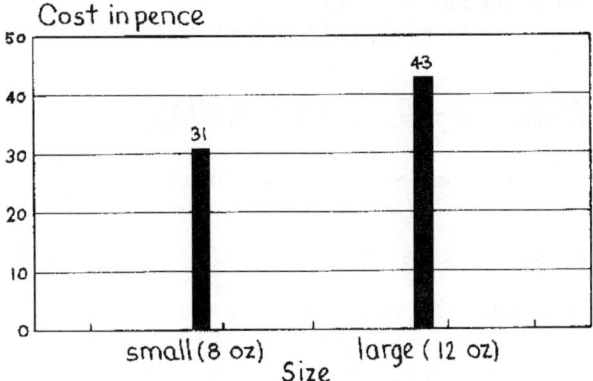

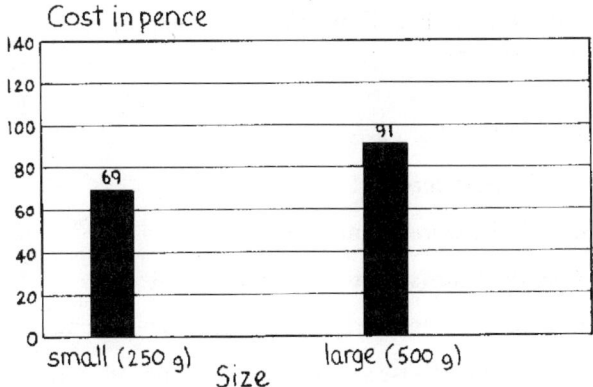

Figure 17.10

10. Have the children draw some more cost graphs of related items (figure 17.10).

11. Copymasters 17.3 and 17.4 provide more practice in estimating by rounding off to the nearest pound.

Check-ups

1. Can the children record pounds and pence in decimal form and recognise the equivalence of, for example, 38p and £0.38, 186p and £1.86, 8p and £0.08?

2. Can the children estimate totals and differences for items when 'shopping'?

3. Can the children find totals and differences using a calculator and explain why the answers are correct?

4. Can the children work out simple money problems including giving the correct change?

New Curriculum Mathematics for Schools Key Stage 2

Section 18

AT 1 3c, 3d, 3e. AT 5 3b, 3d, 4d.

Pages 79–80 Data Handling

Pages 79 and 80 Collecting Badges

Purpose

To give the children further practice in the collection, recording and presentation of data.
To give the children experience of statistical simulation.
To provide the children with opportunities to make and justify estimates of probabilities in a range of events.
To encourage the children to make statements about the likelihood of an event, based on experience.

Recommended material

1. **Copymasters 18.1–18.3**.
2. Dice or spinners marked 1–6.
3. Badge Cards (**Activity Cards 18.1–18.2**).
4. Coloured counters or beads and opaque bags.
5. Spinners (those supplied by Taskmaster, ref. T825, are recommended) and overlays with 2, 3, 4, 5 and 6 equal sectors.

Pre-page activities

Note Many of the collecting activities suggested in this section can be done over a period of time by different groups of children, all contributing to a class graph (figure 18.1). Discuss the graphs 'as they grow'. Although each individual child may not have completed all the activities, have them look at each other's results and compare the graphs. Which graphs are similar? Which graphs are more widely or more narrowly spread? When looking at the graphs, encourage the children to make statements about the likelihood of events (see activity 1 below).

1. Have each child complete a likelihood chart (Copymaster 18.1), encouraging them to use their knowledge of mathematics and probabilities in doing so. Have them illustrate on their charts sentences such as 'I know there is an even chance of getting a head or a tail when I throw a coin', or 'The chance of getting a six when I throw a dice is one out of six, which is much less than half', or 'I know it is

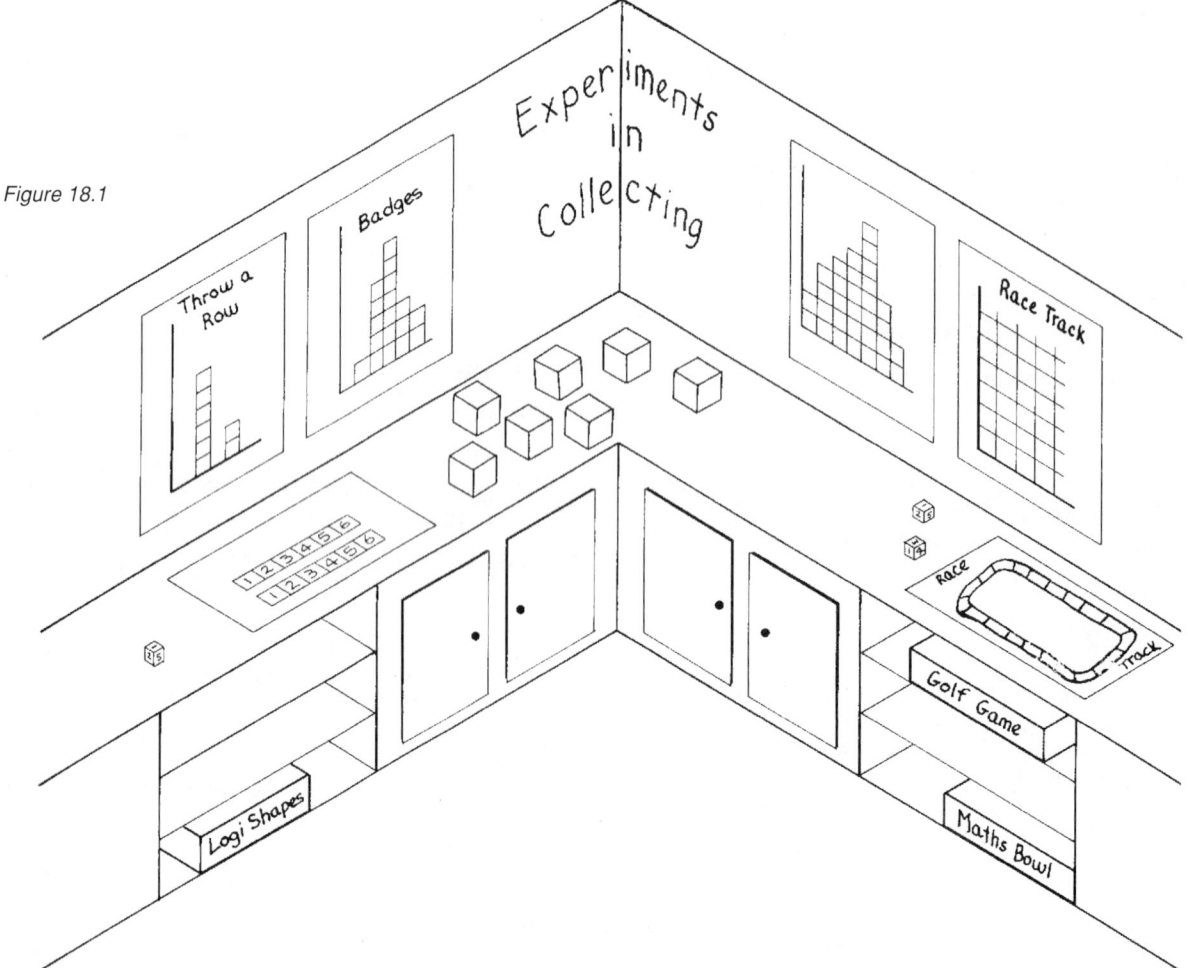

Figure 18.1

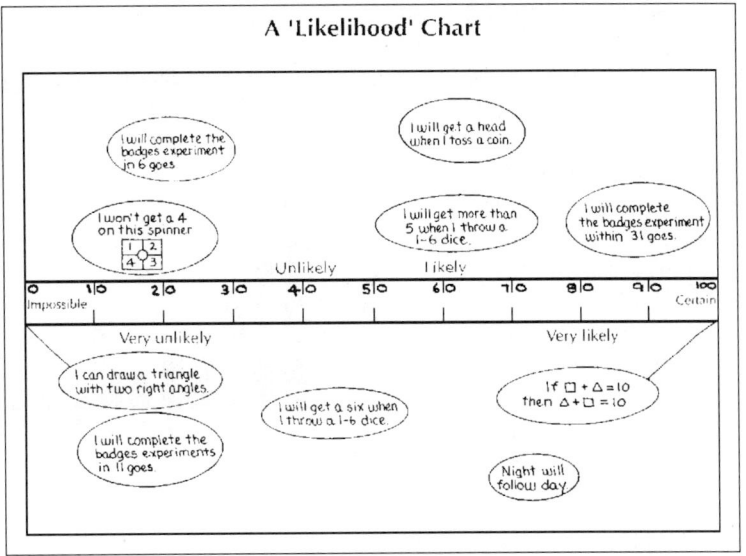

Figure 18.2

impossible to draw a triangle with two right angles' (figure 18.2).

2. Let the children use Copymaster 18.2 to play the Throw a Row game, recording on a class graph the number of 'goes' taken to complete the game. In the game two children take it in turns to throw a 1–6 dice and cross out on their 'mat' the number they obtain. The winner is the first to cross out all the numbers. Have the children play a speeded-up version of the game where each player may cross out a number of his/her choice before starting to play. Discuss their choices with them. Get the children to compare the data from the shortened game with that from the longer game. A 1–6 spinner may be used instead of the 1–6 dice.

Key page points

Page 79 This page asks the children to interpret a graph and complete the thought bubbles for the children shown in the illustrations. In encouraging them to comment that 'twelve in 100 bought ten packets to get a set of six badges from the 36 packets', we are laying the foundations for future work on percentages. By focussing on the numbers who took, for example, less than ten packets (i.e. 30%) to complete the set, we are leading to the considerations required later on for cumulative frequency graphs. Activity Cards 18.1 and 18.2 can be used for the children's experiments in questions 2 and 3. Have the children spread the 36 'cereal packet' cards on the table so that the 'badges' are hidden. They should then 'purchase', i.e. turn over, one card and then another, etc., until a complete set of six badges has been obtained. The number of cards turned over can then be recorded on the class graph, and a comparison made with the graph on the page, which shows the result of 100 attempts.

Page 80 Copymaster 18.1 can be used for the first three activities on this page. To complete the chart in question 1, the children should fill in the blanks in the bubbles and link each statement to the appropriate point on the likelihood chart. The 'swapping' in activity 4 is 'cooperative collecting' in which the children work in pairs, using Activity Cards 18.1 and 18.2, each one passing on to the other any duplicates which the other still needs. Have the children decide on the rules to be operated, e.g. whether they should work together until one set of six is collected, or continue until they have both collected a set of six badges. Figures 18.3 and 18.4 show the kind of result to expect in each of the two situations.

The last activity involving restocking should be done as a simulation using a 1–6 dice. This will avoid the need for the 'purchaser' to replace and shuffle the cards each time. You will have to explain to the children that, rather than draw an

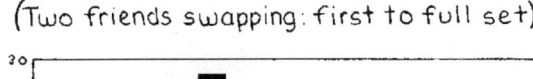
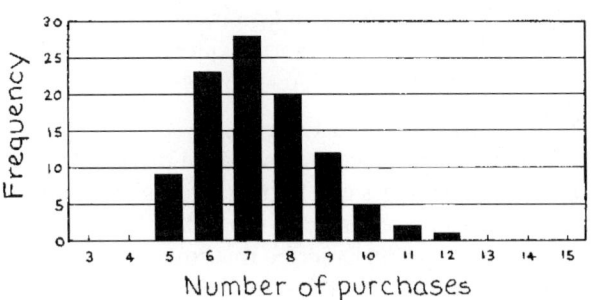

Figure 18.3

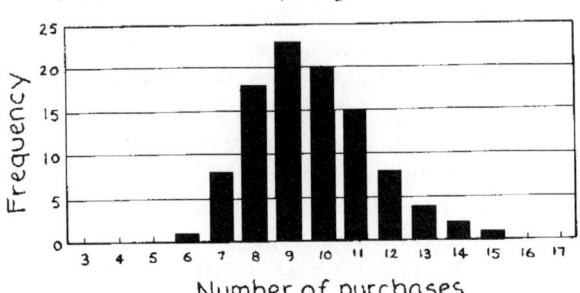

Figure 18.4

animal on each face of a cube, the numbers on the dice can represent the animals. The children will need to record how many throws of the dice they must make before 'collecting' one of each number. (Contrast this with Pre-page activity 2, where the children had to 'collect' numbers 1–6 in the Throw a Row game.) To make a comparison with the graph on page 79 of the Pupils' Book easier, it would help if a graph of 100 experiments could be constructed. This will be completed more quickly if a group of children, or indeed the whole class, contributes to the graph. A likely shape for the graph after 100 experiments is shown in figure 18.5.

Figure 18.5

Further activities

1. Make a classroom display of products which encourage purchasers to collect cards, badges, tokens, sporting personality books, etc. Some will have the straightforward goal of collecting enough tokens to claim a 'gift'; others will have an element of chance. Encourage the children to look for disclaimers and guarantees of equal distribution on these sort of offers. Have them comment on the various promotions.

2. A pet food manufacturer at one stage ran a competition by asking 'Is there a prize in this can?' Customers had to open the can and look at the inside of the lid to see if they had won a 'valuable' prize. Describe this situation to the children and have them make a simulation of it. Get them to place 100 red counters in a bag to represent a random set of cans, and then replace a given number of them with blue ones, to represent cans with prizes. Clearly the manufacturer will intend the competition to produce a low percentage of winners. However, the children can experiment by including in their bag, say, 30 blue counters and 70 red counters. They can then invite their friends to dip into the bag and draw out a counter, repeating the experiment until a blue counter is drawn out. (Have the children replace the counter after each draw.) They should then make a graph of their results to

(a)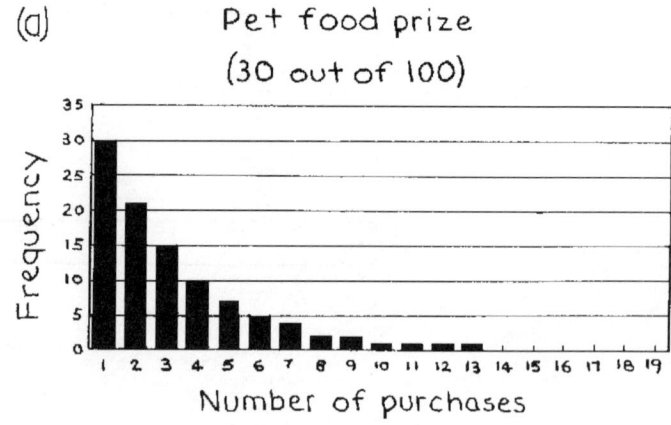

(b)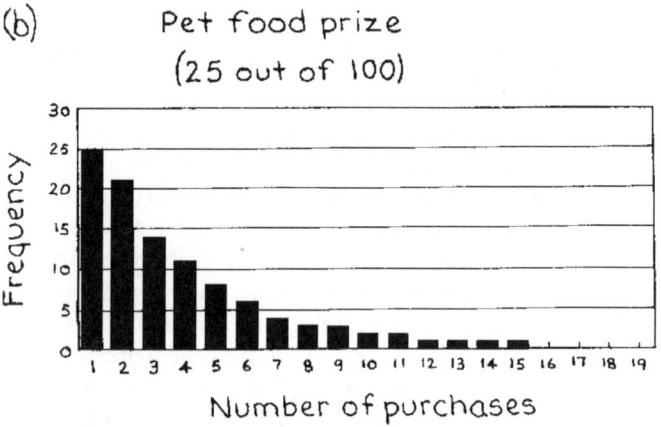

(c)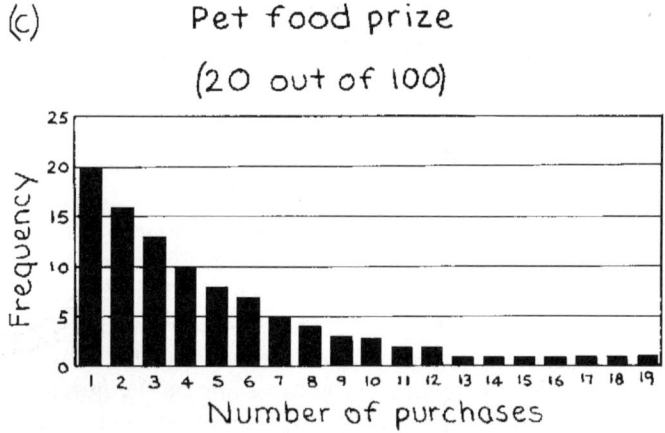

Figure 18.6

show how many 'cans' were bought before a prize was won. The graphs in figure 18.6 show possible results with 30, 25 and 20 'winning' counters included in the 100. Have the children say what proportion of 'winning/losing' counters they would include if they were offering, on the one hand, a sweet as a prize, and on the other hand an expensive car!

3. Using the 'badge' cards provided on Activity Cards 18.1 and 18.2, ask the children to collect a set of two from 12 cards, a set of three from 18 cards, and a set of four from 24 cards. The children should first predict and then make a

graph of the number of cards needed to be taken in order to complete the sets (figure 18.7). Have the children report on their findings. Can they suggest a 'best' number to collect? Is any number too small or too large?

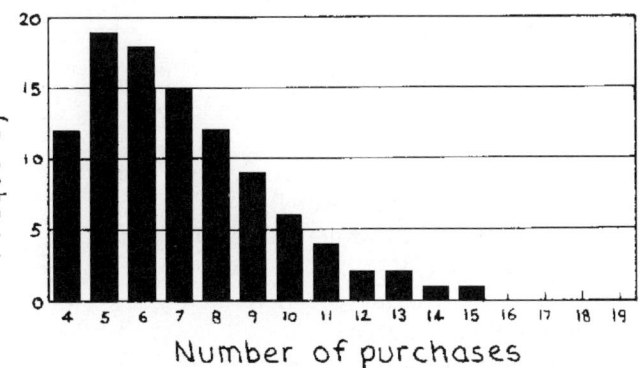

Figure 18.7

4. Provide the children with copies of Copymaster 18.3. Ask them to study and comment on the two graphs on the left of the sheet, and have them make some general observations about what design of spinner might produce these results. The blank spinner overlay can be cut out and used by the children to design their own overlays. It should fit the spinners recommended for this series. The children should then test their spinners and draw graphs of the results.

Check-ups

1. Can the children organise a practical statistical investigation, collecting the data, drawing a graph of the results, and making predictions using their results?

2. Can the children give estimates, in words, of probabilities in a range of events? Can they justify their estimates?

3. Can the children compare graphs by making statements such as 'in this one, 30 out of 100 achieved less than 10, whilst this shows that 16 out of 100 achieved 9', and show that they understand the difference?

Answers

Section 1

Pages 2–3

1. Ming

x	2	3	4	5	2	4
2	4	6	8	10	4	8
3	6	9	12	15	6	12
4	8	12	16	20	8	16
5	10	12	20	25	10	20
2	4	6	8	10	4	8
4	8	12	16	20	8	16

Hannah

x	2	3	4	5	3	3
2	4	6	8	10	6	6
3	6	9	12	15	9	9
4	8	12	16	20	12	12
5	10	15	20	25	15	15
3	6	9	12	15	9	9
3	6	9	12	15	9	9

2. Multiplication Race Track Game
   Extra Numbers: 2, 4.
   The graph shows that [100] games were completed because 2 + 7 + 17 + 23 + 22 + 15 + 8 + 4 + 1 + 1 = 100. The tallest column was at [9] throws. [49] of the players took less than 10 throws. The shortest game took only [6] throws. The longest game took [15]. The difference between the highest and lowest score is [9] because [15] – [6] = [9].

3. Multiplication Race Track Game
   Extra Numbers: 3 and 3.
   The graph shows that 100 games were completed because [2] + [6] + [11] + [17] + [20] + [19] + [14] + [7] + [3] + [1] = 100. The tallest column is at 7 goes. [20] players scored 7. It was the most popular score. The shortest game took only 3 throws. The difference between the highest and lowest score is [9] because 12 – 3 = [9]. [89] of the players took less than 10.

Page 4

1. digital
2. 30
3. more than 10 but less than 20
4. as few as [1] or as many as [9]
5. Open-ended.
6. Between 40 and 50 of the people surveyed preferred each type of watch.
   Between 10 and 20 adults preferred digital watches.
   About 30 more adults preferred analogue watches than children.
   Between 30 and 40 children were surveyed.
   Between 90 and 100 people were surveyed.
   Between 50 and 60 adults were surveyed.
   About 20 more adults preferred analogue watches to digital watches.
7. Open-ended.

Page 5

1. The house representing 100 sales is clearly more than twice as big as the house representing 50 sales.

3. about 15 squares
   about 60 squares
   about 4 times as many squares

4. Any representation where the second is about twice the size (area) of the first. A possible solution might be:

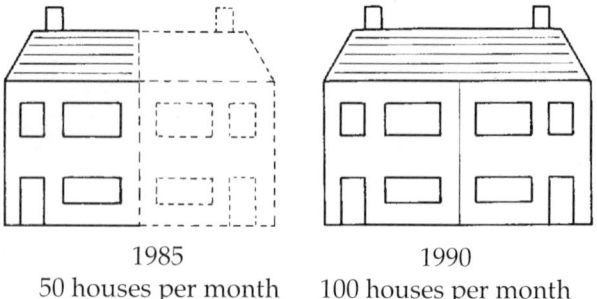

1985　　　　　　　1990
50 houses per month　　100 houses per month

Page 6

Have the children base their answers on the Scrabble distribution chart (figure 1.10) and information given on pages 18–19 of this Guide. For example, for French an acceptable distribution would be as shown on page 18 with 1 fewer 'e' and no 'blanks'.

Answers

Page 7

5	t	c	l	m	u
4	q/z	s	w	o	d
3	y	x	i	p	v
2	f	e	k	h	n
1	a	j	b	g	r
	1	2	3	4	5

1. On a lovely day in winter Naseem and Sue went out to play in the snow.
2. Let us make a snowman said Naseem. He can wear your hat.
3. We can make snowballs as well said Sue. Let us see who will be the first to knock his hat off.

   Now make up a code and write a message for your friend to decode.

Section 2

Page 8

1. Open-ended. Sample answer:
   28p + 30p = 58p
   58p + 7p = 65p
2. Open-ended. Encourage the children to explain their reasons.
3. (a) 66p (b) 60p (c) 95p
   (d) 86p (e) 87p (f) 69p
4. 89p, 60p, 71p, 92p, 88p
5. Open-ended.

Page 9

1. Open-ended. Sample answer:
   72p − 8p = 64p
   64p − 40p = 24p
2. Open-ended. Encourage the children to explain their reasons.
3. (a) 11p (b) 11p (c) 42p
   (d) 45p (e) 6p   (f) 24p
4. 32p, 24p, 48p, 20p, 43p
5. Open-ended.

Page 10

Open-ended.

Section 3

Page 11

1. (a) 20 (b) 50 (c) 100
   (d) 200 (e) 600 (f) 1000
2. (a)

Number of choc ices
230
380
800
460

   (b) 8 boxes
3. (a) 3 (b) 43 (c) 56
4. (a) 3 (b) 5 (c) 6
   (d) 4 (e) 7 (f) 10

Page 12

1. (a) Naseem:
       units   → 4
       tens   → 2
       hundreds → 3
       score   → 324
   Jamie:
       units   → 3
       tens   → 2
       hundreds → 4
       score   → 423
   Gwen:
       units   → 3
       tens   → 4
       hundreds → 2
       score   → 243
   (b) Jamie
   (c) Gwen
2. (a) Fiona:
       units   → 4
       tens   → 1
       hundreds → 4
       score   → 414
   Tony:
       units   → 4
       tens   → 3
       hundreds → 3
       score   → 334
   Kumar:
       units   → 4
       tens   → 2
       hundreds → 4
       score   → 424
   (b) Kumar
   (c) Tony

Page 13

1. (a) 2 hundreds 4 tens 6 units

129

New Curriculum Mathematics for Schools Key Stage 2

       200 + 40 + 6
       246 units
  (b) 4 hundreds 0 tens 3 units
       400 + 3
       403 units
  (c) 4 hundreds 1 ten 5 units
       400 + 10 + 5
       415
  (d) Gwen

2. (a)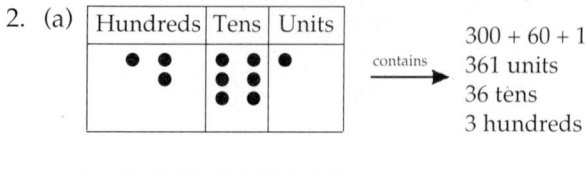
    contains 300 + 60 + 1
    361 units
    36 tens
    3 hundreds

  (b)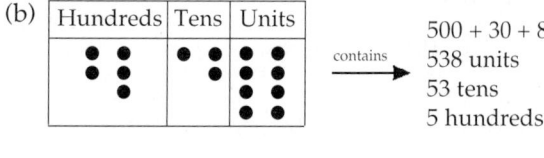
    contains 500 + 30 + 8
    538 units
    53 tens
    5 hundreds

  (c)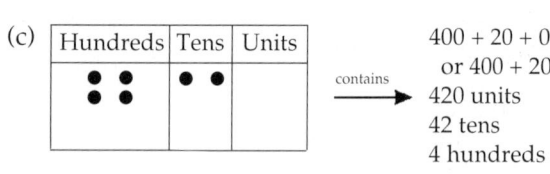
    contains 400 + 20 + 0
    or 400 + 20
    420 units
    42 tens
    4 hundreds

  (d)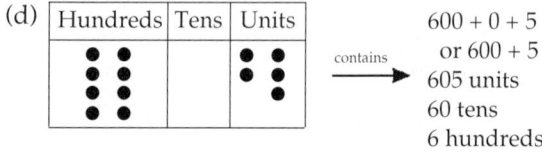
    contains 600 + 0 + 5
    or 600 + 5
    605 units
    60 tens
    6 hundreds

  (e)
    contains 400 + 70 + 4
    474 units
    47 tens
    4 hundreds

3. (a) 765
  (b) 235

Page 14

1. Sue: 112
  John: 121
  Gwen: 211
  Kumar: 202
  Fiona: 220
  Jamie: 22
  Ming: 301
  Tony: 103
  Naseem: 130

2. 301, 220, 211, 202, 130, 121, 112, 103, 22
  or 22, 103, 112, 121, 130, 202, 211, 220, 301.
  Ming won.

3. Open-ended. Sample answers:
  (a) Enter [1][0][0] M+ [1][0] M+ [1] M+ [1] M+ MR
  or Enter [1][1][1] M+ [1] M+ MR
  (b) Enter [1][1][0] M+ [1][1][0] M+ MR
  or Enter [1][0][0] M+ [1][0][0] M+ [1][0] M+ [1][0] M+ MR
  (c) Enter [1][1][0] M+ [1][0] M+ [1][0] M+ MR
  or Enter [1][0][0] M+ [1][0] M+ [1][0] M+ [1][0] M+ MR
  (d) Enter [1][1][0] M+ [1][0][0] M+ [1][0][0] M+ MR
  or Enter [1][0][0] M+ [1][0][0] M+ [1][0][0] M+ [1][0] M+ MR
  (e) Enter [1][1] M+ [1][0] M+ [1][0] M+ MR
  or Enter [1][0] M+ [1][0] M+ [1][0] M+ [1] M+ MR
  (f) Enter [1][0][0] M+ [1][0][0] M+ [1][0][0] M+ [1][0][0] M+ MR

Section 4

Page 15

1.
Omega Time	Gardex Time	Spaceage Time	Mariner Time
11:30	12:00	12:45	10:15
12:00	12:30	13:15	10:45
12:30	13:00	13:45	11:15
13:00	13:30	14:15	11:45
13:30	14:00	14:45	12:15
14:00	14:30	15:15	12:45
14:30	15:00	15:45	13:15
15:00	15:30	16:15	13:45
15:30	16:00	16:45	14:15
16:00	16:30	17:15	14:45
16:30	17:00	17:45	15:15
17:00	17:30	18:15	15:45
17:30	18:00	18:45	16:15
18:00	18:30	19:15	16:45

2. 6 pairs with the following times:
  5 to 12   23:55
  10 past 5   17:10
  nearly half past 8 20:26
  or 26 minutes past 8
  quarter past 10   10:15
  12 o'clock   12:00
  half past 1   13:30

3. 9

4. This is an open question and could depend on how accurate the children's watches are.

Page 16

1. 25 minutes
2. 5 minutes

3. 20 minutes

4. 10 minutes

5. 10 minutes

6.
City Centre to Trentham and Return	City Centre to Leek and Return
dep. 0715	dep. 0710
arr. 0740	arr. 0730
dep. 0745	dep. 0800
arr. 0810	arr. 0800
dep. 0730	dep. 0725
arr. 0755	arr. 0745
dep. 0800	dep. 0755
arr. 0825	arr. 0815
dep. 0745	dep. 0740
arr. 0810	arr. 0800
dep. 0815	dep. 0810
arr. 0840	arr. 0830

7. 0700

8. 0715, 0730, 0745

9. 4

10. 4

Page 17

1. Two flights will get you there in time: the 0730 and the 0830.
   There are two flights after 4 pm.
   There is one at 1730 and one at 1930.
   At 0710 or 0810 depending on the flight.
   Each flight takes one hour.

2. (a) 3 hours 50 minutes (e) 3 hours 40 minutes
   (b) 7 hours 35 minutes (f) 6 hours 40 minutes
   (c) 7 hours 35 minutes (g) 3 hours 50 minutes
   (d) 3 hours 50 minutes (h) 7 hours 5 minutes

Pages 18–19

1.
1st	2nd	3rd	4th	5th	6th	7th	8th
A	G	D	C	F	E	H	B

2. A depart 1100
   G arrive 1835
     depart 1500
   D arrive 2125
     depart 0045
   C arrive 0755
     depart 1255
   F arrive 1815
     depart 0015
   E arrive 2355
     depart 2100
   H arrive 0205
     depart 0500
   B arrive 0620

3.
London–New York	7 hours 35 minutes
New York–San Francisco	6 hours 25 minutes
San Francisco–Tahiti	7 hours 10 minutes
Tahiti–Auckland	5 hours 20 minutes
Auckland–Sydney	3 hours 40 minutes
Sydney–Hong Kong	9 hours 5 minutes
Hong Kong–London	17 hours 20 minutes

Section 5

Pages 20–21

1. Sample explanation: 'First I made a model using blue cubes to represent the 182 plastic bottles collected and yellow cubes to represent the 143 glass bottles. Then I joined ten '10' strips to make another 100 piece, and then I put all the cubes together to find the total.'

2. $143 \rightarrow (100 + 40 + 3)$
   $+182 \quad +(100 + 80 + 2)$
   $(200 + 120 + 5) \rightarrow (300 + 20 + 5) \rightarrow 325$
   Ming expected this result because he knew that $100 + 200 = 300$.

3. B, D, C, A

4. $145 \rightarrow (100 + 40 + 5)$
   $+196 \quad +(100 + 90 + 6)$
   $(200 + 130 + 11) \rightarrow (200 + 140 + 1)$
   $\rightarrow (300 + 40 + 1) \rightarrow 341$

Pages 22–23

1. C, B, A

2. $145 \rightarrow (100 + 40 + 5)$
   $+236 \quad +(200 + 30 + 6)$
   $(300 + 70 + 11) \rightarrow (300 + 80 + 1) \rightarrow 381$

3. Sample explanation: 'First I made a model using blue cubes to represent the 245 plastic bottles and yellow cubes to represent the 323 glass bottles. Then I put the cubes together to find the total.'

4. $323 \rightarrow (300 + 20 + 3)$
   $+245 \quad +(200 + 40 + 5)$
   $(500 + 60 + 8) \rightarrow 568$

5. 538

6. 481

7. Wednesday 521, Thursday 498

Page 24

1. 409, 454, 490, 445, 637, 700, 673, 610

2. 135 + 45 = 180
   235 + 45 = 280
   335 + 45 = 380
   435 + 45 = 480
   535 + 45 = 580

New Curriculum Mathematics for Schools Key Stage 2

123 + 32 = 155
223 + 32 = 255
323 + 32 = 355
423 + 32 = 455
523 + 32 = 555

109 + 28 = 137
209 + 28 = 237
309 + 28 = 337
409 + 28 = 437
509 + 28 = 537

3. Open-ended. Sample answer:
   265 + 18 = 283
   365 + 18 = 383, etc.
   Explanation: 'I added 100 to the first number each time and the total was increased by 100 each time.'

4. 969, 500, 538, 500, 576, 500, 564, 500

5.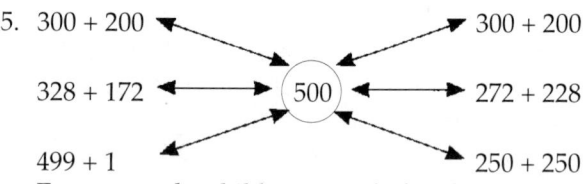
   Encourage the children to include other number sentences.

Page 25

1. (a) 557 kg (b) 595 kg (c) 882 kg (d) 833 kg
   Encourage the children to find the sum in at least three different ways.

2. (a) 153 kg + 213 kg = 366 kg
   (b) 214 kg + 162 kg = 376 kg

Page 26

1. (a)   130 km   (b)   157 km   (c)   261 km
       + 179 km   + 233 km   + 238 km
         309 km   390 km   499 km

   (d)   107 km   (e)   66 km   (f)   164 km
       + 121 km   + 157 km   + 261 km
         228 km   223 km   425 km

   (g)   190 km   (h)   124 km   (i)   249 km
       + 241 km   + 241 km   + 88 km
         431 km   365 km   337 km

   (j)   88 km
       + 249 km
         337 km

2. Open-ended. Encourage the children to include journeys involving the addition of more than two distances, for example:

   Plymouth to Southampton   238 km
   Southampton to London   124 km
   London to Cambridge   + 88 km
                      Total   450 km

Page 27

618   455
+ 271   + 201
889   656

238   685
+ 326   + 242
564   927

226   463
+ 574   + 476
800   939

167   276
+ 259   + 437
426   713

802   217
+ 193   + 553
995   770

374   165
+ 289   + 369
663   534

2. Sample story: Last week Ben delivered 259 morning papers and 167 evening papers. Altogether last week he delivered 426 newspapers.

Section 6

Page 28

1. The lattice points are:
   (0, 6), (1, 5), (2, 4), (3, 3), (4, 2), (5, 1), (6, 0)

   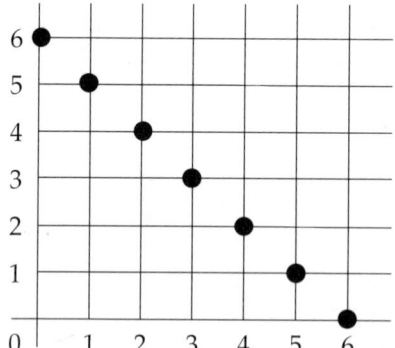

2. The lattice points are:
   (0, 0), (1, 1), (2, 2), (3, 3), (4, 4), (5, 5), (6, 6)

   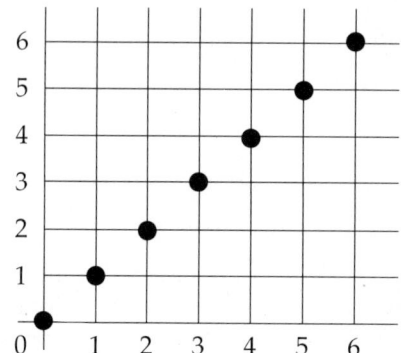

3. The lattice points are:
   (0, 0), (1, 2), (2, 4), (3, 6), (4, 8) ...

Page 29

1. (0, 1) moves to (7, 1); (1, 5) moves to (8, 5)
2. (1, 1) moves to (1, 4); (5, 2) moves to (5, 5)
3. (1, 0) moves to (1, 5); (5, 1) moves to (5, 6)
4. (1, 3) moves to (5, 6); (5, 2) moves to (9, 5)

Page 30

1. (a) 7 units (b) 7 units
   (c) 7 units (d) 7 units
2. (12, 4)
3. Add 7 to the first number of Tony's pair.
4. Red: (2, 5) Tony; (2, 9) Gwen
   Blue: (5, 7) Tony; (5, 11) Gwen
   Green: (7, 4) Tony; (7, 8) Gwen
   Yellow: (4, 2) Tony; (4, 6) Gwen
   The new square is vertically above Tony's square with the same orientation.
5. Open-ended.

Page 31

1. (a) horizontal (b) vertical
   (c) vertical (d) inclined
2. When vertical and horizontal lines meet they make a **right** angle.
3. Open-ended.

Section 7

Pages 32–33

1. The ten hottest places on the map are:
   1 Las Vegas
   2 Miami
      Tampa
   4 New Orleans
      Dallas
      El Paso
      Salt Lake City
   8 Atlanta
   9 Seattle
   10 Los Angeles

2. The ten coldest places on the map are:
   1 Minneapolis
   2 Buffalo
   3 Chicago
      Detroit
      Denver
   6 New York
   7 Kansas City
   8 Washington
   9 Salt Lake City
   10 Atlanta

3.

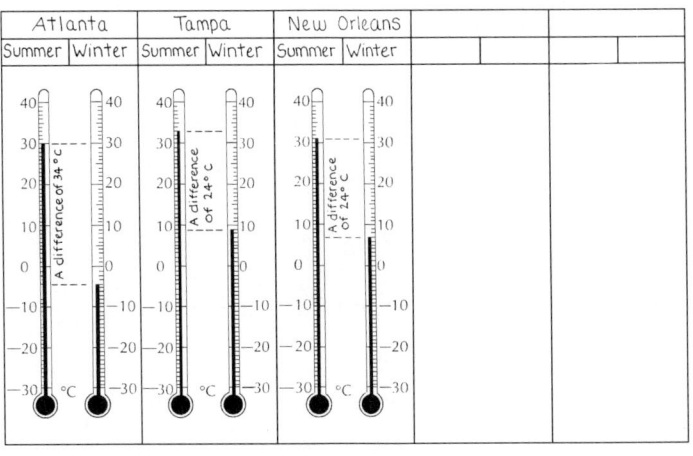

New Curriculum Mathematics for Schools Key Stage 2

4. Minneapolis
5. San Francisco
6. The response depends on the current temperature.

Page 34

1. 6 + 5 = 11   9 + 5 = 14
   7 + 5 = 12   10 + 5 = 15
   8 + 5 = 13

2. 6 – 5 = 1   9 – 5 = 4
   7 – 5 = 2   10 – 5 = 5
   8 – 5 = 3

3. 5 – 5 = 0   8 – 8 = 0
   6 – 6 = 0   9 – 9 = 0
   7 – 7 = 0

4. Example answer:

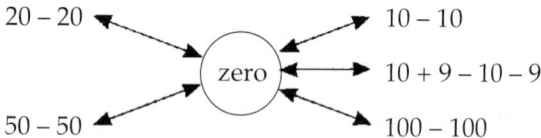

5. 5 – 6 = ⁻1
   5 – 7 = ⁻2
   5 – 8 = ⁻3
   5 – 9 = ⁻4
   5 – 10 = ⁻5

6.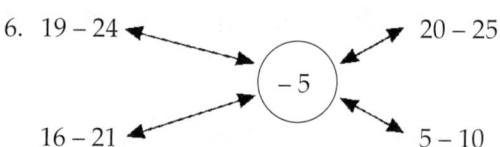

Encourage the children to include a variety of different number sentences.

Section 8

Page 35

1. cube
2. cuboid
3. 6
4. 24
5. 5
6. 20
7. square pyramid
8. triangular pyramid and square pyramid
9. cube and cuboid
10. cube (probably also triangular prism)

Page 36

1. (a) octagon, triangle
   (b) hexagon, rectangle or square
   (c) trapezium, rectangle or square
   (d) trapezium, rectangle or square
   (e) trapezium, triangle, rectangle or square
   (f) trapezium, rectangle or square

2.
	Vertices	Faces	Edges
(a)	24	14	36
(b)	12	8	18
(c)	8	6	12
(d)	8	6	12
(e)	6	5	9
(f)	8	6	12

Page 37

1. (a) 4 ways   (b) 2 ways
   (c) any number of ways (an infinite number)
   (d) 5 ways

2. Top left: cylinder, sphere, cone
   Top right: cube, square prism, square pyramid
   Bottom left: cuboid, prism (any type including cylinder)
   Bottom right: triangular prism, triangular pyramid

Section 9

Page 38

1. There are six possible outfits:
   black skirt with red sweater
   black skirt with blue sweater
   black skirt with green sweater
   yellow skirt with red sweater
   yellow skirt with blue sweater
   yellow skirt with green sweater

2. 3 sweaters and 2 skirts produce 6 outfits.

3. (a) Ming: 3 tops and 4 trousers produce 12 outfits.
   (b) Sue: 4 tops and 4 trousers/skirts produce 16 outfits.
   (c) Gwen: 4 tops and 3 skirts produce 12 outfits.

Page 39

1. There are six possible different meals:
   hamburger/chips and ice-cream sundae
   hamburger/chips and trifle
   pizza and ice-cream sundae
   pizza and trifle
   ham salad and ice-cream sundae
   ham salad and trifle

Answers

2. 3 first course choices and 2 second course choices produce 6 meals.

3. Breakfast:
   Cornflakes and boiled egg
   Cornflakes and scrambled egg
   Cornflakes and pancakes
   Branflakes and boiled egg
   Branflakes and scrambled egg
   Branflakes and pancakes
   Grapefruit and boiled egg
   Grapefruit and scrambled egg
   Grapefruit and pancakes
   3 starters and 3 main courses produce 9 meals.

   Lunch:
   Chicken soup and curry
   Chicken soup and steak pie
   Tomato soup and curry
   Tomato soup and steak pie
   Vegetable soup and curry
   Vegetable soup and steak pie
   Mushroom soup and curry
   Mushroom soup and steak pie
   4 first courses and 2 second courses produce 8 meals.

   Afternoon tea:
   Cheese sandwich and tea
   Cheese sandwich and milkshake
   Cheese sandwich and orange juice
   Cheese sandwich and coke
   Beef sandwich and tea
   Beef sandwich and milkshake
   Beef sandwich and orange juice
   Beef sandwich and coke
   2 different sandwiches and 4 drinks produce 8 meals.

Page 40

1. Table tennis order of play:
   1. Fiona v Kumar
   2. Naseem v Jamie
   3. Gwen v Ming
   4. Fiona v Jamie
   5. Naseem v Ming
   6. Gwen v Kumar
   7. Fiona v Ming
   8. Naseem v Kumar
   9. Gwen v Jamie
   There are 9 games to play.

2. Outcomes of two 1–6 dice:
   1–1, 1–2, 1–3, 1–4, 1–5, 1–6
   2–1, 2–2, 2–3, 2–4, 2–5, 2–6
   3–1, 3–2, 3–3, 3–4, 3–5, 3–6
   4–1, 4–2, 4–3, 4–4, 4–5, 4–6
   5–1, 5–2, 5–3, 5–4, 5–5, 5–6
   6–1, 6–2, 6–3, 6–4, 6–5, 6–6
   There are 36 different outcomes.

3. Plan for 15-gear bicycle:

   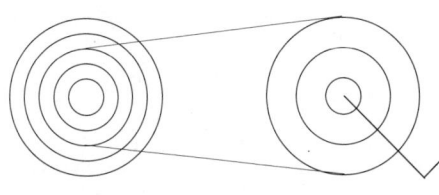

   Rear wheel   Driving wheel
   (5 wheels)   (3 wheels)

4. Two-letter words – product set:
   it   at
   in   an
   is   as

Page 41

1. 4 x 8 = 32
   Sample story: There are 8 boxes with 4 cakes in each. Altogether there are 32 cakes.

2. 4 x 6 = 24   4 x 9 = 36   3 x 8 = 24   4 x 7 = 28
   3 x 9 = 27   3 x 7 = 21   3 x 6 = 18   6 x 3 = 18
   6 x 8 = 48   6 x 9 = 54   4 x 12 = 48   7 x 15 = 105
   Sample example of solving in different ways:
   4 x 12 = (4 x 10) + (4 x 2) = 40 + 8 = 48
   or 4 x 12 = (4 x 7) + (4 x 5) = 28 + 20 = 48

Page 42

1.
Jam tarts		
	contain	
Packs	→	Tarts
1	→	7
2	→	14
3	→	21
4	→	28
5	→	35
6	→	42
7	→	49
8	→	56
9	→	63
10	→	70

Apple pies		
	contain	
Packs	→	Pies
1	→	4
2	→	8
3	→	12
4	→	16
5	→	20
6	→	24
7	→	28
8	→	32
9	→	36
10	→	40

2.
Fruit slices		
	contain	
Boxes	→	Slices
1	→	8
2	→	16
3	→	24
4	→	32
5	→	40
6	→	48
7	→	56
8	→	64
9	→	72
10	→	80

Page 43

1.
Magic pens	
Number of packs	Number of pens
1	3
2	6
3	9
4	12

To be continued by children.

Toy cars	
Number of packs	Number of cars
1	6
2	12
3	18
4	24

To be continued by children.

Stickers	
Number of packs	Number of stickers
1	9
2	18
3	27
4	36

To be continued by children.

2. Open-ended. Sample report (for pens): 1 more pack of pens means 3 more pens each time.
Relationship between the 3 multiplication table and 6 multiplication table: the 6 pattern is double the 3 pattern each time.
Relationship between the 3 multiplication table and 9 multiplication table: the 9 pattern is 3 times the 3 pattern each time.
Relationships between the 3, 6 and 9 multiplication tables: the number of items for any number of packs in the 9 table will be the sum of the number of items for the same number of packs in the 3 and 6 tables.

3. 48
4. 63
5. 27p
6. 45, 21, 72, 54, 24, 63
7. 45, 21, 72, 54, 24, 63

The children should notice the relationship between the sentences, e.g. 9 x 5 = 45 and 5 x 9 = 45.

Page 44

1. 4 x 1 = 4   4 x 2 = 8
   1 x 4 = 4   2 x 4 = 8
   4 x 3 = 12   4 x 4 = 16
   3 x 4 = 12   4 x 4 = 16
   4 x 5 = 20   4 x 6 = 24
   5 x 4 = 20   6 x 4 = 24
   To be continued by children to 4 x 10 = 40 and 10 x 4 = 40.

2. 2 rows of 20 squares   20 x 2 = 40
   20 rows of 2 squares   2 x 20 = 40
   5 rows of 8 squares   8 x 5 = 40
   8 rows of 5 squares   5 x 8 = 40
   4 rows of 10 squares   10 x 4 = 40
   10 rows of 4 squares   4 x 10 = 40

Page 45

1.
x3	3	6	9	12	15	18	21	24	27	30
x7	7	14	21	28	35	42	49	56	63	70
x10	10	20	30	40	50	60	70	80	90	100

2. (a)
x6	6	12	18	24	30	36	42	48	54	60
x3	3	6	9	12	15	18	21	24	27	30
x9	9	18	27	36	45	54	63	72	81	90

(b)
x3	3	6	9	12	15	18	21	24	27	30
x4	4	8	12	16	20	24	28	32	36	40
x7	7	14	21	28	35	42	49	56	63	70

(c)
x2	2	4	6	8	10	12	14	16	18	20
x7	7	14	21	28	35	42	49	56	63	70
x9	9	18	27	36	45	54	63	72	81	90

(d)
x3	3	6	9	12	15	18	21	24	27	30
x5	5	10	15	20	25	30	35	40	45	50
x8	8	16	24	32	40	48	56	64	72	80

(e)
x5	5	10	15	20	25	30	35	40	45	50
x5	5	10	15	20	25	30	35	40	45	50
x10	10	20	30	40	50	60	70	80	90	100

3. 7 x 10 = 70
   7 x 6 = 42
   so 7 x 16 = 112

Page 46

1. Sample mats:

6		14		24
	36	42	45	48
54	81		90	

7		9		16
	18	30	35	40
48	54		60	

18		24		28
	32	42	56	63
64	70		72	

8		12		21
	27	36	49	56
63	72		90	

3. No, different mats win when you start from different positions.

Section 10

Page 47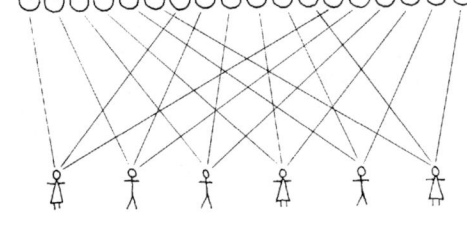

1. 18
    −6
    ─
    12
    −6
    ─
    6
    −6
    ─
    0

    $\frac{18}{6} = 3$ because 3 × 6 = 18

    We have 3 apples each.

2. Picture and number stories as above showing:
   (a) $\frac{32}{4} = 8$ apples each
   (b) $\frac{30}{6} = 5$ apples each
   (c) $\frac{45}{9} = 5$ apples each

3. Picture and number stories as in 1 above showing:
   (a) $\frac{36}{12} = 3$ apples each
   (b) $\frac{36}{9} = 4$ apples each
   (c) $\frac{36}{6} = 6$ apples each
   (d) $\frac{36}{4} = 9$ apples each
   (e) $\frac{36}{3} = 12$ apples each
   (f) $\frac{36}{2} = 18$ apples each

Page 48

1. 24
    −8 1 bag
    ──
    16
    −8 1 bag
    ──
    8
    −8 1 bag
    ──
    0

    $\frac{24}{8} = 3$ because 8 × 3 = 24

    I need 3 bags.

2. Number stories as in 1 above showing:
   (a) $\frac{32}{8} = 4$
   (b) $\frac{80}{8} = 10$
   (c) $\frac{56}{8} = 7$
   (d) $\frac{64}{8} = 8$

3. Number stories as in 1 above showing:
   (a) $\frac{48}{16} = 3$
   (b) $\frac{48}{12} = 4$
   (c) $\frac{48}{8} = 6$
   (d) $\frac{48}{6} = 8$
   (e) $\frac{48}{4} = 12$
   (f) $\frac{48}{3} = 16$

Page 49

1. (a) $\frac{2}{2} = 1$, $\frac{4}{4} = 1$; $\frac{2}{2} = \frac{4}{4}$
   (b) $\frac{4}{2} = 2$, $\frac{8}{4} = 2$; $\frac{4}{2} = \frac{8}{4}$
   (c) $\frac{6}{2} = 3$, $\frac{12}{4} = 3$; $\frac{6}{2} = \frac{12}{4}$
   (d) $\frac{8}{2} = 4$, $\frac{16}{4} = 4$; $\frac{8}{2} = \frac{16}{4}$
   (e) $\frac{10}{2} = 5$, $\frac{20}{4} = 5$; $\frac{10}{2} = \frac{20}{4}$
   (f) $\frac{12}{2} = 6$, $\frac{24}{4} = 6$; $\frac{12}{2} = \frac{24}{4}$

2. Open-ended. Sample answer:
   $\frac{12}{3} = 4$, $\frac{24}{6} = 4$; $\frac{12}{3} = \frac{24}{6}$

3. (a) $\frac{3}{3} = 1$, $\frac{6}{6} = 1$; $\frac{3}{3} = \frac{6}{6}$
   (b) $\frac{6}{3} = 2$, $\frac{12}{6} = 2$; $\frac{6}{3} = \frac{12}{6}$
   (c) $\frac{9}{3} = 3$, $\frac{18}{6} = 3$; $\frac{9}{3} = \frac{18}{6}$
   (d) $\frac{12}{3} = 4$, $\frac{24}{6} = 4$; $\frac{12}{3} = \frac{24}{6}$
   (e) $\frac{15}{3} = 5$, $\frac{30}{6} = 5$; $\frac{15}{3} = \frac{30}{6}$
   (f) $\frac{18}{3} = 6$, $\frac{36}{6} = 6$; $\frac{18}{3} = \frac{36}{6}$

Page 50

1. (a) 8 ÷ 2 = 4   (b) 15 ÷ 3 = 5   (c) 18 ÷ 3 = 6
      4 × 2 = 8   5 × 3 = 15   6 × 3 = 18
   (d) 24 ÷ 4 = 6 (e) 20 ÷ 2 = 10 (f) 30 ÷ 5 = 6
       6 × 4 = 24   10 × 2 = 20   6 × 5 = 30
   (g) 28 ÷ 7 = 4 (h) 21 ÷ 3 = 7
       4 × 7 = 28   7 × 3 = 21

2. (a) 8 × 2 = 16 (b) 9 × 3 = 27   (c) 3 × 8 = 24
       16 ÷ 2 = 8   27 ÷ 3 = 9   24 ÷ 8 = 3

New Curriculum Mathematics for Schools Key Stage 2

Page 51

1. (a)–(f)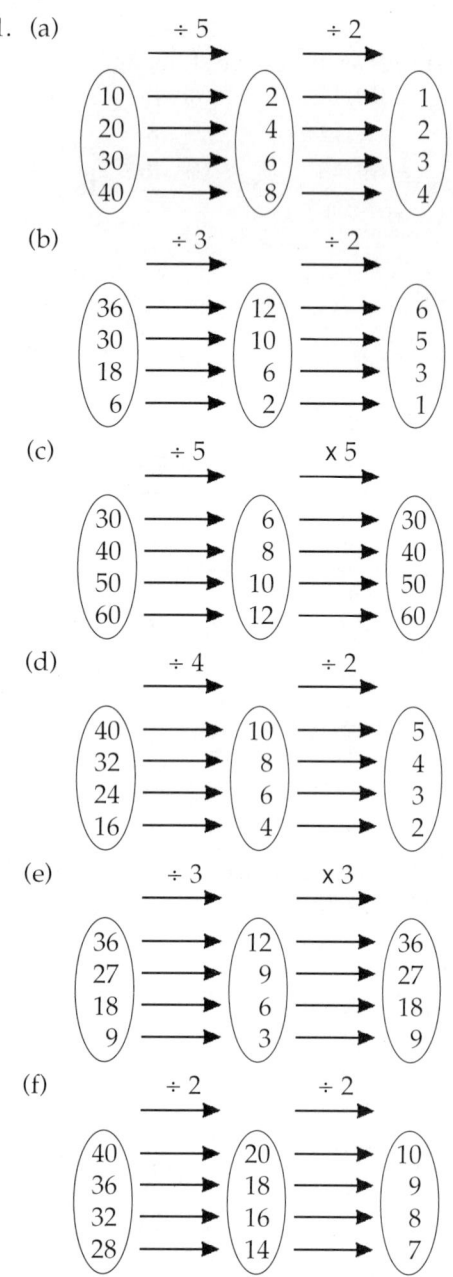

2. ÷10

3. (a) ÷10 (b) ÷6 (c) ×1 or ÷1
   (d) ÷8 (e) ×1 or ÷1 (f) ÷4

Section 11

Pages 52–53

1. Square centimetres are too small a unit of measurement for large areas such as the classroom floor.

2. Square metres

3. 12 metres × 8 metres = 96 square metres or 96 m²

4. She multiplies the length of the room (12 metres) by the breadth (8 metres).

5. Children check this result with their calculators.

6. Children can find the area of their classroom, marking off the metre length and metre breadth using metre sticks and chalk. Work to the nearest whole metre length.

7–9. Open-ended. The work at home could be carried out using paper or card strips cut to 1 metre lengths.

Section 12

Page 54

1. Fiona's pattern:
   1 + 2 = 3; 2 + 4 = 6; 3 + 6 = 9; 4 + 8 = 12;
   5 + 10 = 15; 6 + 12 = 18; 7 + 14 = 21; 8 + 16 = 24;
   9 + 18 = 27; 10 + 20 = 30

2. John's pattern:
   1 + 3 = 4; 3 + 5 = 8; 5 + 7 = 12; 7 + 9 = 16;
   9 + 11 = 20; 11 + 13 = 24; 13 + 15 = 28;
   15 + 17 = 32; 17 + 19 = 36; 19 + 21 = 40

3. Naseem's pattern:
   2 + 3 = 5; 4 + 6 = 10; 6 + 9 = 15; 8 + 12 = 20;
   10 + 15 = 25; 12 + 18 = 30; 14 + 21 = 35;
   16 + 24 = 40; 18 + 27 = 45; 20 + 30 = 50

4. Jamie's pattern:
   2 + 4 = 6; 4 + 8 = 12; 6 + 12 = 18; 8 + 16 = 24;
   10 + 20 = 30; 12 + 24 = 36; 14 + 28 = 42;
   16 + 32 = 48; 18 + 36 = 54; 20 + 40 = 60

Page 55

1. Position number: 5   6
   Number of rods: 25   33

2. Position number: 1 2 3 4 5 6 7
   Number of junctions: 3 6 10 15 21 28 36

3. (a) 4, 9, 16, 25, 36, 49

   (b) 4, 10, 18, 28, 40, 54

4.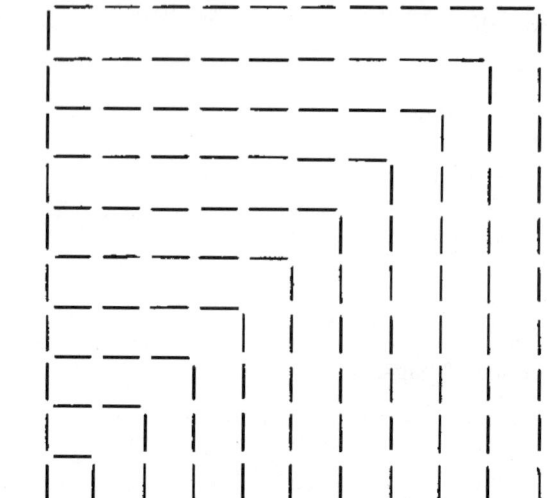

138

Answers

Section 13

Pages 56–57

1. Sample explanation: 'First I made a model using red cubes to represent the 243 vehicles using leaded petrol and green cubes to represent the 119 vehicles using unleaded petrol. Then I exchanged one strip of ten red cubes for ten single cubes. And then I compared the sets to find the difference.'

2. $\begin{array}{r}243\\-119\end{array} \rightarrow \begin{array}{r}(200+40+3)\\-(100+10+9)\end{array} \rightarrow \begin{array}{r}(200+30+13)\\-(100+10+\ 9)\\\hline 100+20+\ 4 \rightarrow 124\end{array}$

3. D, B, A, C

4. $\begin{array}{r}335\\-147\end{array} \rightarrow \begin{array}{r}(300+30+5)\\-(100+40+7)\end{array} \rightarrow \begin{array}{r}(300+20+15)\\-(100+40+\ 7)\end{array}$
    $\rightarrow \begin{array}{r}(200+120+15)\\-(100+\ 40+\ 7)\\\hline 100+\ 80+\ 8\ \rightarrow 188\end{array}$

Pages 58–59

1. C, B, A

2. $\begin{array}{r}329\\-135\end{array} \rightarrow \begin{array}{r}(300+20+9)\\-(100+30+5)\end{array} \rightarrow \begin{array}{r}(200+120+9)\\-(100+\ 30+5)\\\hline 100+\ 90+4 \rightarrow 194\end{array}$

3. $\begin{array}{r}247\\-135\end{array} \rightarrow \begin{array}{r}(200+40+7)\\-(100+30+5)\\\hline 100+10+2 \rightarrow 112\end{array}$

4. Decide which is the greater of the two numbers. Compare the units digits and the tens digits of the two numbers. If the units digit or the tens digit of the smaller number is greater than the units digit or tens digit of the larger number, then exchange is required.

5. Round off to the nearest hundred and find the difference, e.g.

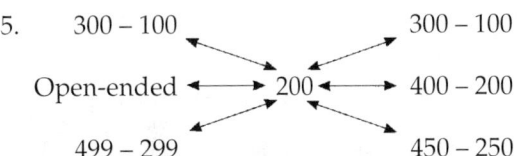

Page 60

1. 201, 201, 201, 201, 299, 299, 299, 299

2. 985 − 165 = 820   985 − 165 = 820   985 − 165 = 820
   885 − 165 = 720   985 − 265 = 720   885 − 265 = 620
   785 − 165 = 620   985 − 365 = 620   785 − 365 = 420
   685 − 165 = 520   985 − 465 = 520   685 − 465 = 220
   585 − 165 = 420   985 − 565 = 420   585 − 565 = 20

3. Open-ended.

4. 200, 345, 200, 209, 200, 416, 200, 453

5. 300 − 100   300 − 100

    Open-ended ↔ 200 ↔ 400 − 200

    499 − 299   450 − 250

   Encourage the children to include other number sentences.

Page 61

1. Sue by 1, Jamie by 140, Jamie by 91, Sue by 600, Jamie by 116

2. 564,   198,   401,   230,   163
   310,   234,   250,   367,   316
   The results show related sentences,
   e.g. 874 − 310 = 564
         874 − 564 = 310

Page 62

1. 136 g

2. 12 g, 80 g, 125 g, 45 g, 75 g, 41 g, 193 g

Page 63

1.

Difference	A300–B4	727–200	727–100	737–400	737–300
A300–B4	—	149	190	166	187
727–200	149	—	41	17	38
727–100	190	41	—	24	3
737–400	166	17	24	—	21
737–300	187	38	3	21	—

2. (a) As 336 + 146 = 482 use one Airbus A300–B4 and one Boeing 727–100
   (b) As 336 + 187 = 523 use one Airbus A300–B4 and one Boeing 727–200
   (c) As 187 + 146 = 333 use one Boeing 727–200 and one Boeing 727–100
   (d) As 336 + 149 = 485 use one Airbus A300–B4 and one Boeing 737–300
   (e) As 170 + 149 = 319 use one Boeing 737–400 and one Boeing 737–300
   (f) As 336 + 336 = 672 use two Airbus A300–B4
   (g) As 336 + 187 + 146 = 669 use one Airbus A300–B4, one Boeing 727–200 and one Boeing 727–100
   (h) As 187 + 146 + 170 = 503 use one Boeing 727–200, one Boeing 727–100 and one Boeing 737–400

New Curriculum Mathematics for Schools Key Stage 2

Section 14

Page 64

1. 2 beakers hold 1/2 a litre.
   3 beakers hold 3/4 of a litre.
   I think 1 beaker holds 250 ml.
   I think 2 beakers hold 500 ml.
   I think 3 beakers hold 750 ml.

2. This is an open question as egg cups vary in size, but 6 is an approximate answer.

Page 65

1.

	250ml	500ml	750ml	1L
John		✓		
Kumar	✓			
Fiona	✓			✓
Sue			✓	✓
Tony			✓	

2. John: 20p
   Kumar: 10p
   Fiona: 50p
   Sue: 70p
   Tony: 30p
   Total: 180p or £1.80

Section 15

Page 66

1. Laura receives 90p
   Tony receives 70p
   Emma receives 50p
   Simon receives 30p
   Encourage statements such as:
   Laura receives 3 times as much as Simon, Tony receives 20p more than Emma, etc.

2.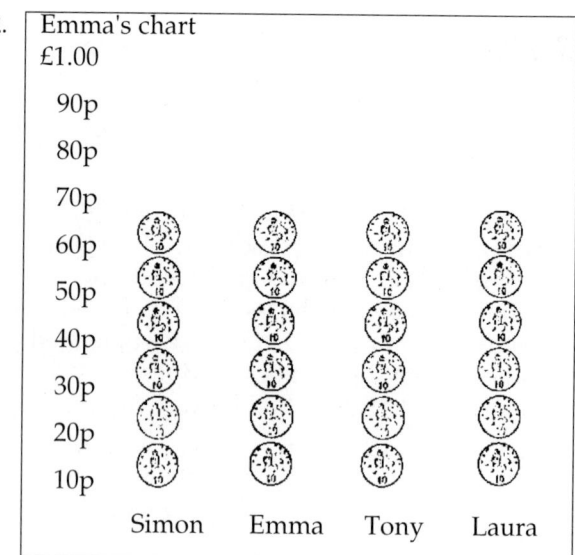
   Encourage statements such as:
   All the children now receive 60p.
   Simon is 30p better off.
   Emma has gained 10p.
   Tony has 10p less.
   Laura is 30p worse off.
   The graph has levelled off, etc.

3. (a) Patels 60p each
   (b) Smiths 60p each
   (c) Roberts 50p each

Page 67

1. Books
2. Toys
3. £20
4. £4
5.

6. £5
7. Open-ended.

Answers

Pages 68–69

1.

	Group		Number of tubs of leaves					
			Monday	Tuesday	Wednesday	Thursday	Friday	Total
1	Ming, Jamie		1	2	1	1	3	8
2	Hannah, Sue, Kumar, Tony, Naseem		4	6	2	2	1	15
3	Macer, Joel, Linda, Neil, Kirsten		2	3	1	3	1	10
4	John, Jenny, Chris, Ron, Anne, Greg, Kay, Andy, Paul, Laura		3	8	2	3	4	20
	Total		10	19	6	9	9	

2.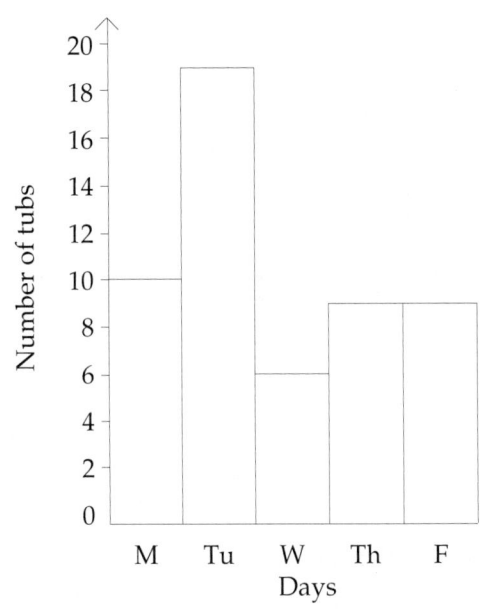

3.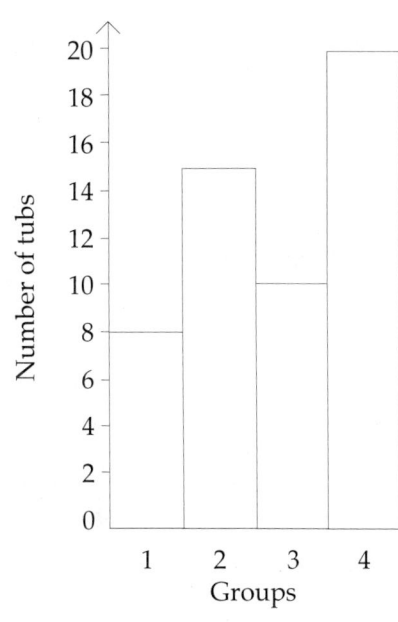

4. Encourage statements such as:
Altogether the children collected 53 tubs.
They collected about the same each day except for Tuesday, when they collected nearly twice as many. Perhaps it was windy in the night, etc.

Group 4 collected the most tubs, 20.
Group 2 did next best with 15.
Group 3 got 10 and Group 1 got 8.
Group 4 collected 12 more tubs than Group 1, etc.

5.

Group	Number of children	Number of tubs of leaves						Number of tubs each
		Monday	Tuesday	Wednesday	Thursday	Friday	Total	
1	2	1	3	0	1	1	6	3
2	5	3	5	2	2	3	15	3
3	5	2	6	4	3	5	20	4
4	10	1	7	3	4	5	20	2
		7	21	9	10	14		

6.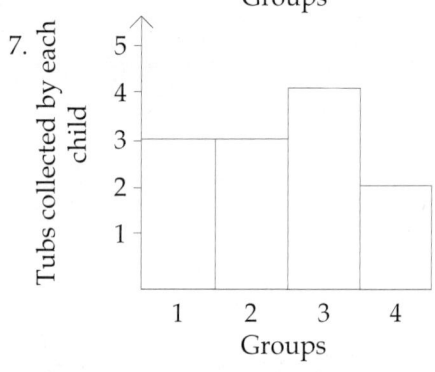

7.

8. Encourage statements such as:
   Groups 3 and 4 collected the most with 20 tubs each.
   Group 1 collected the least with 6 tubs. Group 2 collected 15.
   It looks as though Groups 3 and 4 did a lot better.
   The second graph shows that the children in Groups 1 and 2 collected 3 tubs each but Group 4 only managed 2 tubs each. The second graph looks a lot more even that the first. This is because it takes account of the numbers of children in each group while the first one did not.

9. Group 3

Section 16

Page 70

1. $425 \to (400 + 20 + 5) \to (400 + 10 + 15)$
   $-218 \quad -(200 + 10 + 8) \quad -(200 + 10 + 8)$
   $\qquad\qquad\qquad\qquad\qquad\qquad 200 + 0 + 7 = 207$

2. John knew he had to exchange because he needed to take away 8 units from 5 units.

3. 122

4. 47

5. 10p x 425 = 4250p or £42.50

Page 71

1. Open-ended.

2. (a) $342 \to (300 + 40 + 2) \to (300 + 30 + 12) \to (200 + 130 + 12)$
   $-156 \quad -(100 + 50 + 6) \quad -(100 + 50 + 6) \quad -(100 + 50 + 6)$
   $\qquad\qquad\qquad\qquad\qquad\qquad\qquad\qquad\qquad\qquad 100 + 80 + 6 = 186$

   (b) $452 \to (400 + 50 + 2) \to (400 + 40 + 12) \to (300 + 140 + 12)$
   $-266 \quad -(200 + 60 + 6) \quad -(200 + 60 + 6) \quad -(200 + 60 + 6)$
   $\qquad\qquad\qquad\qquad\qquad\qquad\qquad\qquad\qquad\qquad 100 + 80 + 6 = 186$

   (c) $562 \to (500 + 60 + 2) \to (500 + 50 + 12) \to (400 + 150 + 12)$
   $-376 \quad -(300 + 70 + 6) \quad -(300 + 70 + 6) \quad -(300 + 70 + 6)$
   $\qquad\qquad\qquad\qquad\qquad\qquad\qquad\qquad\qquad\qquad 100 + 80 + 6 = 186$

   (d) $672 \to (600 + 70 + 2) \to (600 + 60 + 12) \to (500 + 160 + 12)$
   $-486 \quad -(400 + 80 + 6) \quad -(400 + 80 + 6) \quad -(400 + 80 + 6)$
   $\qquad\qquad\qquad\qquad\qquad\qquad\qquad\qquad\qquad\qquad 100 + 80 + 6 = 186$

Answers

Page 72

1. 201, 201, 201, 199, 199, 199

2. Open-ended. Sample answers:
   180 – 5 = 175
   190 – 15 = 175
   200 – 25 = 175

3. 431, 155, 241, 155, 234
   155, 441, 155, 152, 155

4. Open-ended. Sample story: There were 387 magazines for sale at the book stall. 232 were sold, leaving 155.

5. Open-ended.

Page 73

1. 116
2. 133
3. 165
4. 144
5. 123
6. 114
7. 384, 567, 635
   166, 138, 6

Page 74

1. Open-ended.
2. 813, 759, 765, 777, 599
   142, 297, 209, 327, 177
3. Open-ended.

Section 17

Page 75

1. £6 + 50p + 20p + 10p = £6.80

2. The calculator or the clock

3. Sue has £4.76.

   Ming has £6.97.

   Naseem has £3.07.

   John has £3.77.

4. Ming has most. Naseem has least.

5. Sue could buy the calculator.
   Ming could buy any one of the three items.
   Naseem and John could not afford to buy anything.

Page 76

1. Gwen has rounded down the figures, Sue has rounded up, while Ming has rounded off to the nearest £1.

2. £5.35

3. Ming's.

4. Probably Gwen's.

5. Sue's.

6. (a) £3.75   (b) £3.44   (c) £6.63
   (d) £8.21   (e) £5.44   (f) £5.45

7. (a) Rounding down = £2 + £1 = £3
      Rounding up = £3 + £2 = 5
   (b) Rounding down = £1 + £1 = £2
      Rounding up = £2 + £2 = £4

Page 77

1. Jane has rounded down the figures, Sue has rounded up, while Harry has rounded off to the nearest £1.

2. £1.50

3. They were all either 50p above or 50p below.

4. Open-ended. Sue's method is probably safer when shopping but Harry's is more likely to be accurate.

5. 75p

6. £2.25

7. (a) £2.24   (b) £3.65   (c) £5.64

8. Open-ended.

Page 78

1. £14.25

2. Megan has rounded down the price before multiplying, while Gwen has rounded up.

3. Gwen's.

4. (a) £7.05   (b) £48.90
   (c) £22.60   (d) £43.04
   (e) £64.62   (f) £37.80

5. (a) £1.80 x 4 = £7.20
      £2.60 x 4 = £10.40
      £7.20 + £10.40 = £17.60

   (b) £1.30 x 6 = £7.80
      £2.40 x 6 = £14.40
      £7.80 + £14.40 = £22.20

Section 18

Page 79

1. (a) Only 2 in 100 bought 6 packets.

   (b) 52 out of 100 bought less than 12 packets.

   (c) It's very likely that most will buy less than 15 packets.

Page 80

1–2.

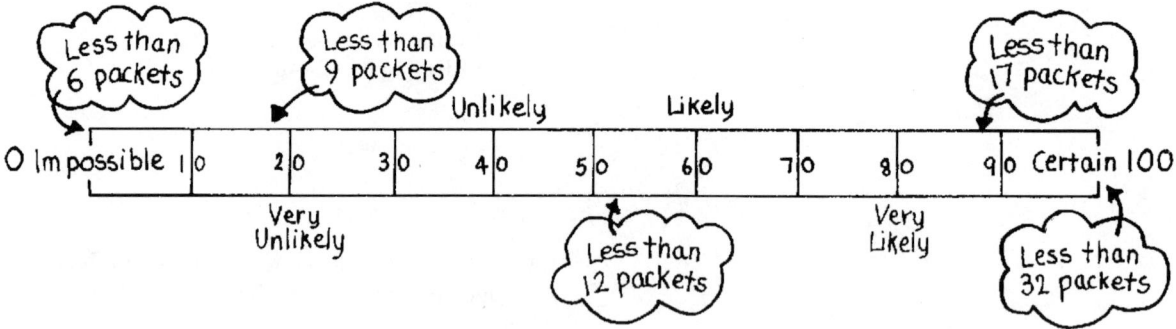

List of Activity Cards and Copymasters

Activity Cards

2.1–2	Shopping Triples	9.9–10	Safari Park
3.1	Hundreds, Tens and Units Triples	9.11–14	Multiplication Dominoes
3.2	Place Value Strips	9.15	Factor Dominoes
3.3–4	The 'Nearly' Game	9.16–21	Cross the Board
4.1	Taxi Driver Cards	10.1	Story Pairs
4.2	Digital Touch and Say	10.2	Sharing Touch and Say
4.3	World Time Touch and Say Pairs	10.3	Double Function Pairs
4.4–5	The 'Nearly' Time Game	10.4	'Any Left Overs?'
5.1–4	Addition Algorithm Cards	13.1–4	Difference Algorithm Cards
5.5	'Nearly' Addition Triples	13.5	'Nearly' Difference Triples
7.1	Temperature Touch and Say	14.1	Capacity Touch and Say
7.2–3	Negative Number Dominoes	14.2	Pouring Pairs
7.4–5	Watch Your Step!	17.1–3	Decimal Money Position Value Cards
9.1	Multiplication Touch and Say	17.4–5	The Money 'Nearly' Game
9.2–3	Party Time Flowcharts	17.6	Supermarket Checkout Cards
9.4	'Tell Me a Story'	17.7–8	Supermarket Triples
9.5–8	Go for Goal	18.1–2	Badge Cards

Copymasters

1.1	Pictogram Pictures	6.3	Numbered Lattice 2
1.2	Class 5's Yogurt Survey	6.4	Parallel Lines
1.3	Letter Frequency (English)	6.5	Face It
1.4	Letter Frequency (French)	6.6	Out and About
1.5	Letter Frequency (German)	6.7	Sets of Parallel Lines
1.6	Outcome Charts	7.1	Above and Below
1.7	100 Cut-out Letters	7.2	Mountain Hotel
1.8	Multiplication Race Track	7.3	Logic Number Chains
1.9	Traffic Survey 1	7.4	More Logic Number Chains
1.10	Traffic Survey 2	7.5	Thermometer Charts
1.11	Traffic Survey 3	7.6	The Crazy Holiday Game
1.12	The 5–10 Multiplication Game	7.7	Break the Code
2.1	Cartoon Frames	8.1	The Solid Shape Quiz/Boxes Results Sheet
2.2	Sue's Game		
2.3	The Clay Pigeon Shoot	8.2	Rotate to Fit
2.4	Golf Score Cards	8.3	Identical Shapes
2.5	Bingo	9.1	1–100 Square
2.6	Find the Sums	9.2	Multiples
2.7	Find the Differences	9.3	Write a Story
3.1	Base 10 Cards	9.4	A Multiplication Square
3.2	Hundreds, Tens and Units	9.5	Multiplication Strips
3.3	Three out of Five	9.6	Arrays
4.1	Time Lines	9.7	Mats for Multiplication Bingo
4.2	Timetables	9.8	Multiplication Grids
4.3	At the Travel Agent's	9.9	Calculator Apples
4.4	Flight Timetables/The Watchmaker's Shop Window Chart	9.10	The Multiple Flowchart Game
		9.11	Factor Dominoes
4.5	The Video Recorder	9.12	Number Sentences
4.6	At Camp	9.13	Match the Strips in Threes
5.1	Four in a Line	10.1	Mappings
5.2	The Puzzle of the Decorated Pebbles	10.2	More Mappings
5.3	'Nearly'	10.3	Calculator Chains
6.1	Random Noughts and Crosses	10.4–5	'Between-ness'
6.2	Numbered Lattice 1	10.6	House Numbers

New Curriculum Mathematics for Schools Key Stage 2

11.1	Plans	**15.5**	The Leaf Collection
12.1	Isometric Grid	**15.6**	Holiday Pocket Money
12.2	Growing Patterns	**16.1**	Rearranging Digits
12.3	Matchstick Patterns	**16.2**	Related Sentences
12.4	Criss-cross Patterns	**16.3**	Paving the Garden
12.5	Numbers in Rows and Columns	**16.4**	Rounding off to 100
12.6	Patterns from Five Columns	**17.1**	Calculators
13.1	Calculator Trail	**17.2**	100 pence
14.1	Yours and Mine	**17.3**	Rounding off to the Nearest Pound
14.2	Find the Costs	**17.4**	More Rounding off
15.1–2	More 'Between-ness'	**18.1**	A 'Likelihood' Chart
15.3	Sharing Equally	**18.2**	Throw a Row
15.4	Holiday Pocket Money Gallery	**18.3**	Design an Overlay

Glossary

Algorithm   A set of rules, a routine, for carrying out a calculation. See for example pages 20 and 21 in Pupils' Book 2 and Section 5 (page 40) in this Guide.

Analogue computer   A computer which represents numbers by means of physical quantities, such as voltage, or in the case of a non-digital clock, angular rotations of gear wheels, which it then manipulates so as to carry out numerical calculations.

Average

(arithmetic) mean   The number obtained by adding together a collection of numbers and dividing the result by the number of numbers in the collection, e.g. the average or arithmetic mean of 3, 3, 4 and 8 is $(3 + 3 + 4 + 8) \div 4 = 4\frac{1}{2}$. See for example page 67 in Pupils' Book 2 and Section 15 (page 108) in this Guide.

median   The 'middle' number of a collection of numbers, obtained by first putting them in ascending or descending order, and then in the case of an odd numbered collection, picking out the middle number, or in the case of an even numbered collection, finding the number halfway between the two middle numbers, e.g. the median of 2, 7, 3, 5 and 8 is 5, and the median of 2, 7, 3 and 5 is 4.

mode   The number which occurs most often in a collection of numbers, e.g. the mode of 2, 2, 3, 3, 3, 5, 7, 4, 3 and 9 is 3, or the 'tallest' column on a block or bar graph. (If there is no such unique number in a collection or more than one 'tallest' column on a block or bar graph, then a more complicated definition is needed; at this stage we avoid such situations.) See for example pages 2 and 3 in Pupils' Book 2 and other block/bar graphs in both the Pupils' Book and Teacher's Guide.

Commutative law   The rules for addition and multiplication which tell us that the ordering of the numbers in these operations does not matter, i.e. that for all numbers a, b: $a + b = b + a$; and $a \times b = b \times a$. (Note that the same rules do not apply to subtraction or division.) See for example page 43 in Pupils' Book 2.

Digital computer   A computer which performs calculations by representing numbers in discrete forms, for example by means of 'switches' which are either 'on' or 'off'.

Distributive law   The rules for the use of brackets when addition and multiplication are used together, i.e. for any numbers a, b, c:
$$a \times (b + c) = (a \times b) + (a \times c).$$
See for example page 41 in Pupils' Book 2 and Section 9 (page 64) in this Guide.

Function   A rule which assigns to a given number a second uniquely defined number. See for example page 51 in Pupils' Book 2 and Section 10 (page 80) in this Guide.

Mapping   Another word for function, often used to refer to the whole operation of the function. Thus the function 'multiply by 2' is said to map, or be a mapping of, the integers to the even integers (or a function from the integers to the even integers). See for example page 51 in Pupils' Book 2 and Section 10 (page 80) in this Guide.

Pupil Record Sheet – Pupils' Book 2
New Curriculum Mathematics for Schools Key Stage 2

Name of Pupil _____

Section	Topic	Pupil Pages / *Teacher Pages*	ATs	Date Comp.	Activities / Comments
1	Data Handling	2–7 / *13–19*	AT 1 3a, 3b, 3c, 3d, 4c. AT 3 3a. AT 4 4d. AT 5 3a, 3b, 3d.		
2	Tens and Units	8–10 / *20–25*	AT 1 3a, 3b, 3c. AT 2 3a, 3e.		
3	Position Value (H.T.U.)	11–14 / *26–32*	AT 1 3c. AT 2 3a, 3c.		
4	Time	15–19 / *33–39*	AT 1 3a, 3b, 3c, 3d. AT 2 3e. AT 5 3a.		
5	Addition (H.T.U.)	20–27 / *40–46*	AT 1 3b, 3c. AT 2 3a, 3d, 3e, 4a. AT 3 2b. AT 5 3a.		
6	Shape, Space and Position	28–31 / *47–52*	AT 1 3c, 3d. AT 3 4a. AT 4 2b, 4a, 4b.		
7	Negative Numbers	32–34 / *53–57*	AT 1 3a, 3c, 3d. AT 2 3e. AT 3 2b. AT 5 3a.		
8	Shape, Space and Position	35–37 / *58–63*	AT 1 3b, 3c, 3d. AT 4 2a, 3a.		
9	Multiplication	38–46 / *64–79*	AT 1 3a, 3b, 3c, 3d. AT 2 3b, 3c. AT 3 2b, 3a.		

Pupil Record Sheet – Pupils' Book 2
New Curriculum Mathematics for Schools Key Stage 2

Name of Pupil _____

Section	Topic	Pupil Pages *Teacher Pages*	ATs	Date Comp.	Activities / Comments
10	Sharing	47–51 *80–86*	AT 1 3a, 3b, 3c, 3d. AT 2 3b, 3c, 4a. AT 3 2b, 3a, 3b, 4a.		
11	Measurement: Area	52–53 *87–89*	AT 1 3a, 3b, 3c, 3d. AT 2 3c, 3e, 4e. AT 3 2b. AT 4, 4d, 5d.		
12	Pattern	54–55 *90–95*	AT 1 3a, 3c, 3d. AT 3 2b, 3a, 4a.		
13	Difference (H.T.U.)	56–63 *96–103*	AT 1 3a, 3b, 3c, 3d. AT 2 3a,3d, 4a, 4b. AT 3 2b, 3a, 4a. AT 5 3b.		
14	Measurement: Capacity	64–65 *104–107*	AT 1 3a, 3b, 3c. AT 2 3e, 4c. AT 3 2b. AT 4 4d. AT 5 3b.		
15	Data Handling	66–69 *108–111*	AT 1 3b, 3c, 4a. AT 2 3c, 3d, 4a. AT 3 4b. AT 5 3a, 3b, 3c, 3d, 4c.		
16	Take Away (H.T.U.)	70–74 *112–116*	AT 1 3a, 3b, 3c, 3d. AT 2 3a, 3d, 4a, 4b, 4d. AT 3 2b, 4a.		
17	Money	75–78 *117–123*	AT 1 3a, 3b, 3c. AT 2 3b, 3c, 3d, 3e, 4a, 4c, 4d.		
18	Data Handling	79–80 *124–127*	AT 1 3c, 3d, 3e. AT 5 3b, 3d, 4d.		